SON and FATHER

*Before and Beyond
the Oedipus Complex*

Peter Blos

THE FREE PRESS
A Division of Macmillan, Inc.
NEW YORK

Collier Macmillan Publishers
LONDON

The Free Press
A Division of Macmillan, Inc.
866 Third Avenue, New York, N. Y. 10022

Collier Macmillan Canada, Inc.

Printed in the United States of America

printing number
1 2 3 4 5 6 7 8 9 10

Library of Congress Cataloging-in-Publication Data

Blos, Peter.
  Son and father.

  Bibliography: p.
  Includes index.
  1. Fathers and sons. 2. Father and child. 3. Child
analysis. I. Title.
BF723.F35B57 1985   155.4′32   85–15882
ISBN 0–02–903680–1

To

Betsy Thomas

Contents

PART ONE

The Son-Father Relationship from Infancy to Manhood: An Intergenerational Inquiry

CONTENTS

Preamble: a Clarification of Terms

Since I shall use terms that differ in their definition from the ones traditionally and conventionally used in psychoanalytic discussion of a subject
such as the one I shall present, it behooves me not only to clarify their
implied meaning but also to explain why I depart from their common
usage, before I can set out on a discourse on those issues which are my
substantive concern. I shall preface the clarification of terms by a general
intimation of the overall theme which I set out to develop. The subject
of my presentation and its specific content and scope have had their
own evolution which deserves a brief comment.*

Decades of psychoanalytic work with adolescents whose developmental progression had come to an impasse in their confrontation with
the tasks of their age made me aware of the influence which the so-
called preoedipal experiences exert on the conflict formation and conflict
resolution in the realm of adolescent object relations and personality development.

---

* A more detailed account of the path which my theoretical formulations have taken
over time will be found in Part Three.

3

Exploring the epigenesis of male object relations from infancy to maturity made me aware with increasing clarity that the complexity of the boy's relationship to the father of his infancy and early childhood had been codified in psychoanalytic theory in too monolithic and confined a form to do justice to observations of child and adolescent development. My present effort aims at a modification and revision of these standard conceptualizations of the Oedipus complex. Anticipating the thesis which I shall present in the subsequent discourse, I state briefly the proposition that the formation of the male personality and its deviations are influenced as much by the Oedipal, i.e. triadic, stage of development as they are by the proedipal, namely, dyadic emotional attachment of the male infant to his father. Considering the etiological significance of both stages— dyadic and triadic—as equal, the uniqueness of the Oedipal stage lies in the fact that it gives a final organization and closure to the infantile period, readying the child for a confrontation with new tasks of growth. These can briefly be stated as attending to the business of middle childhood, namely, to a comprehension of the world in an ever expanding, socially shared and communicable symbolism, usually identified with "school" and "learning", or with ego expansion and structuring. Given the urgency of these tasks, the closure of the infantile period always remains incomplete, with much unfinished business that was shelved. In analytic language we would say that unresolved residues of infantilism are repressed during the decline of the Oedipus complex, only to be revived and taken under final review at adolescence. More about this later.

The triadic stage is traditionally referred to as the Oedipal stage; the word "triadic" emphasizes the characteristic constellation of three parties simultaneously involved in emotional interaction. From the child's point of view each party pursues his or her aim of need gratification in a circular transaction. Gender specificity represents an integral aspect of the Oedipal stage and gives it its unique and stage-specific character. The child's wishes and conflicts of this stage have become general knowledge. At the present time, almost 100 years after the first formulation of the "Oedipus complex,"* this term has become part of the common vocabulary of educated men and women of the Western world. Its definition can be found today in any standard dictionary of the English language. In its barest outline it alludes to the child's desire to take the place of the same-gender parent in relation to the opposite-gender parent. This desire, which is kept from fulfillment by physical immaturity and the incest taboo in human society, was unwittingly consummated by the

* This term appeared for the first time in print in a paper published by Freud in 1910. "The concept had, of course, long been familiar to him" (Standard Edition, 11, p. 171, footnote 1). A clear reference to the concept of the Oedipus complex can be found in Freud's writing as early as 1897 (Standard Edition, 1, p. 255).

adult Oedipus, whose life is part of Greek mythology and told in two tragedies by Sophocles.

In contrast, the dyadic stage of child development refers to a time antedating the oedipal stage. The term employed to denote the earlier stage emphasizes the significant interaction occurring between two parties: child and mother or child and father. Both interactions are linear. What appear then as significant for the dyadic stage are the attachment and avoidance emotions between two partners, infant-mother or infant-father, with the possible affective and physical distancing at any time from the third partner, whose obligatory involvement and participatory presence are characteristic of the Oedipal stage. Due to this trilateral constellation and the presence of an antagonistic and an attractant affect aimed at one of the two partners in the child's simultaneous relatedness to both, this stage is called the triadic stage of object relations. This rigid definition of stages is not quite true to life. When we refer to a stage in the sequential order of progressive development, we mean a preferential trend rather than an exclusive presence, taking for granted that the blending and fusion of stages is the rule before a stage-specific mode of object relation is consolidated.

The exclusive and earliest bonding is reflected in the mother-child unit, the archaic dyad, the oneness of the symbiotic stage (Mahler, 1975). The dyadic stage continues the earlier one-to-one attachment, but now this is extended to both parents in an interchangeable dualism. Their gender difference is acknowledged, but the attachment emotions are equally experienced in relation to each of both parents. Their distinction, besides gender, is marked by the sensations of pleasure or pain which each parent is liable to evoke in the dyadic child. Each parent can be the representation of one or the other at different moments in time; a turn to the other is the always available recourse the child will have in his avoidance of frustration, disappointment, or fear generally referred to as pain. By using the terminology just mentioned, I dispense with the conventional use of the term "preoedipal" because this term conveys no precise meaning beyond the fact that the event alluded to occurred chronologically before the Oedipal stage. This reference, so it seems to me, is too vague and global, covers too many developmentally heterogeneous phases of early life, to serve any useful purpose except in relation to a general temporal allocation, as historians use the designation "B.C." or "pre-Columbian." If the adjective "preoedipal" is employed in this historical sense, it serves a useful descriptive purpose for the global dating of infantile development; I shall continue to use the term "preoedipal" without assigning to it any stage-specific designation. I might mention in passing that as late as 1931 Freud spelled this term "pre-Oedipus phase" (1931, p. 226). This corresponds to the usage I wish to restore to the term, namely its use to comprise all events of infantile development which come before the triadic, i.e. oedipal, constellation, or before the Oedipus complex proper takes shape.

The Oedipus Complex: Comments on the History of the Concept

My investigation in early, i.e., dyadic, object relations is restricted, as indicated above, to the male gender. The fact that my chosen subject is one of momentous importance in human life requires no persuasion or testimony. Within the scope stated above, I propose to investigate the developmental history of intergenerational, reciprocal integration between sonship and fatherhood. Every father has first been a son; arriving at fatherhood and having a son weaves his own sonship existence into the new context of a generational continuum. This investigation grew from my clinical research extending from boyhood—including infancy and early childhood—to manhood, in other words, from being a male infant to becoming a man.

I will attempt here to translate my observations into theoretical and clinically useful propositions. In so doing, I will suggest modifications of some tenets of classic psychoanalysis in order to accommodate my propositions to a larger developmental framework. What encourages me in this endeavor is the fact that the psychoanalytic edifice, standing on solid conceptual foundations, is designed never to reach an endpoint of completion in its towering structure. The open-endedness of psychoanalytic theory is rooted in one of its basic assumptions, which postulates that the principle of causality is secondary to that of overdetermination. This is to say that any discovery which establishes a hitherto unsuspected or unknown causal linkage in the operation of the human mind initiates at the moment of its inception the potential for its self-elimination, partially or totally. This could not be otherwise, because any newly discovered causality elicits the potential discovery of a new set of determinants, capable of establishing a superseding causality which sets the advance of the cognitive spiral into motion *ad infinitum*. It follows from this conceptual framework of psychoanalytic thought that it not only is hospitable to, but indeed invites, conjectural, controversial, and revisionistic propositions of the kind I intent to present.

The discovery of the Oedipus complex and of its fateful role in life and particularly in neurosogenesis has led to an ever deepening investigation of its complexity. Gender polarity represented from the beginning the core configuration in Oedipal conflict formation; this fact is still discernible today in oedipal terminology when we speak of the "positive" and "negative" Oedipus complex. Again I have to pause and delay my substantive presentation in order to query some conventional oedipal terminology. Reference to "positive" or "negative" defines the gender of the object toward which the child's wishes and affects are directed. They are called positive if they are other-gender directed and negative if they are same-gender directed. The use of the identical adjective for either terminological or purely descriptive reference is deplorable and avoidable; indeed, a correction or updating of terms would be timely. The simple question arises, why not use a term which addresses itself directly to the overriding gender issue if the gender connotation is all that the word is supposed to convey? It would be particularly desirable if the term were only used to denote the gender orientation of the child to mother or father in the dyadic and triadic constellation of object relations. The words "positive" and "negative" carry pejorative connotations. In fact, the judgmental implication conveyed by these words did originally motivate their choice. The child's other-gender preference—boy of mother, girl of father—anticipates the direction of libido development which will lead in later life (adolescence, adulthood) to a heterosexual identity. In the days when the psychoanalytic term "positive Oedipus complex" was coined, the dictionary meaning of the word contributed to its choice by the following association: what is normal is positive and heterosexuality is normal; the same reasoning applies to the term "negative."* Besides an evaluative, indeed a moralistic, inference as to the words "positive" and "negative," it must be remembered that physics offered its own persuasive terminology in designating as positive and negative the poles of the electric current and of magnetism as well; the simple lesson by analogy would read: opposite poles attract and identical poles repel each other.

The pejorative connotation of the respective terms becomes even more glaring when we are reminded that they were often used interchangeably—and still are at times—with "active" and "passive" or with "male" and "female." In light of my investigations into the individual, evolutionary history of the "negative" complex, it appears obvious that the male child's "negative" complex of the dyadic phase is of a most positive nature for his personality development. We have also never doubted that the infant boy's imitation or primitive identification with the early mother is foremost of the active modality. His relationship to the dyadic father modulates this early modeling after the active mother, paving the way to the oedipal stage. By no stretch of the imagination can the "negative" complex of the male toddler be called passive or inverted, nor can we deny that passive strivings are present in relation to both parents. We only have to turn our attention to the little boy's father-merger wishes in conjunction with his envy of the mother's faculty to produce a baby in order to find evidence of the more or less simultaneous presence of the preoedipal active and passive drive polarities. They do not stand in conflictual antagonism, nor are they mutually exclusive at

---

* The term "inverted" has been used synonymously with "negative," but dropped out of usage over time. Its misleading innuendo of inversion (homosexuality) rightfully disqualified this term from general acceptance.

this stage of development, which we identify with bisexuality. Freud (1921) has commented on the little boy's demonstrative desire to be close to his father and elicit his appreciative responsiveness. He continues by saying, "This behavior has nothing to do with a passive or feminine attitude toward his father (and toward males in general); it is on the contrary typically masculine" (p. 105). The trends I have spoken of never fade into oblivion altogether; indeed we can trace them as normal admixtures throughout the boy's triadic stage, and after that among the vagaries of adolescent object relations and ultimately in the adult male's normal love life.

In discussing the history of the terminology, we have to remember that Freud in his treatment of women came to realize that the Oedipal schema of neurosogenesis did not comfortably fit in with his observations in their treatment. At this point I shall mention only briefly the fact that women's early and never abandoned mother fixation had to be acknowledged by Freud as the core of their neurosis. That this derivation of their illness was in conflict with the psychoanalytic etiology of the neurosis—more about this later—led into a theoretical dilemma. In order to adhere to the accepted theory, Freud decided to extend the "Oedipus complex" to include the dyadic stage of object relations and include the preoedipal realm in the oedipal schema. Freud referred to this broadened concept as the "complete Oedipus complex." By this extension the terminology with its pejorative innuendo was pressed into a procrustean bed. We have only to remind ourselves of the little boy's so-called negative dyadic attachment and idealizing relationship to his father as a most positive one which ultimately will lend direction and vigor to his adult heterosexuality.

On the basis of the arguments which I have advanced, I suggest a terminology which relinquishes the awkward and outgrown adjectives "positive" and "negative" and introduces a perhaps clumsy neologism, but one which at least defines the respective issues of gender reference with a more literal precision. Keeping this intention in mind, I propose the following terminology: (1) dyadic allogender complex (for preoedipal positive complex), (2) dyadic isogender complex (for preoedipal negative complex), (3) triadic allogender complex (for positive Oedipus complex), and (4) triadic isogender complex (for negative Oedipus complex). I know how formidable a task it is to change traditional, cherished, and familiar terminology in any science; nevertheless I venture a try. I am not the first to deplore the oedipal terminology. Ruth Mack Brunswick (1940), a close co-worker of Freud, did so long ago and was ignored at the time.*

---

* In order to acquaint the reader gradually with the new terminology which I propose, I shall use a dual reference in the text. I hope this will make the reading proceed more smoothly.

Freud's first major case history permits us to contrast early and contemporary views of oedipal dynamics. For this purpose I intend to examine one particular aspect of the "Fragment of an Analysis of a Case of Hysteria" (1905), usually referred to by the name of the patient, a girl age 18, as "the Dora case." In this essay Freud attributed the most significant pathogenic valence to the positive* complex and its influence on her illness, even though he gave ample evidence of his suspicion or, indeed, his conviction that the negative complex was at the root of her illness. He stated this clearly in the case study (pp. 60–61), even though this discernment played a minor role in the analytic work with the patient, at least as far as we can glean from the clinical report. The degree as well as the kind of pathogenic valence the clinician assigns to preoedipality, and to one or the other of the two complexes in their dynamic interplay, often remains—so it seems to me—a matter of the predilection or habituation of the analyst. The drive theory represented by the infantile sequence of oral, anal, and phallic zonal predominance has remained in essence unchallenged over time even though it has become increasingly complex in its integration with object relations theory and ego psychology. This is not the place to pursue this issue.

In contrast to the treatment of Dora, the pathogenicity of preoedipal object relations is presently more widely acknowledged in most cases, and not only is it afforded a more prominent place in the etiology of a given neurosis and other forms of mental disturbance, but explicitly and increasingly it has affected the analytic work itself as well as the understanding of child development in general. One must realize that at the time Dora was in treatment, Freud had just arrived at one of his most momentous discoveries, namely, the Oedipus complex as a universal developmental attribute of childhood.** Even though his clinical scrutiny and theoretical conceptualization of the Oedipus complex stood in the forefront of his attention and etiological reasoning in the Dora case, it did not escape his observation that object relations and drive propensities of a different nature, antedating Dora's positive complex, lay at the root of Dora's late adolescent emotional impasse and symptomatology. Freud worked his observation of maternal attachment emotions into the oedipal schema by relegating these emotions to the negative Oedipus complex. In the drive-oriented psychoanalytic language of the time, Freud wrote about his patient Dora to his friend Wilhelm Fliess, ". . . the principal part in the conflicting mental processes is played by the opposition between attraction towards men and one towards women" (1887–1902, letter 141, 1.30.1901). This shifting "attraction," under present-day scrutiny,

---

* In my comments on the Dora case I retain the oedipal terminology, which was used at the time when this essay was written.
** Dora's treatment began in 1900; the case history was published in 1905.

spells out its heterogeneous nature in terms of belonging either to the dyadic or to the triadic stage of object relations.

The polarity of gender—son-mother, daughter-father—has dominated the concept of the oedipal constellation since its inception and has determined decisively the etiological formulation of any given neurotic conflict. However, clinical observations have attributed an increasingly persuasive significance to isogender early object relations. Indeed, both constellations, namely those of dyadic isogender and allogender partnership, have received slowly, at times reluctantly, the recognition of an equal significance in the formulations, theoretical and dynamic, of normal and pathological development. The emphasis of this distinction and its history might sound groundless and overstated to some readers on first hearing, yet we cannot deny the fact that the "positive" complex and its modes of resolution have received far more attention in the analytic literature than has the developmental history, the neurosogenic valence, or the resolution of the "negative" complex.

The Dyadic Stage of the Boy: His Early Father Experience

This extreme sparseness of investigations in male isogender ("negative") object relations from the earliest stages of development onward prompted me to inquire into these neglected issues. My analytic work over many years had convinced me that early isogender experiences not only dominate and shape the son-father relationship at infancy, but influence critically the boy's evolution of his self and object world for a lifetime. The complexity of the son-father relationship has always been known, even if never sufficiently illuminated. Freud has well described the contrasting roles played by the father in the son's life. The oedipal father is by definition the restraining and punishing father under whose threat of retaliation the little boy abandons his competitive strivings, as well as his patricidal and incestuous animus. There has never been any doubt that this depiction of the father is oversimplified and misleading because we know that the typical father also acknowledges and elicits his little son's self-assertion. Being emulated by the son fills the father with pride and joy as does the junior toddler's phallic, narcissistic, and exhibitionistic exuberance.

A well-known comment by Freud will remind us that we revisit old and familiar territory. "As regards the prehistory of the Oedipus complex . . . we know that period includes an identification of an affectionate sort with the boy's father . . ." (1925, p. 250). This early experience of being protected by a strong father and caringly loved by him becomes internalized as a lifelong sense of safety in a Boschian world of horrors and dangers. It seems to me that heretofore the little boy's sense of security and trust has been too exclusively ascribed to the early mother. We have ample occasion to observe in the analysis of the adult man the enduring influence of his early father, the father imago, especially when it remained fixated at the dyadic level and therefore remained excluded from the ongoing process of emotional maturation. As a consequence, the life of the adult male will encompass an unceasing search for substitute father imagos, i.e., object representatives along the father series. The ensuing emotional infantilism frequently exceeds by far the influence which we have become too accustomed to attribute to the search for maternal protection and attachment. A man's overidealization of a male analyst and also of analysis itself reflects frequently the father's role in the child's life during the first two years (Greenacre, 1966). The resistance which is aroused whenever the analytic work threatens to deprive the patient of this father illusion confirms the life-sustaining influence of the early child-father relationship. The patient will not let go of it easily; ". . . the terrifying impression of helplessness in childhood aroused the need for protection—for protection through love—which was provided by the father" (Freud, 1927, p. 30).

The little boy seeks by active and persistent solicitation the father's approval, recognition, and confirmation, thus establishing a libidinal bond of a profound and lasting kind. We have good cause to reason that these signals of approval and affirmation, transmitted by the father's general bearing and responsive presence (not necessarily verbalized), are received by the son during the early years of life and instill in him a modicum of self-possession and self-assertion—distilled, as it were, out of mutual sameness or shared maleness—which renders the wider world not only manageable and conquerable but infinitely alluring, even though there remains a lasting tinge of threatening and bewildering awesomeness about it. At the termination of adolescence a new stage in the life of the growing son appears, when the father's affirmation of the manhood attained by his son, conveyed in what we might call the father's blessings of the youth's impatient appropriation of adult prerogatives and entitlements, reaches a critical urgency. The eloquent and classic pronouncement of this fateful condition we find in James Joyce's 1916 autobiographical work—*A Portrait of the Artist as a Young Man*—when Stephen Dedalus speaks of the terminal exit point of his youth, namely his self-imposed exile from Ireland. The last sentence of the book reads, "Old father, old artificer, stand me now and ever in good stead." This passionate evocation of the good and strong father's spiritual presence, usually conferred by a ritual act of blessing, brings vividly to mind the story of Jacob, who—with the conspiratorial help of his mother—had tricked his blind father into conferring on him the special blessing of the first-born son, his older brother, Esau. This blessing, dishonestly received, was borne with remorse and shame until expunged in the night when Jacob wrestled with the angel: "And Jacob was left alone and there wrestled a man with him until the breaking of the day." Jacob did not let go of his contestant, crying out, "I will not let thee go, except thou bless me. . . . And he blessed him there" (Genesis 32:26, 29). Jacob had "seen God face to face"; the honestly obtained blessing became the turning point in his life's fortune. Might we not recognize in the biblical story of Jacob a paradigmatic reflection on one component of the son-father relationship which needs to be settled before childhood can be brought to a natural termination?

The profound role which I assign to what I like to call a "blessing" conferred by the father on the son was eloquently expressed in a conversation I had lately with a troubled young man. After he had entered a promising "money making" career and did well in it, he felt inspired to shift to a considerably less renumerative but for him a far more meaningful job in the field of social service. He turned to me at this moment of indecision after having been my patient several years ago during his troubled college years. In his quandary about a career change he had first turned to his father for counsel; there he received the categorical advice to choose the career with the larger monetary promise. His father refused— so the son lamented—to even acknowledge or consider his son's search for personal meaning and human involvement in his life's work. In disappointment and despair he exclaimed, "All I wanted was my father's blessing." Only then, he felt, was a free choice within his reach.

Charles Darwin found himself in a similar predicament after his futile efforts to become a medical man or, subsequently, a clergyman had turned his father's expectations regarding his son into bitter disappointments. When, at the age of 22, young Darwin received an offer to join the *Beagle* trip, he was eager to accept the assignment, but his father refused to give him his permission. Faced with this paternal interdiction, young Darwin was ready to refuse the position of naturalist on the *Beagle*, which promised him a way out of his morass of forfeited careers. Fortunately for Darwin's life and for the advance of scientific thought, Josiah Wedgwood, his uncle, intervened and pleaded with the father for his nephew's liberty to accept the offer. The father relented and gave his "blessing," that protective magical spell, to his son, who, relieved of an impending disharmony with his father, could now embark on the five-year voyage of the *Beagle*, from 1831 to 1836. This trip initiated the scientific adventure during which Darwin's genius ripened and unfolded on a scale which decisively changed man's view of his world and of himself.

I return to the discussion of the dyadic characteristics of the affectionate bond between son and father which proves to be of such a lasting influence in the life of every man. Some questions force themselves upon us: Where do the origins of those attachment emotions lie? At which stage of object relations do they flourish? Under what conditions do these hallmark emotions of the dyadic isogender complex decline and what are the transformations they undergo? One receives the impression from the literature that this complex declines because of the ascendancy of the triadic allogender complex, or that the fully developed triadic configuration effects by its sheer ascension the resolution or transformation of the complex which precedes it. Of course, we know that no developmental stage vanishes in such a manner. Yet until recently very little attention has been paid to the process or the timing of this particular kind of isogender attachment resolution. We are presently justified in saying that pathogenic specificity of this closeness derives from an unaltered perpetuity in the son-father relationship, the beginnings of which are to be found in a quasi-maternal bonding by substitution. Residues of this early father experience lend individual uniqueness to subsequent adolescent and adult object relations; they range over a wide spectrum and affect a man's idiosyncratic relationship to men and women throughout his life.

It is no idle speculation if we contemplate the possibility that the little boy in his effort to distance himself from the symbiotic mother turns to the father, replicating initially a dependency and closeness which he tries to transcend by the change of object. Might we speak here of a secondary symbiotic state and ask the question whether such a condition, if transitory and fleeting, is not a normal trend in the advance toward object constancy? Giving a positive answer only begs the question as to the degree and timing of isogender attachment emotions which offset normality from abnormality in the development of the male child.

The Influence of Infant Research on the Psychoanalytic Theory of Development

It is a well-known historical fact that with the establishment and growth of child analysis the frontiers of psychoanalytic practice and, consequently, of theory building were pushed out farther and deeper into the realms of infancy as well as adolescence, namely, into those two epochs of life during which psychic structure formation, initiated by physical maturation, proceeds on a grand scale. Detailed and direct child observation provided a wealth of new and subtle details with regard to psychic differentiation and developmental moves, thus making more precise and complex our previous knowledge of psychic structure formation as derived from explorations of adult mental life and from the reconstructions which such explorations permit. These investigative penetrations into the developmental terrains of both infancy and adolescence delivered findings that enriched the general body of psychoanalysis and consequently widened the scope of our science.

Instead of relying largely on the reconstruction of infantile trauma and object relations, of internalization processes, of psychosexual and ego development gathered from the analysis of adults, it became possible to observe them in their germinal states and follow their growth. Observing first hand what had previously been largely inferred enhanced our knowledge of a more exact schedule—comprising sequences and timing—of infantile and adolescent development.

As a first consequence of psychoanalytic infant research, the so-called preoedipal mother moved prominently into the center of the stage, eclipsing oedipality to a considerable degree as an etiological determinant of normal personality formation as well as of many mental disturbances and aberrations which we observe later in life. By virtue of distinguishing more clearly the determinants which predate the oedipal stage in pathogenicity generally, the limits and the criteria of analyzability became more sharply delineated and also more inclusive of earlier developmental stages. What I want to emphasize at this point is the importance of the dyadic father in the life of the male child. Here we find ourselves in territory not yet fully charted but with sufficiently explored contours of the terrain to know in which directions to advance our search. The findings just alluded to have not only changed our knowledge of timing as to paternal gender recognition but also to stage progression and sequence in psychic differentiation as exemplified in the infant research of Mahler et al. (1975). These findings defined the symbiotic stage and the processes of separation-individuation from which issues the emotional capacity of object relations proper and the dyadic stage in particular. Included in this infant research were relevant observations which illuminated the dawn of parental imitation, internalization, and identification. The dating of core gender identity to an earlier period relegates many classical psychoanalytic tenets of psychosexual development to the archives of our science. We can no longer—and have not been able to for quite some time—adhere to Freud's statement (1933), about the little girl entering the phallic phase, that "we are now obliged to recognize that the little girl is a little man" (p. 118). In other words, we have come to accept the fact that femininity cannot be defined or understood by its negative apposition to the male, nor can it be taken to represent at its core a secondary and defensive formation (Blos, 1980).

This matter is mentioned here in order to explain and justify the fact that the investigation before us is devoted exclusively to the male child—the son—without juxtaposing the female child—the daughter—which would have given my deliberations a more comprehensive scope. I avoided this inclusiveness because the adherence to the male child as the prototype and model for the early differentiation of the genders has obscured for too long the gender specificity of developmental lines in boy and girl. More will be said about this later; at this point I wish to emphasize only my belief that the developmental lines of the male and the female child are each sui generis. What attracted my attention most persistently were their differences rather than their similarities; the latter had been subjected to comparative studies for a long time. In my adolescent research, I have always been careful not to speak of the adolescent in general, but to speak of the adolescent process as it is typical for the male or the female and for a particular adolescent phase as well. This point of view attributes to the sexes their respective ontogenetic autonomy and is—so it seems to me—in harmony with the social and intellectual forces of the contemporary women's movement, which has unquestioningly exerted its influence on the reexamination of gender biology, gender role, and gender identity.

The Resolution of Infantile Attachment Emotions

I might state at this point that I have devoted the major portion of my professional life to the investigation of the adolescent process. Adolescence thus became the focus of my clinical observations from which my theoretical constructs radiated backward and forward into the protoadolescent and the meta-adolescent stages of life. I refer here to my adolescent research because the theme of this investigation is launched from these observations and their theoretical inferences. Edging my way into the substance of this presentation, I state now a proposition which I advanced some years ago. While I share the well-established opinion that the male child arrives at a resolution of the allogender ("positive") Oedipus complex prior to his entry into latency, beyond that I have postulated that his isogender ("negative") complex, having its origin in the dyadic stage of object relations, survives in a repressed, more or less unaltered state until adolescence (Blos, 1974). Developmentally speaking, the necessity arises to differentiate between a dyadic and a triadic, isogender and allogender ("positive" and "negative") complex. This distinction will gain in clarity during the course of this exposition.

   Whatever course the individual resolution of the allogender ("positive") Oedipus complex will take, its achievement is reflected in the formation of a new structure, the superego. Dual parental, namely dyadic, determinants are always recognizable in the final superego structure; they are referred to as residues of the archaic superego which was built on the fear of loss of love and not yet on feelings of guilt. What appears, however, to acquire prominence in the male superego is the dominant voice of the father principle, which reaches back in time to the earliest state of paternal recognition. In origin these early, namely dyadic, superego components are essentially different from those that obtain from the oedipal stage. We are familiar with the latter—the proverbial voice of conscience, the influence of feelings of guilt, and the fear of punishment. Quite to the contrary, the dyadic components in superego formation derive from a stage at which the father experience was not yet instinctually conflicted because it was a precompetitive, idealizing experience of the "good father," the "powerful father," the little boy's first "comrade in arms." Both father and mother complex operate at this early level more or less reactively and compensatorily rather than in an antagonistic libidinal entanglement. The prototypical dyadic split into a pleasurable and an unpleasurable constituent of each parental figure precludes by its very nature the formation of an internal conflict, because the antagonistic components basic to conflict formation have not yet reached the capacity of emotional interaction, arousing anxiety. This preconflictual state is further upheld by the attribution of pain to the external world, the "not me" realm of perception, and the attribution of pleasure to the "me" experience, inclusive of the pleasure object; within this dawning affective awareness lies the emergence of the self. Implicit in this developmental step is the disidentification from the mother to which Greenson (1968) has assigned a special importance in the case of the boy child. Stoller (1980) speaks of a "proto-identification" (p. 596) of the infant with the mother as favorable for the girl but unfavorable for the boy's development of his core gender identity.

The attainment of a stabilized gender identity is not reached before the child is about four years old. What infant researchers have concluded from direct observation I came to verify from my work with adolescents. There I have observed in normal and abnormal states of regression* a reflection of the young child's rather unconflicted tolerance of bisexuality, a state antedating stabilized gender identity at about the age mentioned above. This early bisexual fluidity is stabilized during adolescence in re-. gressive stages when it is normally transcended in the forward sweep of maturation and in the formation of an irreversible sexual identity. Abelin (1977) affirms that the boy has disidentified with the mother before the advent of the rapprochement subphase; i.e., ". . . his father has become the primary attachment object" (p. 146). Absence of the father seems to affect boys more adversely than it does girls. I believe that gender identity formation is fostered in the boy child by the father's presence as well as the mother's love of and affirmation of her husband's maleness; both countervail the son's modeling of his core gender identity on the mother.

Precursors of this process are apparent from early infancy on; they become organized and stabilized in psychic structure with the decline of the oedipal phase. All this is well-established psychoanalytic knowl-

* By "normal" regression I mean "regression in the service of development" (Blos, 1967).

edge. It is also a well-known fact that the two components of the complex, isogender and allogender (negative and positive) are inseparably intertwined but nevertheless distinguishable by the preponderance or dominance of one or the other in their constant ebb and flow. Alongside these differentiating processes in the male child, the isogender ("negative") complex is not subjected to as radical a transformation during prelatency as the allogender ("positive") one is. In other words, its definitive transformation into psychic structure is delayed until adolescence. The steps by which this transformation is accomplished will be illuminated in the latter part of this essay.*

The Dyadic Father in the Emotional Life of the Adolescent

With the advent of sexual maturation at puberty arrives the biological imperative for a definitive, stabilized sexual identity; we do not refer to this position as synonymous with gender identity. The former presupposes sexual maturity, including sex-specific role competence, while the latter / refers to the firm realization of being a boy or a girl. As a coefficient of the biological imperative we can isolate, observe, and define adjunct identities of a social, cognitive, and self-representational nature. They form in their synergic evolution the postlatency or pubertal personality, setting in motion the adolescent process of psychic restructuring which affects every facet of the adolescent's life and promotes forcefully the terminal resolution of the isogender ("negative") complex, dyadic and triadic in origin. What had appeared to me earlier in my work as the resuscitation of the allogender ("positive") complex, which by deflection, transformation, and displacement turns in an apparently predetermined fashion to extrafamilial heterosexual object finding, gradually acquired in my clinical judgment the character of a largely defensive operation. Here I have in mind the fact that the boy's dyadic relationship to his father, which has oscillated for at least a decade between submission to him, self-assertion vis-à-vis him, and sharing in his grandeur, is drawn into the sexual realm with the advent of puberty. The regressive pull to the dyadic father is counteracted at this advanced age by sexual gender assertion. I came to see ever so clearly that this defense springs into action in the wake of a resurgence of the boy's isogender ("negative") complex, which reaches, at puberty, the apex of its conflictuality.

The defensive state I speak of is transitory in nature and declines with the definitive resolution of the isogender ("negative") complex at the closure of adolescence. I am fully aware that this exposition does

* See the discussion under "The resolution of the boy's dyadic father complex," page 41.

not tell the whole story, but I highlight here intentionally what appears to me a neglected stage in the ontogeny of mature male object relations and of the mature self as well. This particular comprehension of male sexuality at adolescence gained further clarity and plausibility for me from the analytic observation that inordinate, compulsive heterosexual activity or, conversely, anxiety arousal due to heterosexual inaction or passivity subsides markedly with the resolution of the isogender ("negative") complex. I noticed that the decline of this conflict introduces a kind of heterosexual attachment behavior which possesses a different quality; to this we refer as a mature (or more mature) love relationship in which the defensive nature of the attachment has dropped away and recognition as well as appreciation can be extended to the partner as a whole person whose uniqueness of personality is not begrudged because it does not provide perfect need gratification but demands mutual adaptation as a creative act. Erik Erikson (1956) has referred to this emotional competence as the stage of intimacy. When the defensive quality of the immature bonding between sexually mature partners has gradually dissipated, then the formation of the adult personality is reasonably assured.

A developmental process which I have condensed here by sketching its essence is, in fact, an emotional journey of more or less extended duration. Indeed, this journey remains often more or less incomplete and makeshift accommodations must do for better or for worse; in other words, more often than not, psychological security can only be secured and maintained by psychological compromise formations or by characterological stabilizations. Should these fail to produce a psychological homeostasis, then the termination of adolescence constitutes a critical and contributory stage in the formation of the adult neurosis. It is the persistent incapacity of the young man to surmount his isogender ("negative") complex which leads to the consolidation of the manifest and definitive neurosis of his adult life. By inferring that a workable resolution of the Oedipus complex during the postoedipal years of childhood is no assurance of yielding to mature object relations over time, I affirm the opinion that not until the closure of adolescence can the dyadic bonding of the boy to his father be transcended for good. Concomitantly I postulate that the structuralization of the adult neurosis cannot be thought of as completed until adolescence has passed. Adolescence cannot remain an open-ended developmental process; this is to say that the incapacity to respond to the biological timing for transcending the adolescent process by bringing the last phase of childhood, namely adolescence, to a close represents by its very nature an abnormal developmental condition to which I have referred as aborted adolescence.* I shall not elaborate here on the far-reaching consequences

---

* I am fully aware of Arlow's (1981) well-stated admonition: "Theories of pathogenesis, like any other scientific hypotheses, have to be judged by their ability to comprehend in the most parsimonious fashion the data of observation" (p. 505).

of the adolescent process, delivered or aborted, on the ultimate attainment of emotional maturity or abnormality, but take to the path that promises to bring my discourse closer to the core of my investigation.

In accordance with the oedipal schema just outlined and its dyadic antecedent stage as well, I am now ready to say that the resolution of the dyadic and triadic object relations integrated in the Oedipus complex advances in a biphasic fashion: the resolution of the allogender ("positive") component precedes latency—in fact, facilitates its formation—while the resolution of the isogender ("negative") component has its normal timing in adolescence or, to be more precise, in late adolescence when it facilitates the entry into adulthood. This schema was elucidated by my analytic observation that the flight of the adolescent boy to the father, is generally disavowed or disclaimed by a negativistic involvement with him and becomes defensively manifest by rising oppositionalism and aggression. This behavior is commensurate with the intensity and urgency of the son's need for a protective closeness to the dyadic father vis-à-vis the magnetic and mysterious female to whom he is irresistibly drawn with the advent of puberty. We recognize here the toddler's turn to the father as an ally in his effort to grow up or, in other words, to resist the regressive pull to the reengulfing, symbiotic mother. This adolescent drive constellation just mentioned is too frequently and readily identified with a homosexual proclivity; such a simplistic equation demands a vigorous disclaimer. What we observe is the male's defensive struggle against passivity in general, not against homosexuality in particular. I must admit at this point my omission of well-known and relevant facts concerning the boy's competitive, antagonistic, and rivaling struggle with the oedipal father, which is part and parcel of the boy's global forward move toward the stabilization of sexual identity. We are well aware that adolescence is the stage in life when the universal polarities of active and passive are in conflict and in final collision on a Promethean scale.

Having acknowledged that adolescence is the obligatory stage for the resolution of the isogender complex, we cannot be surprised that isogender emotions are resurrected in the final settlement of this issue. These emotions become attached to genital urges due to the advent of sexual maturation and gather momentum genitally from still unfocused channels of excitations.* What we observe is a pseudo-homosexual transient stage without manifest nor stabilized, conscious homosexual orientation. In fact, heterosexual activity of a purely impulsive and impersonal

---

* It is a well-known fact that any affective stimulus can arouse during adolescence a sexual response. The reported circumstances of first involuntary ejaculation are frequently of an entirely "asexual" nature—examination fear at school, climbing a rope in gym class, and many more innocuous circumstances, as reported by Kinsey (1948). See also Blos (1962).

nature, referred to as sexual experimentation or the proverbial "one night stand", is at its height. I have observed that the experience of a romantic infatuation, the wish for intimacy and the enchantment of love, can arouse in the young man the danger signal of a looming dependency and emotional surrender (castration fear) which defensively evokes homosexual imagery, as well as homosexual dreams and disturbing preoccupation with homosexual thoughts or, indeed, same-sex activity such as mutual masturbation or, with advancing adolescence, heterosexual "trophy hunting" engaged in by a bunch of friends. The resolution—either spontaneously or therapeutically—of infantile anxiety residues in relation to the "re-engulfing mother" clear the way for the advance to mature heterosexuality.

In the analysis of the adolescent boy it is imperative that the double-faced defensive struggle—against submissiveness and passivity as well as against self-assertiveness and patricide—becomes disentangled. Should this effort fail, then both sides of the struggle will obstruct and confuse synergically the progression to emotional maturity. It is a commonplace observation in the analysis of the adolescent boy that his attentive perseverance on the conflict with the female—be this mother, sister, girl friend, or "chick" (the proverbial "sex object")—keeps his affectionate, i.e. libidinal father attachment effectively in abeyance. The patient himself does usually his share to keep the focus of attention on heterosexuality by preoccupation and avoidance. At any rate, the adolescent's incessant alternation between defensive and regressive object involvement is profusely demonstrated by his proverbial shift of mood, attitude and behavior in general. It did not escape my attention that the regressive emotional, non-erotic pull of the adolescent boy to the early father—forcefully obscured at this age by repression or reversal—is a manifestation of unsettled residues of the common father complex, aggravated at this age by the powerful hold which the female acquires on his emotions and sexual drive. The degree of anxiety attached to this fear of subjugation or dominance by the female is proportionate to the intensity of the adolescent's regressive needs or, conversely, regressive pull.

The Resolution of the Father Complex in the Male

The paradigmatic constellation of infancy, played out in the polarities of gender and of active-passive modalities of functioning, is repeated in male puberty vis-à-vis the female. The adolescent boy in analysis with a man reveals in the transference his rescue wish and rescue anxiety in relation to the father. If he mirrors the father's or analyst's habits (e.g., smoking a pipe), interests (e.g., music, psychology), and many other qualities, this is not only a defense against physical paternal merging by imitation of or identification with traits, habits, or characteristics, but is simultaneously a stepping stone to the adolescent desexualization of the infantile paternal bond; as such it represents the workings of the second individuation process of adolescence (Blos, 1967) and the forward move toward adult autonomy. Therefore, interpretations of these kinds of transference manifestations have to be given sparingly and judiciously, in fact only when they obstruct developmental progression. We should never forget that the analytic situation by its very nature puts the adolescent boy into a relatively passive and receptive position, figuratively and literally, which is bound to awaken latent passive trends. This fact renders the analysis of the transference particularly precarious, because interpretations can easily elicit resistance to or active rejection of the analyst's "caretaking offerings." Such reactions disguise only thinly the repudiation on a symbolic level of nursing (made to feel better) or penetration (infusing the mind with new ideas) more generally speaking, a repudiation of passivity or submissiveness. The analyst's accepting and nonjudgmental attitude is often experienced by the male adolescent patient as an expression of the analyst's own need and wish for a conflictless interaction with his patient via an interpretive defusion of interpersonal emotions. Pitfalls of this nature are kept from getting out of hand (for example, by acting out) as long as the therapeutic alliance remains operative or, in other words, as long as the therapeutic process remains essentially ego-syntonic for the patient. Parenthetically, acting out, inside and outside the transference, is not always a sign of antitherapeutic behavior; it may well be a form of communication, albeit a nonverbal, gestural one. I shall illustrate this point by a clinical episode.

A late adolescent boy had reacted for some time to my interpretations of his violent behavior toward his parents, especially the father, as proof of my taking sides with them and as an expression of my judging his accusatory and demeaning comments about them as "amoral and demented." This reaction reached paranoid proportions. I abstained from interpreting his acting out in the transference because I knew that interpretations inflamed his defensive rage toward submissiveness and if repeated too often lost their credibility. During a session, which I shall now describe, the patient accused me in a highly agitated state of thinking of him as a helpless and weak child who was scared to stand up against his father. He was obviously trying to pick a fight with me and stand his ground. When his shouting attack mounted and threatened to get out of hand, I told him firmly in a loud voice that he had to stop telling me what was on my mind or leave. His outburst suddenly subsided; he became calm and pensive. After a long silence, he said quietly:

"I just remember a dream I had last night. I am wrestling with my father—not fighting, just wrestling. Suddenly I feel that I'm coming—I cannot control it. I get panicky and I yell, 'No, no—I don't want to make up with you'. I repeat these words again and again, getting more and more panicky. I can't stop the orgasm. I have it." After the recall of this dream neither patient nor analyst had much difficulty in recognizing son and father engaged in sporting playfulness, which was a rare event in the boy's early and middle childhood. "I hardly ever played with my father. He was not there, especially when I was afraid of my mother. I saw just enough of him—or perhaps more than enough of my mother— to know how much I missed him." The dream reflects the son's present struggle between a murderous defense against submission and a passionate yearning for paternal acknowledgment of his manhood. The paranoid reverberations of his past, examined in the struggle of his adolescent life, freed the young man from the fixation on the dyadic father and facilitated his advance toward the oedipal position. Alongside this developmental progression the compulsive and defensive need for "having sex" gave way to a wish and a budding capacity to form a relationship of a sexual as well as a personal, emotional, and romantic nature with a girl. This kind of relationship became his ego-syntonic model of a heterosexual partnership, an attainment usually slow in arriving and even slower to be trusted unconditionally in spite of the rejections and disappointments which intimate relationships necessarily entail.

Returning to the discussion of analytic developmental theory, I must admit that much of what I had attributed to triadic relationships in my first realization of the adolescent boy's libidinal attachment to the father had to be relegated to the dyadic phase. In other words, the oedipal father of the isogender complex is intrinsically fused with the father of the dyadic "preoedipal" period. The regressive pull to the father of the dyadic phase becomes apparent when the adolescent boy is viewed in a developmental continuum, as outlined above. Pursuing this course of thinking and developmental allocation in the analytic work with adolescent boys and adult men, it became apparent to me that the loved and loving father of the dyadic and triadic period—in traditional parlance, of the preoedipal and oedipal period, i.e., the father of the "negative" complex—ascends to a paramount conflictual position at the terminal stage of adolescence. Once alerted to this phenomenon, I became used to its omnipresence as a normal constituent of the male adolescent process; gradually I desisted from relegating the manifestations of these inordinate passions to the realm of abnormal development or oedipal psychopathology. It is no uncommon observation, especially if derived from the microscopic scrutiny of the tidal currents of emotions as is possible in analytic work, that isogender libidinal drives break through after their relative calm of the latency years has passed. These urges do not represent *prima facie* a homosexual inclination or disposition, as stated already, but rather confirm that the normal adolescent formation of male sexual identity is on its way. What we observe, then, are the emotional and expressive manifestations of the normal isogender complex in the state of decline.

The above does not intend to say that the boy in latency has no father conflicts, but it does say that it is the oedipal father who is the dominant imago at this stage. Not until puberty and adolescence do we observe the reascendance of the infantile dyadic father imago; in its course, the boy fights his way through the alternatives of passive surrender (dyadic) and rivalrous competitiveness (triadic-oedipal). This is the familiar drama of the decline of the isogender complex. The simple dichotomy which the separation into the above-mentioned stages implies requires a corrective because what we observe is an overlapping or blending of stage specificities. The polarity of active-passive plays a role in both stages. It is the context in which the two modalities of object relations, active and passive, are experienced by the child, which evokes the shift from a dyadic or linear to a triadic or triangular object involvement. Thus novel emotional complexities of a higher order are evoked which justify the differentiation between the two developmental stages, their distinction being basic to my discussion.

I am fully aware that the dynamics which I have outlined above were adumbrated in the past by insightful and intuitive psychoanalysts, even though their awareness was not integrated at the time into the psychoanalytic theory of development, object relations, and neurosogenesis. We had to wait for the systematic work in psychoanalytically founded infant research; its data accrued over time in new developmental schemata which widened the scope of the genetic and developmental point of view in pychoanalytic theory. As early as 1951 Hans Loewald made the following comment of a general developmental nature: "Against the threat of the maternal engulfment the paternal position is not another threat of danger, but a support of powerful force" (p. 15). Margaret Mahler in 1955 confirmed this finding by saying that "the stable image of a father or of another substitute of the mother, beyond the eighteen-months mark and even earlier, is beneficial and *perhaps a necessary prerequisite* [italics mine] to neutralize and to counteract the ego-characteristic oversensibility of the toddler to the threat of re-engulfment by the mother" (p. 209). Both statements refer in equal measure to boy and girl infant; in both statements the observer of infant behavior conceptualizes the toddler's vacillation between a regressive pull and a forward spurt of development, so typical of this age. This stage of growth is abstracted by the infant researcher in the ominous term of "the re-engulfing mother." This term refers to the typical dilemma of the toddler and not to a proprietary assault by a mother on her infant child. Both statements refer to the infant's regressive pull, externalized by the infant's behavior and abstracted by the observer of the infant in easily misunderstood terminology.

Some contributors to this specialized field of infant studies should be mentioned. Ernest Abelin (1971, 1975, 1977) is a psychoanalytic researcher and clinician who has paid particular and enlightening attention to the development of the early relationship between infant and father during the dyadic period. We are also indebted to John Munder Ross (1977, 1979) for his comprehensive overview of the relevant research that deals with the role of the father in the development of the young child from its beginnings and onward through the early formative years. His overview is enriched by his own observations and ideas, which he brings to bear on his critique of the literature. We owe, furthermore, original and extensive contributions, based on clinical work in this field, to James Herzog (1980). These contributions, mostly of rather recent years, had all been adumbrated by the seminal work of Margaret Mahler in infant and child development research which had extended over several preceding decades.*

The Status of the Father Complex in Psychoanalytic Theory

Returning to the mainstream of my deliberations, I remind the reader that I have submitted so far two theoretical statements which are the outcome of my analytic work with adolescent boys. As the next step I endeavor to integrate them into the body of psychoanalytic theory, its schema of development, and the dynamics of neurosogenicity. Let me inject the statement, even though it may be obvious, that I had analyzed children prior to concentrating on writing extensively about adolescence and, furthermore, that my analytic work with men up and beyond the age of 50 permitted me to search for validation, refutation, or modification of my theoretical propositions regarding male development and male adolescence in particular. One of the two propositions, as I have already stated, attributes to adolescence the final resolution of the isogender complex, implying that the resolution of the "complete Oedipus complex"—using Freud's phrase, to which I shall return later—proceeds in a biphasic progression. The basic resolution of the triadic or Oedipus complex is achieved early in life; then it is resuscitated and brought forward in adolescence in order to rework it in the light of sexual maturation. At this stage the dyadic father attachment encounters its fatal clash with progressive development, the Armageddon of the male isogender complex. The other proposition states that much of what had been generally attributed to the revival of the oedipal father in adolescence is more profitably understood—as to origin and nature—if related to the father imago of the dyadic period. Such an adjudication requires evidence to be persuasive.

---

* References to her work are listed in Mahler et al. (1975).

Preliminary to the introduction of clinical evidence I assume that a differentiation—even a tentative and incomplete one—between the son-father relationship of the dyadic period and that of the triadic period should be welcome. The dyadic father takes over from the early mother some significant portions of infantile attachment emotions, inclusive of the split in good and bad object. Should the father at this stage serve only as a simple displacement or replication of the mother, then the relationship can be expected to become pathogenic; this is to say that it prevents, primitivizes, delays, or arrests the normal advance of differentiation in object and self-representations. Entanglements or residues of a symbiotic kind seem to survive encapsulated or cut off from the expanding realm of the ego, lingering in some disavowed region of the mind. The consequences of this condition are clinically observable during development as contributive to characterological or emotional infantilism of various kind and degree. Should the father, however, be perceived and used differently by his son, then a healthy expansion and enrichment of the child's incipient personality becomes discernible. The father assumes for the little boy early in life a charismatic quality in his physical presence, which differs in its constitutional disposition and bodily responsiveness from that of the mother. The respective ways the father and the mother hold the infant or play with him demonstrate well the variance, or disparity, of which I speak. The father of the dyadic period is indeed a facilitator who, in conjunction with the mother, activates the individuation process and finally becomes for his son a savior from the beckoning regression and the threatening reengulfment during the rapprochement subphase (Mahler, 1955). The infant's father experience of this stage emerges slowly with the rudimentary beginnings of a self-representational system in the child's mind; this early father experience is destined to serve as a lifelong protector against the dangers of regression or, more generally speaking, against the existential drift toward predifferentiative oneness, namely merger with the object world, which might be referred to as "individuation undone."

The dyadic father has been called "uncontaminated" due to the fact that he has never been a full-fledged symbiotic partner. He belongs to the postdifferentiation, preambivalent, idealizing stage of early object relations. Jealousy is indeed already noticeable as what might be called jealousy of object availability and as the quest for total object possession. However, the son's turn to the father is not yet affected or burdened by sexual jealousy, patricidal conflict, and retaliation anxiety. These emotional discordances belong to the father of the oedipal era. The triadic configuration confronts the child with the contradictory sexual passions toward the primary caretakers, who have by now become genitally desired and feared love objects. Furthermore, these novel passions are due to the nature of the triadic conflict, endowed with sexual, gender-differentiated strivings toward both parents. The dyadic father of the little boy, if carried forward into the triadic configuration, cannot escape from being coveted by emotions and arousals of a genital kind.

Alongside these typical oedipal strivings with gratificatory and identificatory aims in relation to both parents of the little boy, the dyadic son-father relationship preserves during the oedipal phase the originally idealizing and tender emotional qualities of earlier days. The dyadic father emotion and imagery are never buried or totally absorbed in derivative psychic formations until the closure of adolescence; but even then, traces of the dyadic father realm remain active in determining certain specially valued, attentively guarded, ego-syntonic activities, attitudes, convictions, and beliefs of adult life. Pursuing these general comments further, I venture to say that the boy's dyadic ("preoedipal") father imago takes form as the so-called isogender complex during his oedipal phase, when we might think of it as being organized and structured by the unfolding of the triadic experience. With the fading of the dyadic object relation its actuality fades into the unsubstantiality of an imago, leaving its impact and imprint on a series of transformations; one of these, the adult ego ideal, I shall discuss later at greater length.

The reference to an isogender ("negative") complex assigned to the dyadic ("preoedipal") period becomes subject to conceptual problems. Only in retrospect, from the oedipal vantage point, can we apply the above terminology because the dyadic father bonding is the genetic forerunner from which the definitive isogender, or "negative," complex of the triadic, or oedipal, constellation emerges. It is in this restricted sense that I speak of an early father complex. My adolescent research suggests that this complex survives the oedipal period without being drawn into the process of resolution that brings the allogender Oedipus complex, i.e., the triadic constellation, to its decline. The idea of a belated resolution of the isogender complex at adolescence forced itself on my mind by the eloquent role which this emotional state and its conflictual elaboration play in the analysis of every male adolescent.

When I once made a comment to an older male adolescent about his analysis, speaking in the metaphor of his dwelling in complacent, unconflicted, and timeless comfort in his analytic cocoon, he responded with the recall of a blissful mood, similar to the one that suddenly had welled up in him when I spoke. He remembered the precious occasions when he was permitted as a little boy to sit quietly in his father's study while the father worked at his desk. He reexperienced in the analytic situation the dyadic bliss of such childhood happenings, which over the years had acquired a timeless and intrinsic quality of what life is all about. In pursuit of this recollection the patient came to realize that his lifelong thirst for great accomplishments and fame not only was due to the meekly attempted and prematurely abandoned competition with his father, but—more basically—embodied his passionate quest for his father's love, indeed, for union and oneness with him. When the patient gleaned this insight through the vehicle of transference interpretations, he was deeply moved and said, "It feels like being accepted for the first time in my father's arms or to have a life of my own, not just playing at it." What originally had led to the neurotic stalemate in the life of this youth was his need for the continuation of dyadic bonding, which in turn left only make-believe or inauthentic action open to him in his never ending effort to transcend the fixation on the dyadic father imago.

The dyadic father attachment and the sharing of father greatness became arrested in this case on the level of sharing, mirroring, and imitation. It had never progressed to the level of identification because it remained cathected with object libido and was left therefore outside the realm of the autonomous ego. The son admired the father, who could work, while he himself could only keep frantically busy, propelled by exalted anticipations. What he called "work" remained on the level of "foreplay," to which we might refer in this context as an infantilization of the "work principle." In his despair of never fulfilling his father's or his own expectations, of not being able to give his father or himself the gratification of accomplishment, the young man finally started to blame his father for not using his extraordinary mind to the fullest and doing great things, which in turn would provide the son with hope and trust in himself by reflection. The awareness of his emotional father involvement was summarized by the patient in saying, "If I'll ever be able to let anything or anybody go for good—and what else is growing up all about?—I have first to say goodbye to my father." We might paraphrase his words to read, "Goodbye to my dyadic father." The fact that he could not tolerate the deidealization of the father at adolescence fixated his emotional development at the stage of terminal childhood, i.e., adolescence, consolidating his neurosis on the threshold of adult life. I speak here of the deidealization of the father as a symbolic patricide which sets the son free by setting into motion the deidealization of the self.

The character pathology of this case was one of a pernicious, debilitating pseudo-purposefulness and chronic incompleteness of action. The patient's insight into the problem just outlined led to a forward move toward identifications along the father series in which the analyst was a representative if not indeed the first. It manifested itself in treatment as the therapeutic alliance; instead of constant lateness and missed appointments, the commitment to our work became finally a shared enterprise.

The Reciprocity of Fatherhood and Sonship Positions

At this point I have to introduce a correction in the protrayal of the dyadic son-father relationship, of which—so I fear—I have given too idyllic a picture. What has to be introduced are the father's ambivalent emotions toward his infant son, which throw dark shadows over his infantile exuberance and lust for life. Even when love, pride, and devotion are the father's manifest and self-avowed emotions, negative feelings are bound to drift into the relationship. They remain, as a rule, unacknowledged by the father; they remain unconscious. However, if not neutralized to some degree, they tend to affect adversely the early son-father attachment. The father who harbors feelings of envy and resentment and death wishes toward his son is dramatically represented in the Greek myth by King Laius, who set out to kill his infant son Oedipus by abandoning him with the help of a shepherd in the wilderness to certain death. The inference that the unnatural deed which Laius committed was evoked by the voice of an oracle only speaks of the ubiquitous danger of hostile emotions which the birth of an infant son unleashes in the father. The oracle, then, had only spelled out the King's unconscious misgivings about his son, thus leaving the moral responsibility of murder to the gods, who had given the father a warning in good time to secure his own safety by resorting to infanticide. Should the father's premonitions be acted upon as real and valid, as in the case of Laius, then the father becomes a primary accomplice in the son's fulfillment of the projected role in which he has been cast, resulting in revolt or submission, patricide or suicide. Normally, negative paternal emotions are reduced to insignificance under the onrush of joy and elation elicited by paternity. John Munder Ross (1982) has written a persuasive paper on this issue, designating this particular component of the oedipal configuration as the Laius complex which every son has to face when he becomes the father of a son.

The effects of the father's negative emotions, such as jealousy, envy, and vengefulness in relation to his infant son, are far less well studied and reliably ascertained than the negative emotions of the mother and her potentially deleterious influence on the infant's capacity to thrive, which is nowadays an accepted factor in the etiology of this condition.* Reasoning by analogy leads me to assume that extremely ambivalent feelings of the father toward his infant son evoke correspondingly deleterious effects. I have to leave this issue in the state of supposition because I have no first-hand experience in clinical work with infants, and published data on this issue are beginning only sparingly and tentatively to become available. On the other hand, I can submit clinical evidence of rivalrous, vengeful, and destructive feelings of fathers toward their beloved infant sons.

One representative case observation shall suffice to illustrate the

---

* "Failure to thrive" is an established diagnostic category in infant psychopathology; it refers to a critical deficit in the supply of emotional sustenance, leading to a slowdown of normal physical development and a deterioration of the infant's health.

point; it is derived from my analytic work with a 40-year-old man who had become the proud father of a wanted son. However, the "joyous" event of pregnancy and birth aroused in him recurrent waves of depression. An overpowering jealousy started to rise in him when his wife's body changed shape during pregnancy; the near presence of a rival had suddenly become real. The rival was her child, boy or girl. Nursing became the baby's theft of the breasts, which had lost some of their erotic responsiveness during foreplay, depriving the husband of his rightful possession and pleasure. All through the first year of the baby's life the father was periodically tortured by envy and resentment. Pleasurable fantasies about a motherless household shared by father and son rushed through his mind engendering momentary feelings of bliss. The ego dystonicity of his negative emotions reached a chronic state of dysphoria due to guilt and self-blame. Whenever the baby preferred his mother to his father, he felt rejected and abandoned. Such incidents were particularly painful when the husband was in need of physical contact and comfort. Once when admonished by his wife to be careful in playing with the then junior toddler, the father became depressed for days. Analytic investigation revealed that the innocent admonishment was heard by him as an accusation of harboring murderous intentions toward his son. Occasions when the child turned joyfully to the father aroused in him an upsurge of elation and happiness; these emotions gradually mediated between love and hate.* A repetition of the father's depression due to a flare-up of jealousy and hostility occurred when the child began to walk. Even though the father felt proud and pleased, he conveyed to me a sense of threat which the son's first steps evoked in him; he said, "Now I see him becoming a man." Watching the child standing up and then walking made the father exclaim, "Now there are two erect men ambulating in my house."

Let me briefly mention that the aggressive jealousy toward his wife's pregnant body made him remember his own mother "changing shape" when he was four years old. The depressive feelings of envy and rejection were residual affects related to the birth of his brother (at age four), rekindled by the birth of his son. We often observe that hostile sibling emotions merge with oedipal residues in the experience of fatherhood. In conjunction with the sibling trauma the patient reexperienced via the transference his yearning for the attention of his father, which was thwarted in early childhood by his father's emotional unavailability and

---

* The manifest problem in the child's life was a sleep disturbance. Herzog (1980) has described in detail several cases of sleep disturbances in male infants due to the chronic and gross emotional instability between father and infant son. Goethe's poem "Der Erlkönig," which reflects the son-father dyadic bond, was employed by Herzog (1980) as a literary metaphor of "father hunger" in his elucidation of a sleep disturbance in three infant boys ("Erekönig Syndrome").

paternal ineptness. My patient neutralized both these father defects effectively by father idealization and by establishing the belief that it was
the mother who kept the father from showing his love to his son. The
exoneration of his father and the preservation of the "good father" imago
were transacted via idealization. A vicious cycle was thus set into motion
which had at the core the child's conviction that the mother possessed
the power of controlling the father, the man. The fear of the castrating
mother reinforced without letup the need for idealization of the father
and denial of his hurtful weakness. A basic fear and distrust of women
was thus established and remained virulent way into his adult years.

In pursuit of these issues it became apparent that the man envied
women's procreative capacity ("to create a perfect organism that lives");
he felt incomplete, imperfect, and wanting. Experiencing these emotions
brought to the fore the most violent rage at his father, who, so he came
to realize, had never supported or acknowledged—to which I had, earlier
in this essay referred to as "blessing"—his masculine identity. He came
to discover at this advanced age the disavowed incompetence of his father,
his weakness, selfishness, and fake generosity. To quote: "My father was
a coward. He sacrificed me to my mother, never protected me from her,
was never there when I needed him. How I tried to please him, always
be perfect, be a good boy, but—I could never win him over. I loved
him. I always saw him as wise, strong, and stable. He was the only one
who could have rescued me, but he was too weak, too afraid of my
mother." When these buried emotions finally burst forth, they erupted
in a melange of murderous rage, yearnings for love, feelings of resentment,
of loss, abandonment, and finally mourning. Deeply shaken by the onslaught of these bewildering affects, tears came to the man's eyes, proving
to both of us the genuineness of his lost and found emotions.

The resolution of the dyadic father fixation initiated the gradual
forward move into the oedipal position. Instead of the infantile polarities
of good or bad, there appeared now a "whole person" recognition of
the father. The son began to acknowledge the fact that his father "could
work extremely well" despite the domestic difficulties with a troublesome
wife. The primitive, illusory dichotomies of the father imago were lifted
to the integrative perception of a higher developmental level, the triadic,
oedipal stage.

Contemplating this case in conjunction with other cases of fathers
who had very young children while in analysis, I am ready to state that
fatherhood arouses emotions from the father's own sonship experience—
dyadic and triadic—which has to be brought into intergenerational harmony with the actuality of having become a partner—the senior male
partner, to be correct—in a new family. When Therese Benedek (1959)
spoke of parenthood as a developmental phase, the conditions she had
in mind included the one which I have described in terms of a mutually
formative experience between father and infant son.

The theoretical inferences which I have stated so far in this essay throw light on many facets of normal adolescent behavior. Whenever I meet an adolescent who habitually moves subtly and facilely between mother and father, replacing without conflict, discomfort, or self-consciousness one for the other, I conclude that this youth is still—loosely or fixedly—in the developmental position of a dyadic son. Indeed, such subtle and facile shuttling from one to the other for libidinal or gratificatory contact reflects an ominous undifferentiated inconstancy of relatedness. The immaturity of this libidinal modality in object relations lies in the fact that the parental object representations are unstable, transient, and permutable. They are formed gratuitously by the adolescent's momentary need and the availability of a particular gratifier, rather than being forged by the immutable individuality of subject and object as well as by their unique grammar of interaction. A repetition at adolescence of such ad hoc plasticity and looseness of object relations, which belongs to the dyadic stage, is an indicator that some crucial genetic determinants of the adolescent disturbance under scrutiny lie in the region of that dim past. Early splitting of the object into a good and a bad one is not repeated in normal adolescence. A residual derivative of it might be found in the proverbial adolescent mood swing, affecting the love-hate fluctuations in relation to self and object. The use of polarities in the dire search for certainty and groundedness while the adolescent psychological turbulence lasts has impressed observers of this age for a long time. We find a conceptual equivalent of this trend in the assignation of such polarities as bright versus stupid, modern versus old-fashioned, loose and open versus rigid or "tight-assed," and many more, to one or the other parent or the parents' institutional substititions (teachers, political leaders, law enforcement people, etc.). The use of such rigid dichotomies reveals the adolescent's effort to transcend the reanimation of early part-object relations by bringing evaluative, i.e., conceptual, order into the outer world and thereby preventing a dangerous distortion of the sense of reality. Within the realm of these conflictual polarities the adolescent normally never loses touch with the devalued and rejected parent. This stands in contrast to the dyadic infant, for whom the attention to one parent obliterates momentarily the existence of the other, a condition typical for the infant of the stage preceding object constancy.

The juxtaposition of adolescent behavior to the findings of infant research has enriched our therapeutic ingenuity by spelling out new developmental, genetic determinants, besides having alerted us to new therapeutic modalities of adolescent-specific techniques. I like to point out in connection with these thoughts that emotional transactions via polarities, such as splitting, are adverse, indeed, contradictory and antagonistic to the object relations of the triadic phase. Abelin (1975) introduced a special terminology for this particular preoedipal constellation which involves interchangeably—at least in its early stages—both parents; he speaks of early triangulation, the endpoint of which lies in the attainment of stable mental representations comprising father, mother, and self. The completion of this internalization process leads into the triadic modality of object relations with which we have been thoroughly familiar for a long time. What Abelin calls "early triangulation" is essentially different from the triadic constellation: it is composed of a simultaneous polarity, or double dyad.

I have been vexed for some years by the fact that the role of the isogender ("negative") complex during male adolescence has not received more determined clinical and theoretical attention, commensurate to its importance, by the psychoanalytic establishment. It is a matter of record that the clinical phenomenology of the isogender complex during adolescence remained allocated to the Procrustean bed of the triadic Oedipus complex and assigned at the pubertal crisis to the conflict of either heterosexual or homosexual incest. A personal note is called for at this moment because the opinion has been expressed, at various occasions of scientific discussion on the subject of adolescence, that my developmental theory concerning male adolescence has been unduly influenced by my extensive, indeed exclusive work with male adolescents. I feel obliged to mention that my work with adolescents has been evenly distributed between boys and girls in my analytic practice and that a comparative point of view has always governed my clinical observations.

Case Illustrations about the Theorem
of the Adolescent "Crossroads"

We are well acquainted with the proverbial crossroads at which the adolescent finds himself. The reference to "crossroads" in this context should remind the reader of the spot on which Oedipus, traveling to Thebes, entered into mortal combat with Laius, his father, whose carriage stubbornly blocked the son's way. Of course, neither one of them knew who the other one was. Who would break down in the confrontation? The contest and clash of wills, as told in the Oedipus myth, reflects in paradigmatic essence the universal crisis of the adolescent boy: two sets of enticements and urges are beckoning him in opposite directions. They are those of emotional retreat to earlier childhood positions, when parental idealizations rendered life dependable and predictable, and those of aggressive self-determination and independence, leading into the unknown and unpredictable future. Within the adolescent states of resoluteness and indecision, it becomes an unforgivable offense and betrayal to the son when, in the process of paternal deidealization, he discovers his father dressed up like the proverbial emperor in his new clothes. Along the torturous passage through the adolescent labyrinth, there arises the wish that the father would once again protect his son against the gloomy sense of loneliness and abandonment which attends paternal deidealization, a loss as well as a potential liberation suddenly adumbrating with radiant hopefulness the termination of childhood and the dawn of adulthood. Both these developmental advances evoke the state of adolescent mourning: "Le roi est mort, vive le roi."

Two comments are in order here. One refers to a component of the common oppositional and self-assertive stance of the son vis-à-vis the father as a defense against passivity. This dynamic explication is convincingly supported by the fact that the analysis of repressed passivity transmutes disorganized and disorganizing oppositionalism into adaptive and organized behavior, solidifying in its course a stable as well as harmonious sense of self. The second comment refers to the theme which I shall call the search for the loving and loved father. This facet of the boy's father complex assumes in adolescence a libidinal ascendancy that impinges on every aspect of the son's emotional life. This longing as observed in male infants has been called "father hunger" by Herzog (1980), "father thirst" by Abelin (1977). The terminology itself implies the assumption of both authors that the affect of father yearning is experienced in infancy within the oral modality. Its resuscitation in adolescence appears in various guises to which I have alluded in the past (Blos, 1974). At any rate, we often have good reason to be astounded by how effectively the analytic work with the adolescent boy's father complex brings about a noticeable advance in the youth's heterosexual identity. It is the analytic work on the resolution of the isogender complex which occupies during male adolescence, recurrently and often precipitously, the center of the therapeutic stage on which the process of psychic restructuring is played out. In other words, the resolution of the Oedipus complex finds its ultimate completion at adolescence in the resolution of the preoedipal, i.e., dyadic, father relationship. This statement does not alter or invalidate the overriding importance of the boy's conflict with the oedipal father (the "murderous confrontation at the crossroads"), but addresses itself to an intrinsic component of the male father complex as a whole.

Clinically, the above theorem is not restricted to adolescence, because it assumes, more often than not, a major role in the analysis of the male adult. Not having surmounted or resolved the father complex, as in the case of an aborted adolescence, lays bare its pathogenic role in the neurotic nexus of any adult male patient. I shall illustrate the proposition just outlined from the analysis of a middle-aged man. His emotional bondage to his father was as extreme as his father's uncompromising need that his son submit to his will and live up to his expectations. The son had to play his part as expected and play it well in the role of a coded son-father interaction, staged by the father to reify his own self-fulfilling expectations of a filial image.

Way into manhood the patient was shaken by the fear that the slight-est show of self-assertion vis-à-vis his father would leave him disinher-ited, namely, rejected, abandoned, starving, lost. The love for his father—which indeed was "father hunger"—emerged in the analysis and was dramatically acknowledged. In an outburst of tears and sobbing he stam-mered the words, "I love that man." Consciously, the son resented his father all his life. He was bewildered by a role he was expected to play but which he never could bring off no matter how hard he tried. Entering analysis he announced, "I cannot hate my father for the rest of my life. It kills me." A recent succession of anxiety attacks and a turn to heavy drinking brought this tormented man to psychoanalytic treatment. In contrast to hating his father, he had always adored his mother, about whom nothing disparaging could ever be said. It was only after the analysis of the isogender complex had significantly advanced that he could see her in a light that felt to him in accordance with his genuine recovered perception of the past. He began to express doubts about her loving nature. Scrutinizing his illusory allogender ("positive") complex he found to his astonishment a cold, managerial caretaker who had "never hugged or kissed me." The patient realized that he had cast her in an idealized madonna image when the father had become a lost cause in his need for emotional closeness. Now the adult son could say, "I loved my father too much." He ceased to endear himself to father figures, and concomi-tantly he ceased to canonize women to whom he had been attracted and by whom he was disenchanted in endless succession. With these changes his addictiveness receded and lost gradually its hold on him; so also did his obsessional and ephemeral involvement with women.

This case shows in remarkable clarity the two-tiered nature of the father complex. An early traumatic experience of disappointment in the mother which collected momentum somewhere around the age of three had reached in analysis the surface of consciousness in a quasi-memory which, it seemed, might be either the recall of a fact which had the unrealness of a fantasy or the recall of a fantasy which had the realness of a fact. Regardless of this incertitude, there persevered an inner sense of conviction that "I saw my mother in bed with a man who was not my father." In the light of what I reported above about the father, it is no surprise to discover that the young child's turn to the father set in motion an everlasting disposition to passive surrender, wished for in rela-tion to men, feared in relation to women. In contrast, life as lived looked quite different. He became a conscientious but never fulfilled worker in his father's special career and a lady's man with a ceaseless succession of women. In order to follow in his father's career, he had to give up the future on which his heart was set. He found himself in a dilemma similar to the one in which Darwin was trapped in his early adulthood at the crucial point of his life to which I referred earlier in this essay.

The dyadic father bonding remained in this case the emotional core determinant of the conduct of his life, in conjunction with an idealized madonna
personification of the mother or, in other words, with a denial of her
devalued imago. These two motivations influenced decisively the direction
into which the child's object relatedness was to move. This tenuous compromise lasted until the neurosis erupted after his father's death; at this
point he started analysis.

In the context of this essay it is worth mentioning that the most
arduous effort during the course of treatment was expended in order to
arrive at the patient's ambivalence to his father in its enduring infantile
polarities. These affects came to the patient's awareness in the recall of
his condemnatory and derogatory silent diatribes he aimed passionately
at the father of early childhood during his adolescence and young adulthood when he tried desperately to blot out the intensity of his father
bonding. This piece of analytic work laid bare the man's guarded preservation of the dyadic, idealized father imago, the care he took to protect it
from aggressive deidealization, and, simultaneously, the ceaseless attempt
he made to escape from the regression to the dyadic father who had
never been much more than the boy's illusory realization of a need-fulfilling wish.

In order to convey the thoughts and emotions of that stage of analysis
which dealt most intensively with the father complex just mentioned, I
shall combine the patient's literal utterances in relation to this theme,
scattered over time but unified thematically, in the condensed form of
an extended monologue. In this way the material will speak for itself
and illustrate the theoretical formulations of this essay.

"I loved my father—I know that. What I did not know was that I
also hated him—even worse: I despised him. When I despised him, it
felt like God had come apart. I wanted my father to worship me, come
down on his knees. Oh, 'love' and 'hate' is just speaking in the broadest
terms. There is more. What? The wish to conquer him. He never returned
my love, I never could count on him. I had to worship him, to please
him to make him notice me. When I saw him drunk, when I saw him
be a bigot, a liar, I felt betrayed by him. It was the betrayal of the lover.
There is a great paradox I cannot deal with. I know that my father loved
me, but he only needed me as the son he wished to have, not the child
I was. He needed an audience, he needed praise. When people praised
him, I thought to myself, Dad is a fool. He is dressed up like important,
powerful people who are also fools. Father's smallness hurt me. Oh, this
groveling admiration which gods require! I never realized how much I
worshipped him, needed him like a god. But father expected deification—
he wanted it from me. It's the mortal's paradox that gods can't live up
to their promise, but make an ass of themselves. It was my father from
whom I wanted love and the nutrients of life. It was money he could

give me. It was this golden navel cord that tied me to him. My Lebensangst was due to losing that life blood coming from him. Starvation fear made me subservient to him.* I hate myself for this subservience and weakness. My father never acknowleged me as me. I did not exist in him, I had to be in his presence in order to exist for him. When the baby looks up from the cradle and sees his father for the first time, that's God. He had the power to extinguish me. He loved me in his way, but I was craving for his love as me, not his image of me. As a matter of speech, I feel like saying that my father should have provided for me a sandbox to play in.** I needed his backing and blessing. I always felt I had—or had to have—an angel. Now I know this angel is my father. I also know, Dad, you did the best you could. Well, you can sleep now in peace—I have no ill feelings toward you any more. The war is over." As soon as the patient had spoken these last words, he burst into tears. The nonretaliatory, nonaggressive father deidealization had made mourning possible. The patient was stunned by the upsurge of feelings; when the affective storm took possession of him, there were no words at his command to penetrate the silence.

The Theory of Stage Progression from Infancy to Adulthood

As a cogent complement to my analytic experience just cited, I am reminded of Freud's remark about the girl's resolution of her Oedipus complex. In his work with women patients he was struck by the fact that the allogender ("positive") Oedipus complex recedes into pale insignificance with the deepening of the analytic work, while the isogender ("negative") complex moves significantly into the forefront of the female patient's life. The analysis of the Oedipus complex—and Freud refers here to its allogender ("positive") component as the one subjected to analysis— comes to a standstill. Freud (1924) writes, "At this point our material— for some incomprehensible reason—becomes far more obscure and full of gaps" (p. 177). In the perplexing pursuit of this problem he came to realize that the preoedipal period exerts an influence on the emotional development of women that equals or even exceeds the influence of the allogender ("positive") oedipal position. Freud (1931) states, ". . . it would seem as though we must retract the universality of the thesis that the oedipus complex is the nucleus of the neurosis." He concludes that "this correction" is not necessary if we include in the oedipus complex the isogender ("negative") component of the girl's exclusive attachment to the mother and realize that the girl reaches the allogender ("positive")

---

* This figure of speech is linked developmentally to early infancy, the dyadic, preoedipal stage of object relations.

** This associative figure of speech is linked developmentally to the toddler age, when father hunger is at its height.

position only after "she has surmounted a period before it that is governed by the negative complex" (p. 226). Obviously, for boys and girls, the preoedipal mother attachment is a primary formation, while the father attachment for both is of a secondary nature. We know that—a distinction between boy and girl—only the girl changes the gender of the preferred love object in her progression to the triadic stage; she establishes at this level firm gender complementarity without ever eradicating all residues of the dyadic bonding. I am repeating here what has been said many times before.

What arouses my attention in this context is the fate of the dyadic father in the boy's formation of the allogender ("positive") complex or, more specifically, the fate of the isogender ("negative") complex—its resolution and its neurosogenic valence. It should be obvious that this comment refers to a far broader context than that of homosexuality. In fact, it would be appropriate and clinically supportable if we made a differentiation between the boy's isogender ("negative") complex of the triadic constellation and the boy's dyadic father complex, which belongs to an earlier stage of object relations, as well as discriminate between their respective influences on a man's love life and his sense of self. The use of the term "preoedipal" is ill advised and misleading, unless dynamically defined, because it denotes an intrinsic enmeshment with the oedipal stage proper. Due to this short circuiting of the two heterogeneous stages of dyadic and triadic object relations, their specific modality is blurred by reducing the preoedipal stage to a preparatory and immature condition of the Oedipus complex *in statu nascendi*. Developmentally speaking, every stage is preparatory to what is to follow, which says little about the essential and singular advance in the respective psychic differentiation and its consequent effect on psychic structure formation. Of course, these are the aspects of development on which we still seek enlightenment.

Freud's comment about the girl's isogender ("negative") complex and its overwhelming pathogenic influence as apparent in her neurosis invites its juxtaposition to my clinical experience with the adolescent boy. Here I can report the observation that the isogender ("negative") complex overshadows, transiently but regularly, all other genetic roots of his neurotic maladaptive condition. The multidetermination of his neurosis is repeatedly dominated by the isogender ("negative") complex. The developmental urgency of its resolution forces the issue of the father complex into a position of priority among the problems the adolescent has to attend to. In this respect one can compare the end phase of adolescence to the end phase of early childhood, one being preparatory for the entry into latency and the other one being obligatory for the forward move into adulthood. The psychic restructuring on each level is contingent on the resolution of the phase-specific component of the oedipus complex in its biphasic continuity and resolution.

In order not to be misunderstood I hasten to add that the residues or fixations pertaining to the allogender ("positive") complex are as clearly apparent throughout male adolescence as we have always considered them to be. However, our attention is aroused by the boy's conflictual, i.e., active and passive, father engagement and disengagement, both reflecting a specific quality of emotional exigency and motivational forcefulness. This should not surprise us if we contemplate—as psychoanalytic theory does—that the oedipal stage deals with the deflection of sexual libido from both primary love objects onto one, thus shaping the triadic conflict. Furthermore, it deals ultimately with the problem of libido redistribution as to aim and object, as well as to the transformation of the repressed into psychic structure. The foremost structural achievements in both genders of oedipal conflict resolutions—each with its own timing, i.e., at the imminence of latency and, later, of adulthood—are respectively the superego and the adult ego ideal.

Returning to the focus on the boy, I shall first mention the familiar theorem that the male superego preserves for good the circumstances of its origin, namely, the interdiction of incest under the threat of chastisement; it remains an agency of prohibition. The infantile ego ideal, in its proximity to object idealization and superego dominance, works against a forward move in libidinal disengagement. It preserves the dependence on the "Thou shalt" and "Thou shalt not," both being enforced by the coercing influence of guilt. Object idealization represents the precondition for the child's sense of security and safety, physically and emotionally. Its internalization establishes the infantile ego ideal. In contrast, the adult ego ideal is an agency of autonomous aspiration; as such it is guarded as a cherished and beloved personality attribute whose archaic origin lies in father attachment, father idealization, or briefly the isogender ("negative") complex. I have expressed it in these words (paraphrasing Freud): ". . . the adult ego ideal is the heir of the negative oedipus complex" (Blos, 1979). "Genetically," as Grete Bibring (1964) commented, "it [the ego ideal] derives its strength mainly from positive* libidinal strivings in contrast to the superego, in which aggressive forces prevail" (p. 517). This view is supported by the clinical fact that the adult ego ideal holds unambivalently to its position, once acquired, with steadfast loyalty.

Contemplating the period of the precompetitive son-father attachment as well as the confidence and security which the little boy derives from his father's control and domination, the conjecture presents itself that an indestructible residue of this early father trust carries over into the tumultuous arena of the triadic struggle, namely, into the oedipal stage proper. This is to say that the restraining and punishing father is also the rescuer of the son from being taken over by infantile delusions;

---

* Here the adjective is used in its dictionary definition.

this so-called rescuer is the early personification of the reality principle who makes growing into manhood an attainable expectancy, evoking loving gratitude which, as I see it, is to become immortalized in the adult ego ideal. Here Nunberg's (1932) comment comes to mind: "Whereas the ego submits to the superego out of fear of punishment, it submits to the ego ideal out of love" (p. 146). It seems that without the dual challenge of oedipal anxiety and guilt as well as preoedipal father attachment, the personality development of the boy is endangered; a disposition in the direction of social and libidinal malfunction will be in store for him. The topic of the male child growing up without a father has been widely studied statistically, clinically, and psychologically, supporting some of the inferences which I have outlined.

The description and categorization of consecutive stages in human development always obscure the overlapping and dimming of precise schedules, a fact we take for granted in clinical work. In speaking of developmental progression, we actually think along the lines of preponderances, directivenesses, and relative ascendancies. Having established this caveat, I advance with more ease to the next step in my discussion, which will explore the consequences of what has so far been said for psychoanalytic theory in general and for modification of it in particular. I am aware that the influence of infant research on psychoanalytic theory and clinical analysis was slow in coming and is still considered by some analysts an achievement of importance and interest but of minor or even negligible import for a revision of psychoanalytic theory in general and for the treatment of the neurosis in particular. I would not be surprised if the outcome of my research and its claim for amendments to the classical theory are met with both agreement and incredulity. I do acknowledge the fact that my propositions are not supported by extensive research. All I can ask from the reader is a response of critical attention and a testing by objective observation.

Psychic Determinism before and during Adulthood

The proposition of a biphasic resolution of the Oedipus complex leads to the logical conclusion that the definitive organization of the adult neurosis occurs during the terminal state of adolescence. I am saying the obvious by drawing attention to the fact that contributory and essential influences on the structuralization of a neurotic illness are identifiable all through the stages of protoadolescent development. Evoking the image of the arch, it is also obvious that its construction remains incomplete and its ultimate self-support and solid rigidity are only attained when the keystone is dropped into place. In an analogous fashion, the definitive neurosis, i.e., the adult neurosis, remains incomplete until the closure of adolescence; this moment declares that the psychobiological period called childhood is passed. Whenever a derailment of the phase-specific differentiations in psychic structure or its abnormal consolidation occurs during childhood, the developmental injury meets a last chance of spontaneous healing during adolescence. Beyond that, temperamental ingenuity and ego resourcefulness present a myriad of adaptive potentials, one of which is the neurotic compromise, the neurosis. The many life crises and subsequent neurotic distortions of normal development—one being conceptualized as the infantile neurosis—represent the psychological constituents of the cumulative process in neurosogenesis. It seems to me that their definitive structuralization has to await the termination of childhood at late adolescence. We think today of the infantile neurosis as an ubiquitous, i.e., normal, formation which in most instances is self-liquidating. Anna Freud (1970) has stated this fact succinctly by saying, "Looked at from the developmental point of view, the infantile neurosis doubtless represents a positive sign of personality growth; a progression from primitive to more sophisticated reaction patterns and as such the consequence and, perhaps, the price which has to be paid for higher human development." I venture to attribute an analogous, self-liquidating process of psychic dislocations to adolescence in general, rendering this phase a critical one for the final attainment of an either healthy or malfunctioning adult personality. At any rate, adolescence contributes decisively to the final and lasting structuralization of neurotic illness. Anna Freud (1965) has acquainted us with the perplexing fact—perplexing in light of the prevalent psychoanalytic theory—that a given childhood disturbance lends no predictive assurance as to what the ultimate neurotic disturbance might be in the life of an adult.

The assertion that the decline of the Oedipus complex proceeds in two stages enunciates—in the same breath, as it were—the opinion that psychological childhood comes to its close at the end of adolescence. To this assertion has to be added that the dyadic isogender attachment experience of the male child constitutes a basic determinant in neurotic formations as they appear in his adult life. The crucial impact of the dyadic determinant becomes manifest at the closure of adolescence because the resolution of the isogender ("negative") complex remains the task of adolescence. When I speak of a biphasic resolution of the boy's dyadic isogender ("negative") complex, I postulate that a novel thrust in this effort is at work in adolescence. This theorem stands in contrast to the classical psychoanalytic recapitulation theory of adolescence which emphasizes the overhauling of earlier conflict resolutions by living once more through the infantile conflicts, but now with an ego which is infinitely more competent than the one which had to confront the gigantic perplexities of the oedipal world. In the Brill Memorial Lecture of 1975 I reported the clinical impression that, at the end of early childhood, some oedipal issues—I was then not sure of how to identify them—fall into a stage of suspension which I referred to then as "an oedipal detente." This designation implied that certain oedipal issues, seemingly of a non-conflictual nature, do not press urgently for a settlement or resolution. They fall into the silence of a nondefensive repression, where they remain in quiescence until the somatic stage of puberty forces them into confrontation or open conflict. Then the unsettled and dormant issues of the isogender ("negative") complex acquire a traumatic and conflictual character which accounts for much of the typical mental turbulence of male adolescence.

As I have stated above, adolescence cannot be comprehended by the classical psychoanalytic recapitulation theory because certain emotional experiences and tasks do not find their normal timing until adolescence, when the developmental progression confronts the child with novel conflictual constellations. A major one is singled out for my deliberation here. The event of sexual maturation, i.e., puberty, is the biological signal that the passing of childhood has arrived; any undue prolongation of it becomes an indication of a developmental derailment by shunting processes of growth onto deviant adaptational tracks.

The shift in object choice or the adolescent displacement of the primary love object is well understood in the son-mother relationship. We are also acquainted with the treacherous gender shift in the oedipal object choice of the girl. What is less well understood is the fate of the son's libidinal father attachment. Simple displacement along isogender lines is observed only when a durable fixation prevents libidinal modulation to advance in puberty toward a heterosexual identity. Simple displacement onto object attachments along the father series (dyadic type) will endanger the son's heterosexual identity formation during adolescence or weaken and possibly prevent its formation or irreversible constancy. I shall now discuss the perplexity and predicament which every son faces when he reaches puberty or, more precisely, when the time has arrived for the transformation of the boy into a man, of the son into a potential father.

The Resolution of the Boy's Dyadic Father Complex

I have dealt with this question ever since my curiosity was aroused by the fate of the isogender ("negative") complex in the male or, in other words, by the question, what do we mean by its resolution? Repression of sexual libido and identification with the father principle, both structuralized in the superego, are the well-understood transformations which signal the resolution of the boy's allogender ("positive") complex at the decline of the oedipal stage. This resolution is buttressed by vigorous ego expansion and the conquest of reality, physically and cognitively, during latency. An analogous course to be postulated in the resolution of the dyadic isogender ("negative") complex is neither convincing nor clinically supportable; indeed, a question was left open here which keeps our curiosity still on the alert. The hiatus in our comprehension of this particular issue has its roots in the fact that the isogender ("negative") complex in the boy is usually equated in psychoanalytic writing with passivity and homosexuality. While this correspondence applies more properly to the triadic constellation, it certainly has no sweeping analogue in the boy's dyadic father attachment, even though passive trends are undoubtedly woven into this early bonding. Their descent from the infant's passive position of infantile maternal caretaking is easy to ascertain in the small child's behavior. On the other hand, we observe a gradual modulation of attachment behavior when the little boy shares, imitates, and displays actively the father's masculine posture in its polarity to the mother. The terminology we use in speaking of these phenomena tends to confuse the issue, because the male's "positive" complex is considered to be implicitly active and his "negative" complex implicitly passive.

The adolescent process of the male offered a fertile ground to observe and study clinically the issues just mentioned. I therefore want to report an observation from adolescent analysis which, by its sheer repetitiveness in several cases, brought to my attention the fact that the resolution of the isogender ("negative") complex is often followed by an intense positive father transference.* A patient's search for a model becomes distinctly recognizable. The mere fact of choosing a new model indicates that father deidealization is on its way. To this modulation of the positive transference between male adolescent and male analyst we might apply Winnicott's (1969) term "the use of an object" in order to conceptualize a developmentally normative forward move in adolescent psychic restructuring. There comes a time in adolescent analysis when the patient wishes to relate to the analyst as a real person. We detect in this changing attitude the overture to a changing perception of the paternal imago. The boy begins to perceive his father without the distortions of idealization or vilification; concomitantly, the patient's object relations in his present life become more individualized, less stereotyped and repetitive. I could ascertain a more stable and dependable ego organization. This change became demonstrable by a comparative assessment of his ego functioning during the term of the analytic work.

My critical attention in assessing adolescent change always roams over a wide behavioral repertoire, a few items of which should be named, such as the adolescent's capricious excitability; diffuse and erratic shifti-

---

* Notice in this sentence the confusing and awkward vocabulary which has evolved from the broadening conception of "the complete Oedipus complex."

ness of attention or fanatical constrictedness of interests; excessive idealization or cynical degradation of people and ideas; and, last but not least, a proclivity to random and transient identifications and counteridentifications. All these particularities yield slowly, if all goes well, to a personality of reasonable predictability and stability as to purpose, direction, and goal. With the rising clarity and firmness of "who I am" emerges simultaneously "who I am not." Erikson (1981) has been particularly interested in this aspect of the human personality and put the issue into the following words: "These habitual rejections, in turn, have helped to give a clearer outline of one's own 'true self' or to those variant 'selves' which are either proudly or fatalistically accepted as a self-description within the contemporary world of roles" (p. 331). If I understand Erikson correctly, I would conclude that the integration of these inclusive and exclusive determinations shapes and sustains the sense of identity and that they are the building blocks of the emerging adult character. In giving permanent structure to this internal inclusiveness and exclusiveness, the individual establishes, at the terminal stage of childhood, the awareness of a generational uniqueness between past and future.

With the narrowing down of the possible self-realizations in life, or the surrender of the wide array of choices and the commitment to a selected few, there emerges the emotive state of mourning the passing of childhood. The stark realization of the loss of childhood affords the growing individual a sense of the human condition as well as a sense of the tragic. The protective envelope of childhood, having been discarded, the safekeeping of purpose and meaning of life passes over into the guardianship of the self. I conceive the dynamics of this personality change in the male as intrinsically related to the resolution of the dyadic father relationship, which becomes increasingly divested of infantile bonding or attachment needs. This resolution cannot be effected by object displacement, but only by the formation of a new psychic institution, which is to say by a structural innovation, the adult ego ideal (Blos, 1974).

I think I have made it clear—perhaps redundantly clear—that in my opinion the boy faces in his adolescence the task of renouncing the libidinal bond that he had once formed and experienced in relation to the dyadic and triadic, i.e., preoedipal and oedipal, father. What attract our special attention are the vicissitudes of the "negative" complex from adolescence onward throughout a man's life. Behavioral observation has taught us that the adolescent boy possesses a particular sensitivity to social situations or interactions which contain potential entrapments into submissiveness to males or dependency on them. The same emotional reactions in his relation to females are common knowledge because he often expresses them with remarkable frankness. We know of the many ways submissiveness or dependency, real or imagined, are fought off by the adolescent boy, but we should not overlook the many ways in which

submissive modalities, directly or symbolically, are overtly or clandes-
tinely sought by him. These trends can take the form of admiration,
gratitude, followership, idealization, and the need to please. Analysis of
these trends, expressed in relation to males, father and father substitutes
as well as brother and brother substitutes, reveals a fixation on the dyadic
and triadic father, a condition which can become responsible for deviant
character formation and emotional immaturity; both become clearly discernible during adolescence. We cannot fail to recognize the analogy between, on the one hand, the individuating toddler who turns away from
the reengulfing mother seeking safe refuge in the father as his newly
discovered source of emotional protection and sustenance and, on the
other hand, the pubertal boy caught up in a similar dilemma and engaging
in a similar but extensively disguised self-rescue operation. The two-
tiered identification of the male with the dyadic and triadic father imago
becomes reconciled and stabilized in his adulthood. A middle-aged man
who had arrived in his analysis at such a newfound reconciliation, expressed his awareness of it in the following words: "I have come to believe
that there is a boy and a man in me. The boy seeks the company of
men and the man seeks the company of women."

The Emergence of the Adult Ego Ideal
and the Condition for Its Deterrence

To particularize the inferences just made, I submit a contribution from
the phenomenology of the ego ideal in transition during adolescence. I
have in mind the adolescent boy's proverbial hero worship and his search
for models of emulation, characteristically expressed in his construction
of a personal hall of fame. We observe that the personalities on posters
and record albums, inhabiting the inner sanctum of the adolescent's world,
represent his transient but intense idealizations and transient identifications. These imaginary relationships, while highly emotional, are devoid
of sexual, i.e., genital constituents and are—due to sublimatory transformations—devoid of infantile attachment emotions. The ego-syntonic affects are exclusively those of admiration, idealization, and devotion to
the respective hero's qualities of excellence and perfection, most frequently attached to personalities in the fields of sports, music, and the
stage. The bearers of these qualities are predominantly acclaimed perform-
ers and almost exclusively male. We witness here *in statu nascendi* the
socialization of the infantile ego ideal, and its transformation during adolescence to its mature form, namely, to the adult ego ideal.

A further reason for mentioning what I summarily have called the
adolescent boy's hall of fame lies in its demonstration of that unique
and powerful need for personalized and specialized idealizations which

arises at this age. This trend has been recognized as long as adolescence has been observed or studied; Aristotle (1927) described this adolescent trait in the most eloquent of terms.* Taking a look at the infantile origin of adolescent idealization, I am prepared to say that we can trace this tendency to a dual origin, namely, to the dyadic and triadic, i.e., to the preoedipal and oedipal father as the precursory relationships in the ontogeny of adolescent types of idealization. The role of the early mother in the history of the idealizing trend as a rock-bottom foundation is sufficiently familiar to us and is solidly enough established not to require its retelling in the context of this exploration.

However, it must be mentioned at this point that the adult character pathology of exaggerated loftiness and idealizing distortions of reality as well as of a compelling cynicism and debunking of the world in general constitutes a regressive phenomenon which is embedded in early ambivalences. These veer between the excesses of idealization and those of loss and abandonment. My clinical work encourages me to say that the traits mentioned above extend their roots into the realm of early object relations which leave their imprint on the sense of self and the interaction with the object world. A specific roadblock of massive proportions in the path leading from infantile bonding dependency to the expanding autonomy of the triadic stage demands our attention at this point. I have traced the origin of this predicament to a particular emotional entanglement of father and son, namely, to an overwhelming paternal need for an isogender offspring who will provide him with emotional nurturance which has been brought at last within his reach by the state of fatherhood. We might say that fatherhood as a developmental stage (Benedek, 1959) touches on the parents' experience of their own parental interaction and normally sets the stage on which particular aspects of their own child-parent experience, be they enriching or impoverishing, are played out in the role of parenthood. An ensuing libidinal interaction can lead into a twofold pathogenic stalemate: the father's infantilizing caretaking behavior, in conjunction with the emotional sustenance it affords him, draws the father ever closer to his son; conversely, the infant son becomes abnormally needful of his father's bodily ministrations and demonstrative love, thus turning into an oppressive bondage what was meant to be the liberating father attachment of the dyadic stage. A mutual bondage is thus established, held together by erotically tinged affects and sensations. This kind of emotional overload tends to form the nucleus of a pathogenic fixation. In the intense closeness to his son the father gratifies vicariously and belatedly his lifelong "father hunger." An emotional involvement of this kind always comprises a three-generational network. One might

* Relevant excerpts from Aristotle's writings pertaining to adolescence can be found in my paper "The Generation Gap" (Blos, 1971).

say that the abandoned seduction theory has reentered here along an unexpected course and in an unexpected guise. I refer to the dyadic constellation of the father seducing the son, using the word "seducing" in its wider sense of involving the young child in a kind and intensity of an attractive interpersonal experience which is phase-alien and beyond the child's capacity to cope with; therefore, the experience inhibits rather than promotes emotional development.

I have observed this kind of interaction between father and son in the analyses of several men who derived excessive pleasure from the caretaking ministrations to their infant son and possessed an overwhelming need for tactile proximity to him. I shall refer here to one case in which the child responded to the father's need by becoming a nightly visitor to his bed, always bypassing the mother. No disciplinary interference could influence the now four-year-old child to remain in his bed. The little boy kept responding to the father's unrelenting, unconscious wishes for the physical closeness to him. When the patient's deprivation of physical and emotional contact with his early father emerged in the analysis, the little boy began to listen to the request that he stay in his own room. The nightly commuting to the father's bed faded away with the patient's mounting realization that he gratified vicariously his own dyadic "father hunger" via his little son's bodily closeness. The vicarious gratification which the father experienced blinded this sensitive, caring, and sophisticated man to the inappropriateness of his behavior. Though he was conscious only of his loving intent, he nevertheless began to doubt whether his relationship to his son was a healthy one or might be infantilizing. The rise of this self-questioning awareness went parallel with the analysis of his father complex in the transference. The fear of being thrown out of his treatment in case he should fail to be a good patient (i.e., "bring dreams") mounted to abandonment terror: "How can I live without you?" The lifelong emotional distance between father and son never extinguished the flame of yearning for father contact. With tears and sobbing he came to realize how much and how hopelessly he loved his father. The analysis of the patient's role as son and as father brought belatedly a gratifying measure of harmony into his three-generational disturbance which had induced in him a sense of personal incompleteness, a state of dissatisfaction, and a life of compromise (symptom formation).

During the infantile stages father idealization is intimately bound up with the little child's dependency on external sources for his sense of physical safety and emotional security. I have earlier in this essay described how the male infant turns to the dyadic father for meeting these particular needs. They become dramatically manifest when exclusive maternal dependency (symbiotic stage) reaches the point of discord with the status quo due to the maturational progression of the infant's body and its urges to actualize these needs in an ever wider scope of interaction with his surround. The father of the triadic period is destined to inherit some of the earlier attachment emotions which the dyadic boy had shaped and established in his partnership with the father. This residue of the preoedipal object tie to the father becomes apparent in the triadic constellation when either mother or father becomes intermittently intruder and antagonist, depending on who momentarily is the preferred partner of oedipal coupling. As we know, the ascendancy of the allogender ("positive") complex evokes in its wake a clash with the reality principle, i.e., the child's physical immaturity and dependency on parental care, whose sovereignty, once accepted, leads the way to conflict resolution and mastery within its realm; in this case, changing the self gains priority over the attempt to change reality. It would be carrying coals to Newcastle if I should retell how—in the process of resolution—the superego becomes heir to the allogender ("positive") complex or how at this critical moment of development the multitude of superego precursors become unified and organized in a mental structure.

The Function of the Dyadic Isogender Father in Adolescence and Beyond

Adolescent psychic restructuring always encompasses the boy's emotional history with his preoedipal and oedipal father. The conflict which erupts at this advanced stage is twofold: it has the father not only as adversary and competitor but also as protector, partner, and mentor. While these father roles are rarely revealed by the boy's manifest behavior or his conscious thoughts, they can nevertheless be ascertained in certain facets of his social behavior, relationship with peers, daydreams, and moods (Blos, 1976). The conflict of antithetical positions reaches crucial acuteness at the stage of late adolescence and never fails to constitute a prominent issue in the boy's emotional life. It should be no surprise to observe that the resolution of the isogender ("negative") complex is sidestepped whenever the tenacity of the preoedipal father fixation proves unsurmountable. As always when developmental continuities are disrupted and shunted onto a dead-end track, a deviant kind of adaptation takes over. In that case, we witness such deviances as delinquency, characterological, social, and sexual pathologies, the eruption of a neurosis, or a psychotic break.

In the preceding exposition I have followed the boy's father complex up to the termination of childhood, which is synchronous with the closure of adolescence. In our adult male patients we never fail to observe the continuance of this issue due to the fact that its resolution was aborted or incompletely settled during late adolescence. What I refer to here as failure in the adolescent process cannot be stated in sharply defined, absolute terms, because we observe individually a great variance due to its particular contextual embedment in a developmental medley of preoedipal and oedipal trends, both being simultaneously and antithetically in motion.

Two facts which derived from developmental infant research should be mentioned here. It has been noted that the male toddler turns away from the mother and toward the father earlier than the girl. Furthermore, dyadic father deprivation exerts a far more injurious influence on the boy's subsequent adaptive faculties than is the case with the girl. These findings, borne out in the analysis of adult male patients, often beg the question whether their adaptive failures are due to a basic conflictual constellation and subsequent regression or to a developmental delay or arrest. In a considerable number of my adult analytic male patients, ranging in age from their twenties to their late fifties, the isogender ("negative") complex—in its two-tiered entanglement—appears surprisingly often as the rock bottom of their neurotic disturbance.

I remind the reader here of Freud's 1931 paper on female sexuality, to which I have referred earlier. There he calls attention to some of his women patients' all-encompassing fixation on the early mother which lies at the root of their neurotic illness. One cannot help but wonder why the male's isogender ("negative") complex, being of equal neurosogenic valence, has never received an equal measure of attention. This neglectfulness persisted despite the fact that Freud—as quoted by Ruth Mack Brunswick (1940) in her classic paper (written in collaboration with Freud) on the "preoedipal phase"—had commented at the time, ". . . on the basis of this new concept of early female sexuality, the preoedipal phase of the boy should be thoroughly investigated" (p. 266). This admonition was never fully heeded, unless we declare the preoedipal phase of the boy simply identical with a bisexual phase—a position which is hardly tenable. Clinical observation leaves no doubt that a universal constituent of normal psychosexual development, namely, a homosexual propensity, does not follow the same course or development in men as it does in women. Without doubt, its repression in men is by comparison far more profound than it is in women. Change of object, gender morphology, and cultural imprinting are in all likelihood accountable for this divergence.

The residues of the dyadic, i.e., preoedipal, attachment of son to father, lie, to a large extent, buried under a forceful repression once adolescence is passed. The profundity of this infantile experience, when roused into emotional reanimation during analysis, remains usually inaccessible in its latent intensity by verbalization alone. It finds expression via affecto-motor channels, such as uncontrollable weeping and sobbing, when the patient is tormented by overwhelming feelings of love and loss in relation to the dyadic father. One man in his fifties exclaimed at such a moment, choked by tears, "Why did I love my father so much? After all, I had a mother." In contrast to these affects of passion, the manifest and remembered son-father relationship had usually been distant or hateful, admiring or submissive, governed by a fear of rejection or grudgeful with a sense of gnawing disappointment. This latter sensation follows the boy's alert and sensitive registration of the father's shortcomings which disqualify him as the son's hero or worthy opponent. To these configurations has to be added the little boy's yielding or opposing posture toward the father's unchecked need for libidinal gratification which he seeks in the closeness to his son. In either of the little boy's extreme reactions to paternal seductiveness—surrender or flight—the son remains eternally remorseful over having failed to evoke his due measure of the father's approval, pleasure, and loving support in growing up and becoming his "big boy." Thus is the bewildering paradox of the father complex which I have described. Over time this early experience lays the foundation for a self-image of depressing inadequacy or aggressive self-sufficiency; both coalesce in adolescence into pathological forms of adaptation which become elaborated throughout adult life.

The clinical references in this essay were taken from my analytic work with male patients of various ages. Within the dyadic and triadic father transference, once manifested in treatment, it was possible to work out or resolve enough of their father complex to render their lives reasonably mature, productive, and rewarding. Pertaining to the dyadic father fixation of the male patient, it seems that an isogender transference is of special significance in his treatment because preoedipal memory traces do not readily appear in word representations, but—as already alluded to in my clinical illustrations—require affecto-motor expressions before the symbolic process via verbal communication can serve the work of insight and reconstruction.

A question to be asked here concerns the dyadic father transference when the analyst is a woman. In the literature on this subject, which is extraordinarily scant, our interest is aroused by Laila Karme's paper (1979), which raises relevant questions of clinical importance in this area of unsettled observation as well as conception. The opinion taken as axiomatic for a long time states that "the repetition of the complete Oedipus complex is an essential part of all analyses"* (Glover, 1955). It was, therefore, taken for granted that transference repetitions are not limited by the sex of the analyst. This assumption, which is presently challenged, predates the growing conviction that the dyadic father complex of the male

* The term "complete Oedipus complex" came into use in the psychoanalytic literature in order to extend the definition of the original Oedipus complex to include the dyadic phase (preoedipal), once its importance in neurosogenesis was recognized in its universal, often dominating, role.

patient is not satisfactorily comprehended within the confines of what
has summarily been called the homosexual or "negative" transference.
Is there any substantive difference to be observed in cases where the
male patient's analyst is a woman?

Under these circumstances, we might ask, is the patient's isogender
("negative") complex in the transference the manifestation of a homosexual father fixation, as a prevalent interpretation claims it to be? We have
probably paid too little attention to the threat a woman analyst poses
at one point for her male patient. He reexperiences in her the dyadic
"reengulfing mother" who becomes in the transference the castrating
woman from whom the adult male patient seeks protection in his flight
to the sanctuary of isogender partnership. This position is identical with
what we refer to as the dyadic isogender ("negative") complex. Evaluating
this defensive position from a developmental point of view, we must
affirm its growth-promoting potential. Speaking of the "castrating
woman," we imply a sexual specificity which has become welded at later
stages to the early avoidance of the mother as the tempting source of
passive dependency; this renders her a "feared" object who becomes gen-
eralized and prototyped as "woman."

What Freud (1923) has referred to as "an affectionate feminine attitude [of the boy child] to his father" is not *prima facie* feminine, because
this very position serves to protect the boy's masculinity and his progressive development against stunting or destruction by the "reengulfing"
or "castrating" mother or, more precisely, by the child's fear of his own
menacing surrender to his regressive pull. This normative stage in infantile
object relations I have extensively dealt with in this essay. Extension of
all normative stages beyond their normal timing leads to a lopsided development, namely, to some form of maladaptation. This applies certainly
to the boy's dyadic father complex, which represents his effort to distance
the symbiotic mother. A fixation at this stage leads in the male's allogender
object relations to all kinds of avoidances and fears or to compulsive
affirmations of their opposites. When this fixation is finally drawn into
the physical process of sexual maturation, it is no surprise to witness
that the father complex brings homosexual trends to the fore as an unavoidable complement to a never abandoned father idealization and vigi-
lant resistance to maternal dependency.* This all now awaits its fitting
into the realm of clinical psychoanalysis. I think the question of the
"negative" complex in the transference of the male patient to the female
analyst can only be answered by a woman analyst. I therefore caution
myself not to voice opinions which have no authentic foundation in my
analytic experience by virtue of my being male. I want to mention just
one of Dr. Karne's (1979) findings; she states that in her case ". . . a

---

* This schema offers by no means a valid etiology for male homosexuality in general.

paternal homosexual transference did not develop . . . the maternal transference persisted" (p. 266). No analogous transference limitations or re-
strictions were observed by her within any other gender combination
of analyst and analysand, nor were they reported by other analysts, male
or female.

I have spoken extensively throughout this presentation about the
boy's relationship to the father of the dyadic and triadic stage, about
the continuities and discontinuities in the transition from one to the other,
and, particularly, about the influence of this relationship experience on
the fate of the isogender ("negative") complex on male personality formation. I feel now called upon to give the inferred discrimination between
the dyadic and triadic father some substantive specificity. First and foremost, the dyadic father becomes heir to the infantile split into the good
and the bad primordial mother, into that dual "other" who arouses pleasure or pain, satiation-comfort or need-tension. Mahler (1975) has referred
to this infantile split into part objects as "ambitendency" in contrast to
"ambivalence," because the latter term implies the existence of object
constancy and whole-object representation. Ambivalence proper is not
acquired and fully developed before the triadic stage. Adolescent analysis
has taught me that the preoedipal father provides the boy with a source
of security and the implicit protection against the powers of regressive
needfulness; in addition, the preoedipal father actuates in the little boy
the experience of male congruity and sameness. Partaking in the father's
maleness represents the early stage of gender identity; here lie the tender
roots of identification. In their fully developed strength they will, at a
later time, bring the oedipal stage to its decline. In relation to the preoedipal father we are ready to say that the dominant affect of the little boy
is one of affection, body contact pleasure, involving large-muscle activity
with imitation of movement, and, furthermore, attachment behavior in
continuity and expansion of mother-infant interaction. In the balance
between passive and active trends the latter normally gain in ascendancy
with age, which augurs well for the boy's gender-specific development
during the triadic confrontation. If the father continues to remain subject
to the infantile split in object relations, then a condition arises which
weakens and possibly aborts the oedipal challenge. It has been my impression from the observation of adolescent transferences that the preoedipal
son-father attachment is normally without any narrow genital focus; exci-
tation and pleasure arise as a sensory response of the whole body—especially its musculature—of which the penis is a component, a *primum inter
pares.*

The dyadic isogender attachment emotions do not implicitly promote
a feminine orientation in the boy. Therefore, the determinant of male
homosexuality is not to be found in this stage of development. However,
should a preoedipal father fixation prevent the boy from renouncing the

dyadic bond, then the persevering preoedipal tie becomes alloyed with the sexual passions of the oedipal stage; in other words, the attachment emotions merge with the wish to replace the mother in pleasing the father and to be pleased by him; this can be couched in the wish to have a baby or in its forceful disavowal via overbearing, obstreperous, self-asserting behavior. Under these auspices, a homosexual threat is woven into the ultimate fabric of the boy's postoedipal psychosexual organization. A dyadic father fixation is not, in my opinion, a precursory condition for the homosexual drive to gain ascendancy; oedipal determinants are too well known as contributory factors which act more decisively for such a lasting outcome to be established. Should the fear of the engulfing mother or the castrating female be regressively and defensively revived at this phase, then the boy's flight to the father or, generally speaking, to a male object choice reveals the preoedipal determinants in his sexual orientation. The forcefulness of the dyadic father attachment loses normally its exclusivity, following the example of mother attachment, with the onrush of oedipal object relations. Before closing this discussion on the discrimination between the boy's dyadic and triadic father relationship, I wish to point out that the preoedipal tie is governed by the fear of loss of object availability (i.e., "love") and a delusional sense of invulnerability; the latter is acquired through attachment to the father and secured by emulation of him. In contrast, the oedipal relationship is governed by fear of retaliation and feelings of guilt. In both stages we observe jealousy and envy, yet with a difference: In the early stage, the libidinal cathexis fluctuates to and fro toward one or both parents in an interchangeable and needful turnabout. In the oedipal stage, it advances to significantly more stabilized and differentiated object ties, specific for father and mother, male and female.

The Influence of the Dyadic and Triadic Stages on the Evolution of Cognitive Thinking

In order to convey my observations relative to the development of relations, I have made use of a conceptual differentiation between the dyadic (preoedipal) and triadic (oedipal) stages in their sequential transition and typical specificities. Both stages in their normal development were described in their decisive but not identical influence on psychic structure formation, on the modulation of affective life generally, on the growing complexity of cognition, comprehension, and creative articulation, and, last but not least, on the formation of social, sexual, and self identity formation. That both complexes have been coexistent but qualitatively and quantitatively variable within limits throughout keeps that essential degree of psychic tension alive without which psychic metabolism ceases and the continuity of psychic homeostasis is in jeopardy. The residual reverberations of both complexes can be traced throughout a man's life even though they have become stabilized in preferential object relations, social role, occupation, hobbies, and character structure. Their reflexive maintenance is analogous to the healthy functioning of the body.

In speaking of the two complexes, I have always emphasized the fact that their incomplete and therefore disequilibrating resolution constitutes the "nucleus of the neurosis." Due to the limited attention extended to the isogender, i.e., "negative," complex and the almost exclusive attribution of neurosogenesis to the workings of the allogender, i.e., "positive," complex, a fertile field for analytic exploration lies in front of us. This statement is only relatively correct, because in clinical work the facts to which I have alluded throughout this presentation have never escaped the attention of the discriminative clinician. However, I venture to say that the role of the dyadic father as a factor in male neurosogenesis has received only marginal—i.e., case-specific versus case-universal—acceptance in the contemporary theory of the neurosis. In the field of adolescent disturbances of the boy, there has been a marked acceptance of a pathogenicity which is rooted in the dyadic stage.

There is, however, one more thought which I shall relate before closing this essay. It is a digression of a speculative nature. I mentioned earlier in this essay that the dyadic stage operates in polarities which are reflected in the split into "good" and "bad" objects. The cognitive level of thought, when restricted to the exclusive use of polarities, is of a primitive nature and of limited efficiency because complexities are dealt with in terms of simple dichotomies. The advance to the triadic stage lifts the thought process onto a higher level, or, to be exact, it establishes the precondition for this advance. We might say that the triadic complexity of object relations with the implicit rise onto a higher level of conflict formation produces an infinite multitude of possible constellations within its realm; of these, a selected few are retained and stabilized in the process of transcending the triadic stage.

The oedipal complexity of interpersonal experiences is reflected on the cognitive level in the emergence of the dialectic process. We recognize in this process the triadic nature of thesis, antithesis, and synthesis. The complexity of this thought process permits, by choice or by fortuity, an endless sequence of possible cognitive combinations or permutations, each pressing forward toward a resolution on a higher level of thought. We might speak here of a mental strain or tension in the cognitive sphere as a stimulus to problem solving in thought, or of mental inventiveness analogous to triadic conflict resolution, which was kept in motion by the relentless influx of antagonistic affects, such as pleasurable object possession versus unpleasurable conflictuality, until finally a satisfactory measure of resolution was attained.

From postulating a biphasic resolution of the Oedipus complex it would follow by implication that the so-called higher levels of thought make their appearance at the time of its terminal resolution, which occurs in the adolescent period. This theoretical assumption finds a validation in the adolescent research by Inhelder and Piaget (1958). To quote: "The adolescent is the individual who begins to build 'systems' or 'theories' in the largest sense of the term . . . the adolescent is able to analyze his own thinking and construct theories" (p. 337). The capacity to carry out such mental operations declares the readiness of the adolescent mind to deal with the abstractions inherent in ideologies, philosophy, epistemology, and science. The child does not possess a thought faculty of this kind. The investigators claim that these higher thought constructs serve the purpose of furnishing "the cognitive and evaluative bases for the assumption of adult roles. They are vital in the assimilation of the values which delineate societies or social classes as entities in contrast to simple inter-individual relations" (p. 340).

I have commented on the fact that the primitiveness of thought, anchored in dyadic object relations, stands in stark contrast to the intricacy of the dialectic thought process. The triadic state is concerned with self, object, and identity, as well as with object-directed emotional and sexual issues; it transcends its infantile origin and instinctual involvement by perpetuating its existence in the cognitive sphere, namely, in the interminable effort to comprehend the world and the self in ever more complex terms and configurations.

I have traced in my deliberations the mutual influence of drive and ego development throughout the male child's dyadic and triadic father relatedness as it proceeds within a changing soma and social surround during the first two decades of life. I have made the effort to conceptualize the normal developmental progression in male personality formation with explicit references to the fate of the boy's dyadic father relationship as well as his isogender ("negative") Oedipus complex in general. In a broad sense, I have dealt with the reciprocal integration of sonship and fatherhood. The fact that every father has been a son weaves his own sonship experience into the new context of a generational continuum. These considerations, restricted as they are in scope and gender, assign to the dyadic father complex a nuclear role in neurosogenesis as well as recognize in it an etiological factor in relation to specific forms of psychopathology throughout the male life cycle.

Before I close, I will turn over my voice to a little seven-year-old Puerto Rican boy, a second grader in the New York City public schools, who gave his teacher what he called "A tiny poem to my Dad."

It reads:

You are like a strong kite
*   waiting for the wind*
and the sweet snow that loves me
and the hurt tiger that needs my help.

PART TWO

Some Literary References to the Dyadic Son-Father Connection

Tradition is much more than the memory.
Is it experience, say, the final form
To which all other forms, at last, return,
The frame of a repeated effect, is it that?
It has a clear, a single, a solid form,
That of the son who bears upon his back
The father that he loves, and bears him from
The ruins of the past, out of nothing left,
Made noble by the honor he receives,
As if in a golden cloud. The son restores
The father. He hides his ancient blue beneath
His own bright red. But he bears him out of love,
His life made double by his father's life,
Ascending the humane. This is the form
Tradition wears

from a poem by Wallace Stevens, "Recitation after Dinner"

CONTENTS

Prefatory note

The two essays which follow require a few words of introduction to indicate their intended scope and the purpose of my endeavor in using the literary works which I have chosen. It seems unavoidable that the subject of these essays—by the sheer weight of their acknowledged eminence—will invite in the reader expectations of a far broader reach and compass than I wish to address. The thoughts expressed in what follows may be congenially subsumed under the literary genre of the "aperçu" or "reflection"; they are not to be placed on a par with a treatise in literary criticism which encompasses the author's work under scrutiny in its entirety or in the whole complexity of its possible ramifications. Quite to the contrary, in my literary criticism I try to apply a specific developmental principle to a given text in order to explore its validity and its usefulness for deepening our comprehension of that work.

It should be kept in mind that the thesis I have advanced in the preceding discourse contains propositions of a circumscribed scope, representing specific aspects of male development which are traceable from the cradle to the grave. My findings and formulations pertaining to the son-father relationship in its reciprocal interplay and intergenerational circularity are brought to bear on the three subjects of the discussion which follows.

Embedded in this enterprise lies the conviction that the specificities of male development as described in the opening chapter of this book represent the universal condition of being a male child and becoming a man. In order to describe this specific human condition and relate it to the gender-related aspect of male personality, I have subjected the developmental stages with regard to object relations and psychic structure formation to a detailed study. From the theoretical formulation of male gender-specific stage progression I ventured to establish a congruity with the phenomenology of behavior, thought, and affect as these are typical for the mutuality of a son-father relationship. A connection between clinical observation and theoretical formulation, once established with reasonable accuracy, promised to advance a measure of insight into works of literature wherever the son-father theme makes its distinctive presence felt.

I have selected two works for my interpretive paper, a letter written by Kafka with an addendum on Freud's Schreber Case, and Shakespeare's *Hamlet*. Whatever my findings have to contribute to the clarification of these literary works I express here as additions to an ongoing deliberation on these works—especially *Hamlet*—which have been widely, expertly, and profoundly discussed over time by many eminent minds the world over.

Commentary on Franz Kafka's autobiographical document of sonship

Letter to His Father (Brief an den Vater) 1919*

Introductory comments

Thematic issues of the *Letter*
  Father idealization
  Submission to the father
  Persecutory ideas
  In search of an emotional truce

* The edition used for this study is Franz Kafka, *Letter to His Father*, bilingual edition, translation by Ernst Kaiser and Eithne Wilkins. New York: Schocken Books, 1966.

Introductory Comments

In 1919, when Kafka was 36 years old, he made a desperate effort to bridge the emotional abyss that had existed over a lifetime between himself and his father. The bridge he constructed was in the form of a letter; he hoped that such an indirect voice could bring to his father's attention the most personal and intimate feelings and thoughts about him which he had never been able to express in a face-to-face encounter. The *Letter* comprises 59 printed pages. It reads like a lifelong monologue on Kafka's struggle and ultimate defeat in dealing with the challenges of his sonship. It reads like a last and frantic attempt to unearth a hidden bedrock of good feelings between father and son which neither of them was sure could ever be reached, even though both believed in its existence. The *Letter* reads like the draft of a peace treaty which might succeed in laying the distress of mutual mistrust, accusations, and disharmonies to eternal rest. As it happened, the *Letter* was never delivered to the father because the son chose his mother as his mail carrier; she chose to return the *Letter* to its author in order to spare her husband a confrontation she knew he would have thoroughly disliked. The *Letter* reveals in its extraordinary candor the son's tortured relationship with his father, touching eloquently on the passionate interplay of sonship and fatherhood which I have described in developmental terms in the preceding essay.

The original title in German reads "Brief an den Vater." The English translation "Letter to his father" fails to convey the subtlety of spirit and unique innuendo of the original. Literally translated it would read "Letter to *the* father." "His father" objectifies the addressee as to his genealogical position. "The father" (*"den* Vater") implies that there is only one father, namely *the* father, just as there is only one God. There is ample evidence in the *Letter* that father and God played for the author identical roles, especially in childhood but also later in life. To address the *Letter* to "the father" infuses the salutation with a sense of awe. We might ask ourselves the question, why Kafka did not simply call it "Letter to my father" (in German, "Brief an meinen Vater")? The subsequent discussion may throw light on the use of the impersonal title for this most personal piece of writing. Furthermore, I like to point out that the feeling tone of the German salutation "Liebster Vater" is not quite captured by the English of "Dearest father," because the German contains an admixture of affection which would best be captured by the words "Beloved father"; this salutation, however, conveys in English a too demonstrative emotional intimacy. I admit that these are matters of delicate subtlety where the translator had to avoid either "too much" or "too little." The bilingual edition gives the reader the opportunity to restore by his own discrimination the loss of exactitude generally inherent in translations.

The *Letter* is a human document *par excellence* and occupies a prominent place in the literature of great confessions. For this reason I have chosen it to illustrate the vicissitudes of a specific son-father relationship that failed to keep pace in its emotional growth with the normative stages of childhood and adolescence. As a consequence, the grown son became possessed by his infantile father imago; he could live neither with it nor without it, and thus was restricted and constricted to live lastingly through the tragedy of an unquieted emotional longing and loneliness. If there ever was an unabated father hunger, the *Letter* is its epic documentation. In the most general terms, the *Letter* expresses the tenacity of a son-father attachment which was never consummated or relinquished. The virulent father bonding exerted a devastating influence on the son's growing personality. This the *Letter* spells out in the most lucid of terms, describing the paternal influence on Kafka's self-contempt, his diffidence, his emotional isolation, and his incapacity to marry, to mention a few of the lasting encumbrances on his life. "And because you were the person who really brought me up, this has had its repercussions [everywhere] throughout my life" (33, II).* The father did not bring up his son in a

---

* The arabic number in parentheses after a quotation in the text of this essay refers to the page of the English translation from which the quotation is taken; the roman numeral that follows refers to the paragraph on that page.

literal sense because the child was raised in an intact, established, bourgeois family. What Kafka is saying expresses his lasting impression that his father outweighed any other person's influence on a sense of self which he could consider his own.

Kafka's descriptive rendition of his emotions in relation to his father as he experienced them over a lifetime is executed with such sincerity and unabashed soul-baring frankness that I do not hesitate to use the *Letter* as an authentic comprehensive personal statement which promises to lend corroborative evidence to my propositions concerning the emotional ontogeny of the son-father relationship. In applying to the reading of the *Letter* the developmental concepts I presented at length in the preceding essay, I aim to compose a personality which unifies all the facets of the recorded personal reflections into a convincing and believable *Gestalt* or, in simple words, to make sense of the total, often disjointed and enigmatic, autobiographical account. In this sense, my present intentions parallel those of my clinical work, in which the son-father developmental propositions have guided me in the reconstructive effort of psychopathological aberrations and their therapeutic normalization. I use the *Letter* as a substantiation of these propositions without attempting to reconstruct Kafka's life history in its complexity. I keep the focus of my inquiry carefully limited to the descriptive evidence of Kafka's sonship experience. I do trace the influence of the father complex on his personality development and on the deviancy of his emotional life as far as the *Letter* offers direct documentation of these by the internal consistency of the autobiographical record. However, I do not attempt to write a pathography of Franz Kafka.

I use the *Letter* in the same way I used the creative writings or autobiographical essays of adolescent boys and girls early in my research on adolescence (Blos, 1941)—in order to abstract from their internal consistency, individually and collectively, the general emotional dynamics which govern the adolescent process, regardless of individual life histories. The abstracted developmental and normative processes thus obtained can then be applied to individual lives in order to validate or disprove their normative nature. This approach proved to be a rewarding method in my developmental studies in the past. In a similar fashion I view the *Letter* as a dramatic monologue, written by a tragic writer with an extraordinary introspective faculty and reflective candor who was able to put into words the innermost complexities of his tormented sonship.

Thematic Issues of the *Letter*

Four distinct themes emerge from a reading of the *Letter;* they weave in and out of it as well as intermingle with each other. They are easy to recognize because their variations resound in the son's never ending Jobiade, making themselves heard from whisper to outcry as recurrent leitmotifs. These four mental sets or emotional complexes are illustrated without pause by the letter writer from all possible angles until they stand out in glaring sharpness, chiseled in finest detail with the tools of language forged and tempered in the anguish and despair of Kafka's wish that his father would understand him.

The first theme concerns the fanatical idealization of the father, of whom the son says, "From your armchair you ruled the world" (21, II). The virtues of the father are of such incomparable magnificence that they are rendered unattainable in whole or in part by the son, who is condemned to a state of nothingness. The father's grandeur extirpates all possibilities for the son to even approach any degree of deserving self-respect in any enterprise he entertains or in any aspiration he pursues.

The second theme reflects the absolute immutable centrality of the father in the son's life. To quote, ". . . if the world consisted only of me and you (a notion I was much inclined to have) . . ." (105, I), so Franz concludes, we would be safe in our absolute state of union. This unattainable paradise of mutual affection and harmony is constantly devastated by an unending onslaught of blasphemous, accusatory, vilifying thoughts about the father, delivering the son to the tortures of guilt and shame. Without any escape or reprieve there was no other alternative but to heap and reheap the total burden of guilt and shame upon himself. This he did in bouts of remorse and repentance, asserting repeatedly that the father was innocent, guiltless, and too godlike to be endured. Within this vicious circle there remains the firm belief that the father loves him and that it is the father's jealousy that makes him react to his son's liking of people, things, or ideas as contemptible, worthless, and destined to do him harm.

The third theme touches on the son's constant mental alertness not to be overwhelmed by the man whom he loves beyond reason. The *Letter* gives evidence of the reciprocity and bondage between tyrant and slave, persecutor and victim. There was no possible escape from this persecutory mesh which encompassed fear and wish, both deeply rooted and ambivalently maintained in the context of an all-consuming infantile attachment. "In all my thinking I was, after all, under the heavy pressure of your personality, even in that part of it—and particularly in that—which was not in accord with yours" (23, I).

The fourth theme can be called the invocation of a truce offer, a plea to stop fighting and inflicting hurt on each other. Life seems not possible for Kafka—the child, the adolescent, and the man—if the relationship to his father is irreparably ruptured. The only road to peace seemed to lie in mutual acceptance and forgiveness of crimes never committed and in receiving the father's blessing of his work, his loves and hates, and, above all, his manhood. "My valuation of myself was much more dependent on you than on anything else, such as some external success" (93, I). Nothing could be achieved or enjoyed without the father's blessing. Since neither mutual acceptance of the other's imperfections nor a cessation of mutual disappointments caused by the other was ever forthcoming in Kafka's life, two questions present themselves, the answers to which will be found in the *Letter*. The first one is concerned with retracing the evolutionary history of the father complex in order to identify the particular emotional elements encapsulated in this affective state which dominated Kafka's personality. The other question searches for an elucidation of the son's strategems of escape from his abnormal psychological adaptation. Furthermore, I wish to shed some light on the inner resources which enabled Kafka to salvage that modicum of autonomous selfhood which enabled him to become the extraordinary writer known to the world.

It is the purpose of the discussion which follows to show that a careful reading of the *Letter* provides the answers to these questions. In other words, synthesis of the four themes and of the particular roles they play in Kafka's life gives the author of the *Letter* the complexity and cohesiveness of an integrated, tragically human personality. I should announce at this point that there is no separate summary of the themes because each discussion of a theme contains conceptual threads from the remaining three themes woven into its dominant texture. In this review of his life, which he wrote within the context of his relation to his father, Kafka left to posterity a confessional document—strange, eccentric, often freakishly perverse—which throws light on the unique experience—normal and deviant—of his sonship.

Father Idealization

The son's idealization of the father is counterpoised against his own self-denigration; both these positions are maintained in mutual interdependence, never reaching a resolution or settlement. A similar antagonistic entanglement can be found in the silent vilification of the father in thought which is followed without fail by an overwhelming mental preoccupation with father adulation, self-humiliation, and unconditional attribution of guilt to himself about the disastrous estrangement from each other and the unending disappointment in each other. The father imago acquires at these moments an incomprehensible dimension which is bigger than life. In the desired and feared confrontation which never comes to pass, the father remains unassailable; this state of the father's absolute dominance Kafka expresses in these words: ". . . you were for me the measure of all things" (19, II). What the father said to the child "was positively a heavenly command, I never forgot it, it remained for me the most important means of forming a judgment of the world . . ." (27, I).

In comparison to himself he sees in the father "a true Kafka" (13, I), which is to say a paragon "in strength, health, appetite, loudness of voice, eloquence, self-satisfaction, worldly dominance, endurance, presence of mind, knowledge of human nature, a certain way of doing things on a grand scale" (13, I). This sentence of exaltation is followed by the exposure, with equal eloquence, of the father's "defects and weaknesses" (13, I). These the father was expected to eradicate in order to give back to his son the hero father of dyadic grandeur. The son cries out in the *Letter* that the father should offer to his children "an exemplary life" (83, I) because it is his duty and obligation by his exalted state of having become a father.

In light of what I have presented in the essay on the ontogeny of isogender sonship it appears that the splitting of the father into a protective, godlike and a cruel, dangerous imago, both tyrants of power, reflects a dyadic object relation which is never totally or tracelessly abandoned in a man's life. If there was ever a convincing and articulate expression of dyadic father bondage carried into manhood, the *Letter* conveys it in the most lucid and passionate language. Kafka's father hunger is reflected in the description of a lifelong effort to be and remain emotionally close to his father, thus obtaining the emotional nutrients for growing into a man, made in the father's image and therefore forever one with him. We can deduce from the fact that the role of the father in Kafka's mental life had never essentially changed through the various developmental stages of childhood or adolescence that the flight of the dyadic son from the so-called reengulfing mother to the dyadic father had failed disastrously. What is meant to be a temporary resting place turned into a permanent abode. Whether such a debacle led to an exaggerated protective father idealization and fatal rupture of the infantile mother attachment remains inconclusive from the content of the *Letter*.

I desist from reconstruction where documentary evidence is missing and leave moot questions unanswered. I prefer to adhere closely to the literal contents of the *Letter* as illustrative and cogent references to my studies on sonship. There are, however, a few instances when I cannot help but digress into drawing conclusions of an interpretive and hypothetical nature, taking into account the propositions of my essay on son and father as far as they define general and normative developmental landmarks. I should also mention that I do not attribute a causal and consummate significance to the father's difficult personality as attested to by several witnesses and recounted convincingly in Kafka biographies. Of course, there is no doubt that the father, like any father in a comparative family setting, was influential, for better or for worse, in shaping idiosyncratically the son's personality. However, I shall adhere to the evidence in the *Letter*, which describes one son's evolutionary experience in a particular sonship constellation, reflecting in its uniqueness the normative stages of the son-father relationship, which in this case has gone woefully astray. It is worth mentioning at this point that Kafka's mother does not figure prominently or appear as a distinct personality with a living countenance in the *Letter*, but is always reflected in relation to the father, as, for instance, when Kafka talks about his mother spoiling him and protecting him too readily against the father's harshness, thus forestalling his active father liberation which he so desperately wished to achieve. ". . . the battle that you [father] were waging with us [children] . . . that we were waging with you, and it was Mother on whom we relieved our wild feelings" (61, I); "It is true that Mother was inimitably good to me, but for me all that was in relation to you . . ." (45, III). Even if the father might have been able to make a man of him, "Mother canceled that out again by kindness, by talking sensibly" He continues: "I was again driven back into your orbit, which I might perhaps otherwise have broken out of, to your advantage and to my own. . . . Mother shielded me from you in secret . . ." (47, I). The dynamic constellation which Kafka describes here is identical with the "reengulfing mother" and the dyadic infant's wish for father closeness. He calls his mother weak and too devoted to her husband to assist her son in his efforts to grow up. He uses an incrimin .ting analogy of utmost cruelty in describing his mother's way of supporting her husband's initial combative engagement with his son. He compares his parents' interaction with him to a *"battue,"* a hunt in which the beaters drive the game into the range of the hunters' guns. "Mother unconsciously played the part of a beater during a hunt" (45, III). He assigns a double role to his mother in her influence on the son-father conflict: she offered herself as a target of his "wild feelings," protecting the child from the father's wrath, and, on the other hand, she drove the little boy into the father's domination by laying herself indulgently open to his childish weaknesses which his father abhorred and ruthlessly condemned. Only with "violence and revolution," Kafka argues, would there have been a chance of "breaking away from home . . . assuming . . . that Mother wouldn't have worked against it . . ." (49, I).

The above comments reflect the early triangulation; in fact, they put pointedly into words the small boy's flight to his protector, the powerful father, expecting him to stem the tide against his regression to the symbiotic position. The primitive fear of the reengulfing mother and the danger of becoming abandoned, even sacrificed by her, is reflected in stark imagery by the analogy of the *"battue"* (in German, "Treibjagd"). It is equally correct to say that the wish for, and fear of, being overwhelmed by the godlike father and of being annihilated by him, i.e., incorporated in his orbit, were contributory to driving the child into the engulfing fortress of the mother's realm, from which he finally fled for good into his father's arms. It seems that this early partitioning of the child's world was never abandoned by the growing boy or man, but became more rigidly fixed with advancing age. What is supposed to be a passing juncture of early development established itself as a never settled and therefore permanent disharmony, extending its painful inner divisiveness over all significant aspects of his life. One might well say that life had become a perennial pilgrimage to the shrine of the dyadic father; the *Letter* records the itinerary of these peregrinations, including the last effort to arrive at a lasting reconciliation, an effort which, indeed, was the *Letter* itself. This effort was again, as always before, defeated by Kafka's entrusting the *Letter* to his mother, leaving its delivery to her judgment and responsibility. He thus appointed her as his judge and censor, thereby protecting his father from renewed hurt and dejection, expecting his mother to attend to this task as she had always done in the past. Of course, with this arrangement for delivery, the whole purpose of the *Letter* was lost, namely, for son and father to share the truth about their relationship, which "might reassure us both a little and make our living and dying easier" (125, II). With these words the letter closes. "Dona nobis pacem" son and father never came to sing together.

The theme of dyadic father idealization appears also in the preservation of a father imago of sexual purity, innocence, and marital excellence. Kafka recalls in the *Letter* the time when his father offered words of sexual enlightenment to him when he was an adolescent boy of 16 (pp. 101–105). He was offended, appalled, and horrified that his father could stoop that low and talk about "the filthiest thing possible" (105, I), implying that his son was not worthy of anything better than to live in "physical filth" (105, I), while "you yourself remained outside your own advice, a married man, a pure man, above such things. . . ." In contrast, "marriage seemed to me shameless. . . ." It was impossible for me to apply to my parents the general information I had picked up about marriage. Thus you became still purer, rose still higher . . . so there was hardly any smudge of earthly filth on you at all . . . this purity of the world came to an end with you and, by virtue of your advice, the filth began with me" (105, I). These words expressing insult, abuse, and outrage convey his feeling of having been "pushed down into this filth—just as though I were predestined to it" (105, I). The son had never abandoned the infantile paternal idealization, not even with the advent of his puberty; he felt besmirched and abused by the father in his allusions to brothels, prostitutes, and venereal disease, since he had never acknowledged his father as a sexually active man. Paternal sexual purity was jealously guarded by the son; even though he writes, ". . . there was hardly any smudge of earthly filth on you at all" (105, I), he mentions, half accusatorily and half in awestruck wonderment, the father's "vulgarity" of speech, "your taste for indecent expressions" (45, I), and their unrestricted delivery in his place of business and also at home.

The *Letter* provides convincing evidence of the son's clinging to, and indeed cultivation of, a father who is bigger than life. In other words, he literally clung to the feeling of being small and puny in contrast to the giant father who easily could crush or enslave him. "There was I, skinny, weakly, slight; you strong, tall, broad" (19, II). The child took exquisite pride in the magnificent body of his father; indeed, he shared it or, at least, tried to share it by sacrificing his own body as contemptible and hateful. From a bathing excursion with his father he remembers the utter shame about his body vis-à-vis his father's: "I was, after all, weighed down by your mere physical presence" (19, II). He continues: "I was proud of my father's body. By the way, this difference between us remains much the same to this very day" (21, I). The child's envy and adulation, as well as the wish to be a consensual proprietor of the father's body, had remained unchanged up to the time of the *Letter* at the age of 36. Of course, the dyadic father does look huge and towering to every toddler and is experienced as a source of fear as well as security and pride. The fear is a permanent part of the relationship which ultimately is channeled into the organization of the superego, while the wish for father's protective care and power remains a never fulfilled craving which stands in conflict with the wish for autonomy and selfhood. In fact, the *Letter* opens with the sentence, "You asked me recently why I maintain that I am afraid of you" (7, I). The kaleidoscopic shift of affects in the relationship to his father repeats unremittingly two equidominant trends, namely, the need for a hero father and the terror of being overwhelmed by him and reduced to impotence and nothingness. In this connection Kafka's sibling position might be considered, even though the *Letter* refers to it only in passing and rather cryptically. "I should have been happy to have you as a friend, as a boss, an uncle, a grandfather, even (though rather more hesitantly) as a father-in-law. Only as a father you have been too strong for me, particularly since my brothers died when they were small and my sisters only came along much later, so that I alone had to bear the brunt of it—and for that I was much too weak" (11, II). He goes on to say that he takes after his mother's family, which, in comparison to the Kafka stock, with its might and competence, can only evoke contempt in the father, especially since the child is a boy but not a "real" boy and only in name "a Kafka."

Is it too much to assume that this father two of whose children, both sons, died in infancy heaped naturally all his hope on his one surviving son and his first-born at that? Repeated references in the *Letter* illustrate the father's efforts to mold the child—sensitive and of slight build by nature—into a "real boy" of whom he could be proud. He tried passionately to instill in him physical discipline and a soldiery bearing. "You encouraged me, for instance, when I saluted and marched smartly, but I was no future soldier . . ." (17, II–19, I); ". . . you wanted to bring me up to be a strong brave boy" (15, II). The son never lived down these ordeals of his childhood and the miserable disappointments he inflicted on his father in everything that mattered to him in the life of his only surviving son. From the father's unrelenting and futile efforts to satisfy his cravings for a son whom he could love unconditionally we can fathom the titanic struggle of father and son for mutual role fulfillment. The child had grown morbidly attentive to the father's minute reactions to him; he correctly calls himself "a child, over-acutely observant from sheer nervousness" (81, I). It had always been incomprehensible to the son how to reconcile the father's contradictory behavior: "And here again was your enigmatic innocence and inviolability; you cursed and swore without the slightest scruple; yet you condemned cursing and swearing in other people and would not have it" (35, III). "For me you took on the enigmatic quality that all tyrants have . . ." (21, II).

In order to bring some comprehensibility into this life of confusion, Kafka had divided "the world into three parts" (29, I). In the one where he lived, ". . . the slave lived under laws that had been invented only for me . . . then a second world, which was infinitely remote from mine, in which you lived . . . and finally a third world where everybody else lived happily and free from orders and from having to obey" (29, I). The attachment to the dyadic father, bodily, emotionally, and spiritually had become over the years a way of life, namely, the son's enslavement as the only means of becoming an emotionally meaningful, albeit despicable, object of the father's attention. Little wonder that the letter writer referred to himself as a parasite (125, I) in the literal sense of sucking sustenance from his chosen host. Thus Kafka attributes the following words to the father in his putative reply to the son's letter: "If I am not very much mistaken, you are preying on me even with this letter itself" (125, I). Perhaps it was this kind of self-accusation and the ensuing sense of guilt that aborted the delivery of the *Letter* to the proper addressee.

Despite the images of the tyrant and of the cruel giant crushing the worm of a son, despite the father's terrifying outburst "I'll tear you apart like a fish" (35, IV), there survived unaffected the conviction that the father is "at bottom a kindly and softhearted person . . . but not every child has the endurance and fearlessness to go on searching until it comes to the kindliness that lies beneath the surface" (15, II). The father is repeatedly declared guiltless, like God; the son is exclusively guilty for having turned the father's goodness and caring love into a state of mutual discord and estrangement. The search for harmony and mutual acceptance, both postulated by the son to exist even if never experienced, was sustained by a profound need for each other; for moments this hopeless search slackened by battle fatigue as expressed by the words of the reminiscing adult son: ". . . the child's exclusive sense of guilt has been partly replaced by insight into our helplessness, yours and mine" (33, I). With these words Kafka let the battle stand still at an impasse of resignation which, in a paradoxical way, brings son and father closer to each other in the quiescence of a precarious armistice of attrition; paraphrasing the above lines (33, I), the implied message would read as follows: let us admit to each other that we are both helpless; we are equals and neither one of us is guiltless or guilty. Then we are beyond the rift of big and little, slave and tyrant, because we both are weak (see *Letter*, p. 33). This thought relieved for a moment the sense of separateness and loss which Kafka referred to by saying, "You were such a giant in every respect. What could you care for our pity or even our help?" (41, II). It is clear from the text, that "our" refers to the Kafka children.

An unresolved dyadic father attachment and the preservation of infantile idealization preclude the young child's and the adolescent's capacity to mourn; this affect constitutes the corollary to the first and second processes of individuation; without ability to mourn, these processes cannot take their normal course. Kafka was aware of his failure in the "internal disengagement from you" (71, II).* Generally speaking, the incapacity for internal disengagement from primary objects has always profound and infantilizing consequences for personality development. In the first place, it keeps the faculty of reality testing from progressing in synchronicity with age, thus allowing uncensored intrusions of primary-process thought, imagery, and related emotions to blunt and distort perception and sensation to the point of momentary delusions. Such lasting permeability of ego boundaries accounts for the infantile emotionality documented in the *Letter* where Kafka speaks of himself as "a glum, inattentive, disobedient child, always intent on escape, mainly within one's own self" (41, I).**

Let us now turn to the consequences of a defaulted deidealization.

First a word about the conditions in which idealization originates; they are to be found in the infantile state of identity when it is exclusively derived from the expressed opinions of significant others as they are conveyed to the child. "You are a good boy" makes the child feel good; this goodness becomes a congruent quality of what and who he is. At this state of low-level self-differentiation the input derived from objective

---

* This quote is my translation of Kafka's words "innere Ablösung von Dir," which reads in the official translation "the breaking away from you." My translation reflects Kafka's awareness that the internalized object is of the essence in the process he describes. (See Blos, 1967.)

** Literally translated, this phrase reads, "always intent on an escape, mostly an internal one"; in German, "immer auf eine Flucht, meist eine innere, bedacht." Kafka's polarization of external and internal activity shows such an extraordinary degree of psychological sophistication that it deserves our explicit appreciation.

self-evaluation and from a diacritical faculty is necessarily weak and insignificant. Identity maintenance is, therefore, embedded in anxiety because the preservation, continuity, and durability of the self are largely left to persons or their collective representations, such as social institutions, in the outside world. A legitimate narcissistic gratification, derived from the adult ego ideal whenever it is approximated by the successful endeavors of the ego, was denied to Kafka. Neither his extraordinary work as a writer nor the recognition it earned him in his lifetime gave him the slightest sense of achievement, pride, or autonomy. I shall return to this issue in the discussion of the fourth theme.

Kafka, in self-contemplation, was puzzled by the fact that no other man in the father series was ever chosen or even considered by him as a transiently idealized object, idol, or hero, in order to bring about in a normal way the emotional father disengagement of which he spoke so often with longing. If he had ever thought about it, he writes, ". . . everyday thinking would have taken over and shown me other men who are different from you" (119, II). The father deidealization never ran its normal course because neither internal nor external aggressive and evaluative confrontation with the idealized father imago was within the son's reach. "Between us there was no real struggle; I was soon finished off; what remained was flight, embitterment, melancholy, and inner struggle" (65, I). Under the pressure of an overwhelming need for the preservation of an omnipotent, irreproachable father, a critical evaluation of him and a consolidation of a separate identity remained foreclosed. To be shamed, blamed, and humiliated was preferable to being ignored and wiped out by his father's inattention. "I could enjoy what you gave, but only in humiliation, weariness, weakness, and with a sense of guilt. That was why I could be grateful to you for everything only as a beggar is, and could never show it by doing the right things" (53, I). The masochistic gratification of passively receiving handouts, in conjunction with meek submissiveness, fed a bottomless sense of shame which became the source of his feeling not to exist rightfully in this world. "I was continually in disgrace* . . ." (29, I). "He is afraid the shame will outlive him" (73, I).**

Submission to the Father

Enough has been said about Kafka's lifelong fixation on the dyadic father. The manifestations in his adult life, such as the self-effacing subservience and emotional surrender to his father, aroused in his best friend and

* In the German text, "Schande"; here translated as "disgrace," the word "Schande" refers equally to the sense of shame.

** Kafka quotes here a comment he once made about someone; in the *Letter* he applies it to himself.

later biographer Max Brod (1963) serious worries which prompted him to talk sense into his beloved and admired friend; at least, he tried. In his biography Brod poses—in a tone of exasperation—the rhetorical question "What did Kafka need his father for?" or more directly stated, "Why was he not able to break away from him?" (1963, p. 22). He never could penetrate the density of this enigma. Brod describes his friend's attitude to his father as one of critical rationality overshadowed by "loving admiration" (p. 23), which—so he says—has its equal only with "a woman one is in love with—and therefore has to put up with under all circumstances" (p. 22). Brod touches here on the androgynous constellation of son to father. Brod is undoubtedly right in his surmise, which must have been derived from a wide range of observations to which he, as a close friend, was privy. Brod remained a helpless witness to his friend's incomprehensible, unalterable, emotionally paralyzing predicament.

Little children normally like to please their parents by identifying with their expectations and demands, thus responding to them with a conditioned, selected awareness. This particularized response to the surround starts the child off toward socialization in its broadest sense. His advance along these lines remains contingent on a sharpening distinction between critical reactions of others and critical observations of self. Little Franz failed at this developmental task of early object disengagement, i.e., infantile individuation. This fact, however, did not preclude his becoming an individualist of extraordinary proportions, as attested by his writing.

It cannot escape the reader of the *Letter* that the son speaks of the father and to the father with the most affectionate expressions. It seems that the father had acquired maternal qualities—real or imagined—of tender beauty and perfection, to wit, "You have a particularly beautiful, very rare way of quickly, contentedly, approvingly smiling, a way of smiling that can make the person for whom it is meant entirely happy" (43, II). "Rare as this was, it was wonderful" (43, I). "At such times one would lie back and weep for happiness, and one weeps again now, writing it down" (43, I). He wrote it down at the age of 36 with a sense of bliss, undiminished since early childhood and treasured ever since, like a glowing reminiscence of paradise. Kafka hastens to add that these were rare moments when the father extended "affection and kindliness" to his son; they could only have occurred, so he speculates, at a time when "I still seemed blameless to you and was your great hope" (43, II)—in other words, before the "Fall," or before the primeval innocence was lost due to the intrusion of aggression, fear, and guilt as part of the relationship. In order to relieve the father of any guilt for having crushed his child's spirit, he appropriated all the guilt for having smashed the father's great hope of his becoming a son worthy to be loved by a father of such magnificence.

In the voice of an impeached criminal he defends himself and accuses his prosecutor: I had never charged you "with anything improper or wicked* (with the exception perhaps of my latest marriage plan), you do charge me with coldness, estrangement and ingratitude" (9, I). The juxtaposition of being a pure child who could only be charged with having committed an "improper and wicked" act by announcing as an adult his wish to marry leaves no doubt that the affirmation of his manhood and the gratification of his sexual desires, inclusive of the withdrawal of affection and submissiveness from his father, constituted an unforgivable act of "coldness, estrangement and ingratitude," unforgivable by the father in his adult son. Reflected in the juxtaposition of himself as a child and as an adult, namely, as a child of innocence and as an adult of evil and selfish sexuality (marriage) there appears the self-accusation of improper desires which the adolescent son once extended or wished to extend toward his father in response to his "indecent and evil" (my translation: see footnote) talk by which, so the son felt, the father imposed on him his possessive, emotional demands. Kafka states this clearly by saying that his father expected from him—child or adult—"at least some sort of obligingness, some sign of sympathy" (7, II). The son fled from the father demanding demonstrative love. Regardless of the agonizing discord between them, there existed an incomprehensible and indestructible understanding and attraction between them: "Oddly enough you have some sort of notion of what I mean. For instance, a short time ago you said to me, "I have always been fond of you . . ." (9, III). That is indeed what the son lived for to hear but could not return in kind lest he surrender his self without reservation, forfeiting his separate identity. To divorce himself from his father, to attach himself to a woman and get married, would certainly open the road to madness. "To try to get out of all this [i.e., get married] had therefore a touch of madness about it, and every attempt is almost punished with it" (113, II). Having lived in a permanent chaos of guilt and of craving for his father's recognition and affection, he cries out, "And now marry without going mad!" (121, I).

Kafka tried desperately to illuminate this mysterious bonding and mutual torture of attraction and rejection, to no avail; he contented himself with the insight "that something is wrong in our relationship and you have played your part in causing it to be so, but without its being your fault" (11, I). The irreconcilable conviction of "You caused me harm but you are blameless" highlights the latent accusation of the dyadic father for having committed the monstrous crime of not having loved and protected his little son enough or for having loved him too much in his

---

* The German word in the text for "improper" is "Unanständiges," a word which contains an innuendo of "dirty, filthy, indecent"; the word for "wicked" in the German text is "Böses," a word which is best imparted to the reader in the full extent of its meaning by blending it with adjectives such as "bad, evil, nasty, amoral."

blind and passionate desire to "bring me up to be a strong brave boy" (15, II) or, simply, to "become a person after your own heart" (11, II). Father and son could never reconcile their different personalities or their antagonistic temperaments and libidinal appetites. "In any case, we were so different and in our difference so dangerous to each other . . . that I, the slowly developing child, and you, the fullgrown man . . . you would simply trample me underfoot so that nothing was left of me" (13, I). Kafka lived in permanent annihilation anxiety; in fact, he was driven to put himself right in the path of his father's wrath by making demands on him which the frustrated father always met with an overbearing outburst of loathing and displeasure. In consequence, they both lived in mutual attraction and rejection, fastened to each other's "soul with hoops of steel" (*Hamlet*, I, iii, 63). As a grown man, Kafka never ceased to bemoan his failure to reach his father's heart: ". . . not every child has the endurance and fearlessness to go on searching until it comes to the kindliness that lies beneath the surface" (15, II). There has never been any doubt in his mind that the father is loving and kind, "at bottom a kindly and softhearted person" (15, II); he, the son, has ruined it all by his weakness and submissiveness: ". . . you should stop considering it some particular malice on my part that I succumbed . . . to the effect you had on me" (15, I). In a paradoxical way, the idealized father had to be ceaselessly reaffirmed, regardless of the glaring contradictions which reality offered and which Kafka clearly recognized. The never surrendered split father imago of the dyadic stage worked relentlessly against the integration of a whole-object representation. Did the preservation of the idealized father imago, this relic of the dyadic stage, serve as a bullwark against the possessive or infantilizing woman? Here we can only surmise that this was the case and turn to two cogent themes in the *Letter* for possible enlightenment on this score.

One of the themes refers to the father as being attached to his little son beyond reason, thus arresting or preventing the child's emotional growth; the other theme refers to the fact, expounded at great length in the *Letter*, that a progression to the triadic stage was only tentatively and weakly attempted and definitively foreclosed by an aborted adolescence.

With reference to the first issue it has to be noted that the child as well as the adult Kafka sensed the father's possessive intrusiveness as an expression of his love. He knew that his father "mistrustfully and jealously (I don't deny, do I, that you are fond of me?) . . . assumed that I had to compensate elsewhere for the lack of a family life" (75, I). The son conjectures that the father suffered rejection whenever he turned to his own friends, associates, or interests. The father was jealous of anybody—man or woman—who was liked or loved by his son. ". . . as was so often the case with people I was fond of, you were automatically ready with the proverb of the dog and its fleas" (25, I).* Such demon-strations of the father's jealousy left the son in a state of bewildered isolation and indecisiveness whether to surrender or take flight from the father's intrusiveness and libidinal wishes. We have no evidence from reading the *Letter* that Kafka senior's portrait corresponds to reality, but, on the other hand, we have no reason to doubt that the portrait represents the father as seen and experienced by the son; despite imputed qualities and obvious projections, every distortion and exaggeration contains a kernel of truth, as we are informed by Kafka biographers.

It is no surprise to read in the *Letter* that the child reacted to the father's friendliness with a sense of guilt, since he felt undeserving of it. ". . . friendly impressions brought about nothing but an increased sense of guilt, making the world still more incomprehensible to me" (43, II). This bottomless reservoir of guilt is fed by the constant effort of distancing himself, manifest in thought and behavior, in order to escape from his desire to succumb to his father's overpowering might. "In order to assert myself even a little in relation to you, and partly too from a kind of vengefulness, I soon began to observe little ridiculous things about you, to collect them and to exaggerate them" (43, III). The typical adolescent revelation of seeing the father in the "emperor's new clothes" was never fully acknowledged by Kafka in its naked truth, but was denied and denied again, filling and refilling the reservoir of guilt dangerously close to an overflow level. The vicious cycle just described kept the son in unremitted bondage to his father. The son was helpless vis-à-vis his father's seductiveness. We can only surmise that the mother was equally submissive to him and counteracted the father's imposing and uncompro-mising dominance in the family with indulgence and tolerance.

Whatever the disastrous circumstances in the child's dyadic stage of development had been, the *Letter* does not offer any direct elucidation on that score. However, certain assumptions about the writer, based on developmental principles, attain persuasive credibility. Summarizing them we can say: (1) The idealized dyadic father imago was never surrendered to the voice of reason. (2) The adolescent deidealization of the father had failed. (3) The infantile ego ideal, based on the father's image of an ideal, wished-for son, remained basically unaltered and became a per-manent personality attribute. (4) The polarized dyadic father imago, good and evil, or God and Devil, remained unreconciled for life and established a segmentation of the sense of self. (5) The adult ego ideal was acquired only in isolated fragments, especially Kafka's identity as a creative artist. (6) The function of reality testing remained seriously incapacitated even though only selectively; his father's evaluation of reality remained a con-stant inner reference which never permitted him to hear his own assess-

---

* A German saying: "He who lies down with dogs gets up with fleas."

ment of facts or emotions clearly and without interference by his father's corrective. We might say that in Kafka's case the reality principle had never wrenched itself loose from the infantile father idealization and therefore never acquired mature autonomy.

The second topic listed in the above summary shall now be explored in more detail because it promises to throw light on Kafka's father fixation. Basic to this condition is the fact that the child's dyadic stage was resolved, tentatively and ambivalently, via his identification with the mother and his emotional surrender to the idealized father. A progression to the oedipal triadic stage was clearly attempted, but the state of bondage and attachment to the father always proved insurmountable. Kafka returns in the *Letter* repeatedly to the point that his emotional liberation remains contingent on becoming equal to the father, a step—so he anticipates in all seriousness—which will be punished by madness. Equality with the father can only be attained by marriage and family; this ultimate affirmation of manhood and fatherhood, however, is an act of hubris punishable by madness; only self-emasculation can avert this dreadful fate, condemning the wretched creature to a life of shame. This emotional impasse is dramatically reflected in Kafka's adolescent sexual awakening, when he turned to his father for help, and in the history of his several engagements, marriage plans, and their ultimate abandonment for good at the time the *Letter* was written. These emotional vagaries are recounted in the *Letter* at great length.

Kafka remembers well the walk he took with his parents as a 16-year-old boy when "in a stupidly boastful . . . and stammering manner" he confronted them for "having left me uninstructed" (101, III) and said that due to their neglectfulness as parents, "I had been close to great dangers (here I was brazenly lying . . . to show myself brave) . . ." (101, III–103, I). The father responded to the haughty tirade of accusations by saying that he "could give me advice about how I could go in for these things without danger. Perhaps I did want to lure just such an answer out of you . . ." (103, I). With these last words Kafka admits his wish to involve his father via talking about sexual matters in the rising emotions of his pubertal urges. The father's reference to the use of a condom—not using the word outright, just offering "a piece of advice that might prevent damage to health" (105, II)—and mention of the availability of females in a brothel threw the boy into a fit of shame and humiliation. He was shocked beyond comprehension that his father could advise him to practice "the filthiest thing possible" (105, I). He asked himself if it was possible that his father might have given to himself the same abominable advice before his marriage which he now gave to his son. This "was to me utterly unthinkable" (105, I). For a moment the idealized father was totally destroyed, but denial undid the unbearable disappointment by shifting the blame for the crime to himself; the godhead was resurrected, the world was in order once again. "The important thing was rather that you yourself remained outside your own advice" (105, I). In reestablishing the sexual purity and innocence of his father, the son could not escape the thought that he himself was "predestined" to be "pushed down into this filth" (105, I); his father's monstrous advice, however, was to the son no impugnment of the great man's purity; fate was taking its course. Here we hear the voice of Job, asking God to explain why he was forsaken to live in filth and guilt after a life of faithful obedience, never having doubted God's justice and love.

Kafka relived his pubertal trauma in his recurrent marriage plans. The adult man was certain of his father's jealousy; while he condemns his suspiciousness vociferously, he nevertheless is compelled to renounce his marriage plans, again and again, and yield to his father's secret wishes. In reading the account of the wrecked engagement or marriage plans, one cannot escape the impression that the father's passionate involvement, opposition, or plea for delay was partially the product of the son's fabrications. All these dramatic episodes have the earmarks of a *folie à deux*. Kafka, age 36, recognizes in the father's negative attitude toward his last marriage plans a repeat performance of their devastating, shocking encounter 20 years earlier during his adolescence, at the age of 16. To the father, Kafka muses, he is not 20 years older, but "only more pitiable by twenty years" (109, I).

He keenly senses and clearly states that his father's attachment to him is of such power that no escape from it is possible. This fact is well documented by two passages. One refers to Kafka's announcement of his last marriage plans at age 36, which is the year when the *Letter* was written. The father responds to his son's intention with insulting cynicism, implying that only sexual lust, cleverly aroused by the woman, drove him into wanting to marry her. As quoted in the *Letter,* the father says, "She probably "put on a fancy blouse . . . and right away, of course, you decided to marry her . . . as fast as possible, in a week, tomorrow, today" (107, II). The father, in desperation, proposes—whether seriously or derisively is left uncertain—other possibilities to satisfy such urgent sexual desires. At this moment of emotional excitement he is quoted as saying, "If you are frightened, I'll go with you" (107, II). The reader of the *Letter* is left with the question, where? One wonders. To the woman the son wants to marry or, in the father's version, lusts after? The conjunction in the *Letter* of the marriage incident and the sex talk at age 16 raises and answers the question which arose in the mind of the now 36-year-old man as to what other abominable advice might be forthcoming now, namely, the advice that the son visit a brothel and regain his sane judgment after his lust is spent. This is not stated explicitly in the *Letter,* because all that Kafka remembers of this particular juncture in the conversation with his father is a momentary loss of memory as to what exactly the father had said "in more detail and more plainly . . . perhaps too, things became a little vague before my eyes . . ." (107, II).

The father's intrusion into his adult son's love life was responded to by limp surrender and helpless agony. In Kafka's words, "My choice of a girl meant nothing at all to you. You had (unconsciously) [sic] always kept down my power of decision and now believed (unconsciously) [sic] that you knew what it was worth" (109, I). While he belived in his father's competition with the girl of his heart, he nevertheless could not ignore his father's seductive excitement in response to the marriage plans. Of course, the father supported a son's wish for the independence which comes with marriage and family life. These were pious words, acknowledgements in principle, but—as the shrewdly chosen analogy in the *Letter* reveals—what remained unspoken was all that really mattered, to wit, ". . . in reality it always turns out like the children's game in which one holds and even grips the other's hand, calling out: 'Oh, go away, go away, why don't you go away?' Which in our case happens to be complicated by the fact that you have always honestly meant this 'go away!' and have always unknowingly held me, or rather held me down . . ." (109, III–111, I). The son reacted to his father's hold on him with almost teasing marriage pretenses. "It is precisely this close relation [to the father] that partly lures me toward marrying. I picture the equality which would then arise between us—and which you would be able to understand better than any other form of equality . . ." (115, I). He speaks, of course, of sexual equality, which would rid their bond of its devastating libidinal undercurrents. Then, so Kafka writes, "I could be a free . . . son, and you could be a . . . contented father" (115, I). But he concludes, in typical Kafkaesque logic, "But to this end everything that ever happened would have to be undone, that is, we ourselves should have to be cancelled out" (115, I).

In painful humiliation Kafka wishes that via the *Letter* he could persuade his father to abandon the conviction that the intention to marry was evoked by nothing more than "delight over a blouse" (111, II). In his cynical allusion to the girl's breasts, the father degraded his son's wish for independence to a cheap matter of sexual lust; it was the father's last trump he played in the fight for the repossession of his son's soul. While Kafka sensed clearly the father's unconscious or unknowing (Kafka's words; see above) obsession with his son, he was blind to the counterpart he himself played in making certain that his emotional bondage was never lost. Little forays to gain independence were made but always abandoned. The move toward liberation was canceled out by the wish to remain in prison. Kafka compares the state of his paralyzed will to a prisoner who "had not only the intention to escape . . . but also, and indeed simultaneously, the intention to rebuild the prison as a pleasure dome for himself" (113, II). He states clearly that marrying is "the most honorable independence, it is also at the same time in the closest relation to you [the father]. To get out of all this" [i.e., to marry]" has therefore a touch of madness about it . . ." (113, II). Madness was averted by submission, by the acceptance of emasculation, followed by self-abomination, shame, and guilt.

Kafka speaks of his wish to become an equal to his father by marrying and being the founder of a family. "Marrying is the greatest thing of all . . ." (113, II), but such an act would represent an intrusion into the father's realm and take from him by force what is by natural law his privileged estate. "Marrying is barred to me because it is your very own domain" (115, II). To disregard the sanctity of the borders as drawn by child and father could only be likened to Promethean arrogance. Such hubris provokes punishment by madness or by the infliction of body damage, namely, emasculation. We recognize in the struggle for sexual equality an effort to relinquish the bond to the dyadic, precompetitive, idealized father and seek a foothold on the triadic, or oedipal, level of conflict, namely, rivalry and competition. Entering into rivalry with the father meant giving up the dyadic paternal attachment. Kafka attempted to do this many times in his life, but he always faltered and finally retreated for good. The triadic challenge, i.e., becoming an equal to his father, was never taken up and settled for good, but was repeated up to his last abortive decision to marry. The thought was unbearable that, should he marry, his father might "flee from him, emigrate" (117, I), unable to endure the disappointment; at least, such was the son's belief in the significance of himself in his father's life. This belief had delusional components which made it resist any realistic assessment. The ego of Kafka, the child and the adult, remained threatened by the thought of losing the remnants of an infantile emotional fusion with the dyadic father. We can only infer that the father's powerfulness and magnificence, as seen by the young child, had become a lasting source of protection against dangerous elements in the surrounding world and later increasingly in his private emotional universe, the true nature of which we cannot fathom from the *Letter*.

The almost total absence of any substantive or evocative reference in the *Letter* to the mother represents a gaping void in Kafka's account. One fact, however, is clearly conveyed in the *Letter*, namely, the mother's presence in the home during the years of his growing up. The fact that he entrusted the *Letter* to her for delivery, thus leaving it to her final judgment what would become of it, assigns to her by inference the role of a buffer and go-between for child and father. That she did not pass on the *Letter* to the father tells us nothing about her intention—whether she wanted to protect her husband or her child. Not wishing to speculate where evidence is lacking, I shall move forward to the discussion of other issues in the *Letter* which now clamor for our attention.

Persecutory Ideas

Whatever I have illuminated so far in the discussion of sonship and father-hood in Kafka's life was documented by excerpts from the *Letter*. In this way I hoped to impart authenticity and rationality to the conclusions I have drawn from the text and to support their validity in relation to the developmental theory which I have brought to bear on the Kafka document. Having thus established a body of reasonably well-docu-mented and hopefully convincing psychological opinions, I feel now justi-fied to draw further on the formulations once secured, without feeling obliged to reproduce the textual references already quoted.

The theme which I will now discuss deals with the mutual persecutory entanglement of the son and his father. I will highlight here the child's depression, fear of abandonment, and dread of annihilation by the father. The incompleteness of individuation in conjunction with the clinging closeness to the object, in this case the father, is too obvious to mention at any length. However, the extraordinary developmental history of Kaf-ka's persecution complex deserves a more detailed account; this can best be accomplished by retelling the affective and associative experiences of paternal persecution in their subjective reality over the entire course of his life. The author of the *Letter* leads the way in this effort by illuminat-ing the genealogy of the complex over the various stages of his life, from infancy to near middle age. We cannot fail to notice in the *Letter* that the turbulent and frantic mood swings and the affective extravagances of his early childhood and adolescence remained, singlemindedly and consciously, attached through time to one person only, namely, the father.

It seems that from early life onward Kafka, in his effort to avert his persecutory anxiety, entertained an internal dialogue of argumentation with his father, in turn accusing him and declaring him blameless, yet never losing for one moment the bond of attachment to his savior and annihilator. He argues with the incomprehensible, mysterious, and fasci-nating father (see 20, II) in the same vein as Job argued with God: "God, Do not condemn me; show me why thou contendest with me" (Job 10:2). "Thine hands have made me and fashioned me together round about, yet thou dost destroy me" (10:8). "Thou huntest me as a fierce lion; and again thou showest thyself marvelous upon me" (10:16). "I should have been as though I had not been; I should have been carried from the womb to the grave" (10:19).

The attachment to the father served the little boy—as it does for all little boys—as an anchor which steadied him from drifting into the powerful currents of his needfulness for the reengulfing mother. This usually transient circumstance apparently coalesced in the case under discussion into a complete surrender to the father, who had an uncompromising expectation of the kind of son he wished to possess. This he made unmistakenly clear, by word and action, to the little boy with all the forcefulness of his sanguine paternal passion. The confrontation of the child with a prefabricated model of what his father's son must be led to the surrender of his budding identity to the imposed and imposing dimensions of an exacting paternal template. Not fitting the ideal model of a son became over time an unforgivable failure like having committed a crime. What followed was a ceaseless search for the guilty partner among the two protagonists. This trial lasted a lifetime. Kafka knew that he was a prisoner of his childhood; he expressed it to his friend in the following words: "I shall never grow up to be a man; from being a child I shall immediately become a white-haired ancient" (Brod, 1963, p. 37). Wherever the origins might lie, the *Letter* makes it clear that father love and father hate never became reconciled, nor were they ever reduced to the dimensions of a bearable conflict. The dyadic polarity between the benevolent and the malevolent father was never let go, but adhered to with a perverse tenacity up to the moment of Kafka's writing the *Letter* the age of 36, five years before his death.

There are several passages in the *Letter* which tell of the giant, namely the ruthless father, who is bent on the annihilation of the "parasite" (see 125, I) or the "worm" (see 85, II), namely the disappointing, revolting son. These nightmarish episodes grew into obsessional ruminations with depressive and hypomanic mood swings, extending from ecstatic happiness at the thought of being loved and acknowledged in his being by the father to states of guilt and self-hate. "In the place where I lived I was spurned, condemned, fought to a standstill . . ." (91, I). At these moments the son renounced his devastating accusations of the father for having destroyed his son, declaring them null and void, thus restoring to him his due position as the ruler of the world. In the same breath, the pitiful supplicant readied himself for his share of humiliation by prostrating himself to the mental and physical* annihilation which he, the cowardly and defaulting Prometheus, deserved. The *Letter* mentions repeatedly that in the dark recesses of his heart the father does love his son or he might even love him too much, as would follow from considering the cosmic dimensions of his father's disappointment. The father also expects, so the son feels, signs of love from his son, a realization which immediately paralyzes the expression of any positive feelings and evokes a state of fear if not terror. At such moments, the father appears

---

* Referring to the tuberculosis which finally was the cause of his death, Kafka said, "My head has made an appointment with my lungs behind my back" (Brod, 1963, p. 76).

enigmatic and overwhelming; to figure him out overtaxes the mental strength of his son. In the words of the *Letter;* ". . . if I now try to give you an answer in writing, it will be very incomplete . . . because the magnitude of the subject goes far beyond the scope of my memory and power of reasoning" (7, I). The son could never shake the suspicion that the father concealed an incomprehensible design on his son or harbored a secret purpose which lay hidden beneath his words and actions. The son perceived the father as mistrustful and jealous (see 75, I), and he looked for "some hidden motive*" (41, II) behind the father's behavior. Such hidden motives could arouse a delusional terror, as in the instance when Kafka describes in the *Letter* his father's facial distortions, reminiscent of a devil's mask: "clenching your teeth and with that gurgling laughter that gave the child its first notion of hell . . ." (41, I).

The persecutory allusions in the *Letter* speak of the son's obsessional preoccupation with the father's imputed possessive and intrusive wishes as well as of the son's alert self-protection against his own temptation to let himself be swept into annihilation or absorption by the godhead and thus become one with him in his power and glory. The enmeshment of the persecutor and the persecuted, having its roots in the dyadic father fixation, was tentatively carried forward toward the sexualization of the triadic stage.** A catastrophic break in development probably occurred at this point. A bipolar or bigender identification had rendered the father the dominant "other." Identification with the father on the level of male gender identity and the ensuing oedipal rivalry had become a forbidden and unattainable aspiration; it was comparable to blasphemy in the moral realm. The boy's blasphemous imagination was aroused when taken by the father to the synagogue; he tells of his obsessional defamation of God, "as for instansce when the Arc of the Covenant was opened, which always reminded me of the shooting galleries where a cupboard door would open in the same way whenever one hit the bull's eye; except that there something interesting came out and here it was always the same old dolls without heads. Incidentally, it was also very frightening for me there . . ." (77, II). Judaism as a tradition and ethos remained a lifelong controversy between son and father. Kafka felt that his own

* The word "motive" is in German "Absicht," which is closer to the English word "intention."

** Every clinician who is familiar with the male adolescent process, normative and deviant, has had ample opportunity to observe the persecutory mesh between son and father as a corollary to the resolution of the "negative," i.e., isogender, Oedipus complex. Should these persecutory, quasi-delusional ideas not be self-liquidating by maturation but persevere, then we observe their malignant influence on the formation of the adult ego ideal, on the reliability of reality testing, and on the stabilization of sexual identity. The conceptualization of the nexus in which the just mentioned adolescent personality differentiations are affected by the isogender dyadic relationship and its resolution has been elaborated in Part One.

Judaism "bore your curse within it" (85, I) and that it was poisoned by his father's cynical and hypocritical comments about Judaism to which the boy and later the man had to listen. He spoke of this insidious influence as one that deprived him of his birthright and made him unable to ever establish a Jewish identity of his own (see 75, II). The synagogue scene cited above reflects a vengeful mockery and caricature of the father. Psychologically speaking, the boy's blasphemous vilification of God and Father belongs to that cluster of determinants which usually entice an upsurge of independence. This, however, was too half-hearted a self-assertion to deliver the boy from his infantile father bondage. The experience in the temple reflected the son's ambivilant feelings toward the father, who had neglected to pass on to the son his Jewish heritage, but made instead a mockery of it by his perfunctory and hypocritical attendance at the Sabbath services (see pp. 75–85). Kafka felt "in sober truth a disinherited son" (91, I).

This thought brings us back to the discussion of the infantile bisexual position which was never resolved, keeping the dyadic paternal split defensively intact. Therefore the phase-specific libidinal contribution to the triadic stage could never become attainable. The passions of the oedipal conflict became inhibited or arrested and remained encompassed in a son-father bondage of a sadomasochistic nature; this constellation induces a deviant formation of character. Any praise from the father was rejected as undeserved and therefore false at the core; in a perverse need for masochistic humiliation and self-deprecation (see 89, I) Kafka never ceased to provoke these emotional experiences by exposing himself avidly to their repetition.

An early memory which Kafka describes in the *Letter* bears the hallmark of a paradigmatic event which condenses the essence of his infantile trauma, setting the stage for reliving it yet never arriving at its mastery. "There is only one episode in the early years* of which I have a direct memory" (17, I). He describes the incident: "One night I kept on whimpering for water." When the father's shouts failed to silence the child, "You took me out of bed, carried me onto the *pavlatche* [balcony], and left me there alone for a while in my nightshirt, outside the shut door" (17, I). The "extraordinary terror" evoked by this incident made a lasting impression. "Even years afterwards I suffered from the tormented fancy that the huge man, my father, would" (17, I) do such a thing; it meant to Kafka that "I was a mere nothing for him . . . this sense of nothingness . . . often dominates me" (17, I–II) still. Kafka touches here on the origin, condensed in a single episode (comparable to a screen memory), of his lifelong annihilation anxiety, abandonment, depression, helplessness in the rageful arms of "the huge man"; eventually he let go of all budding

---

* "Early years" reads in the German text "ersten Jahren," which more accurately translated would be "the very first years."

self-assertion. The crushing sense of nothingness left no other escape open to the child but masochistic surrender, begging for "a little encouragement, a little friendliness, a little keeping open of my road" (17, II). Paradoxically, it was precisely the child's meekness, his whining and supplicant manner, that aroused the father's sadistic contemptuousness and emotional brutality. Kafka makes a point of the fact that he was not physically beaten as a child, but rather emotionally neglected and abused by his father (see 41, I). He still regrets that the father was "scarcely able to be with me even once a day" (15, III); he missed the physical closeness to his persecutor, whose infliction of mental pain was like an addiction, more desirable than the father's absence and indifference. He never ceased to place himself in the father's path and receive his insults or humiliating comments, which spoiled everything that might have been a source of happiness or joy: ". . . by virtue of your antagonistic nature, you could not help but always and inevitably cause the child such disappointments . . ." (23, I); ". . . one was utterly defenseless against you" (25, I). He felt always in the wrong whether he obeyed or was contrary. He suffered from shame whether he was submissive and weak or obstreperous and oppositional. He was caught in the snare of his sadomasochistic guilt. Yet he knew well, ". . . if I had obeyed you less, I am sure you would have been much better pleased with me" (33, II). In spite of his knowledge how to please his father and gratify his expectations, the passive masochistic craving always won out at the end. In a perverse way he was the ideal counterpart to the father, who lavishly dispensed his sadistic torment on the son standing weak, paralyzed, and awestruck before the giant and his "engimatic innocence and inviolability" (35, III). The pair formed the perfect match of master and slave. Kafka expressed it in these words: "When I began to do something you did not like and you threatened me with the prospect of failure, my veneration for your opinion was so great that the failure became inevitable . . ." (37, I).

One is tempted to attribute the son's surrender of his desires to the fear of competition with the oedipal father. No doubt this factor plays its part in his chronic submissiveness. However, in the light of my study as presented here, it seems more likely that the perseveration of the idealized father imago and the dependency on it provided the only attainable protection against the imminent danger of being swept into the chaos and terror of ego disintegration. Stating my opinion in this way raises urgent questions; they will be taken up in the discussion which follows.

Creativity, a Way of Life

The question arises as to why Kafka as a little boy fled into the dyadic, isogender protectorate where the father was the absolute potentate and, furthermore, why child and adult never left this domain of mutually torturing impositions. ". . . for me as a child everything you called out at me was positively a heavenly commandment . . . the most important means of forming a judgment of the world . . ." (27, I). To call this impasse a developmental arrest does not address the question as to the point of breakdown along the line of developmental progression, resulting in a pathological father fixation.

My clinical studies on the ontogeny of dyadic, isogender sonship always comprises a two-generational synergic system which I had occasion to observe in the analysis of male adolescents and adult men. My clinical observations coalesced with the well-established findings of infant research* which describe the little boy's passionate turn to the father as the savior from the regressive pull to the reengulfing mother. This normal and shifting dyadic maneuver from one parent to the other is gradually outgrown by the ascendancy of the rapprochement subphase. The establishment of object constancy which follows brings about by its very nature a reduction in the dyadic split into the good and the bad object. It seems to me that at this juncture a break in Kafka's development occurred. The rapprochement subphase was bypassed, with the result that the idealization of the good, namely, the godlike father imago, became established as a lifelong bulwark against regression to the archaic mother.

This defensive stance effected with the arrival of puberty lifelong inhibition in Kafka's relation to women. Even if we take into account constitutional sensitivities and physical inadequacies, to which he refers repeatedly in the *Letter*, there still remains the question what those catastrophic anxieties may have been which derailed the normal developmental course of object relations during the early life of the little boy.

At one point Kafka reflects in the *Letter* on the fact that he had to succumb to the father's powerful presence "particularly since my brothers died when they were small" (11, II). He, the first child and the first-born son, witnessed the death of two infant brothers. The young boy might well have wondered why the mother did not keep them alive or why she gratified the common enough wish of the first-born to remain her only child? We can only surmise that the father in his bereavement heaped all paternal expectations on the one son left to him. Kafka's first brother was born when he was slightly more than two years old and about four years old when this brother died; he was slightly more than four years old on the birth of his second brother, who died at the age of six months. Three sisters were born later, when Franz was six, seven, and nine years old respectively.** Kafka's reference in the *Letter* to the

---

* These studies have been referred to in Part One.

** The dates reported here were taken from R. Hayman's biography of Kafka (1982, pp. 11, 19).

death of his little brothers in conjunction with his father's gigantic power suggests the conjecture that the mother had become devalued as a protector of life in the perception of the small child, who fled for protection into the realm of the idealized father. The infantile fixation became the source of a lifelong yearning for caretaking or mothering by the godlike father imago. Only his father's presence, physically and mentally, would calm his fear of dying. The importance to the father of having a son, and the grief of having lost two sons early in their lives, can be gauged by the quote from Hayman's (1982) Kafka biography: "It can be inferred from Hermann Kafka's [the father] later reactions to the birth of nephews and grandchildren that he must have taken enormous pleasure and pride in the birth of his first son . . ." (p. 12).

The question which logically arises at this point concerns Kafka's struggle to escape from the pathological adaptation in his early life and from the suffering it had caused him ever since. There are three relevant qualities of his personality which repeatedly surface in the *Letter*. The first is his innate gift of writing and imaginative thought. His unique and personal imagination and his verbal gift of expressing it allowed him to cast his inner life into a socialized and communicable form; it broke down the prison walls of his isolation, estrangement, and loneliness. This is the moment to remind ourselves that Kafka's literary facility for infusing his writings with the distinctive emotional state of alienation and the absurd (words that became popular expressions of mood and attitude in the post-World War II epoch) afford him the distinction of having been in the vanguard of existentialist writing. The highly personal idiom of his imagination, which sustained his creative productivity, became a bridge to the outer world, rescuing the endangered artist from a delusional isolation.

Kafka knew well of his father's "aversion to my writing" (85, II), and furthermore he realized that "here I had, in fact, got some distance away from you by my own efforts. . . . To a certain extent I was in safety; there was a chance to breathe freely. The aversion you naturally and immediately took to my writing was, for once, welcome to me" (85, II–87, I). Regardless of where his imagination took him, the father asserted his presence in the act of writing, but it might be concluded that Kafka tried to master his pathological father complex in the literary act and at least succeeded in containing it within manageable bounds. At other times he lived like an escaped prisoner on the loose, searching the world for proof of his guilt; by not having served his time commensurate to his crime, he had forfeited forever his return to the blissful state of innocence. He was possessed by a sense of being "condemned" (see 91, I). No wonder the uncertainty of continued creative resourcefulness haunted the author: ". . . in my writing, and in everything connected with it, I have made some attempts at independence, attempts at escape

. . . it is my duty or, rather, the essence of my life, to watch over them, to let no danger . . . approach them" (117, II). He was aware that his writing represented his most reliable and therefore most valuable self-built, self-regulated, and self-reflective identity without which his psychological survival would have been endangered. Paradoxically, writing not only offered him an escape from the emotional bondage to his father but also kept the writer in constant closeness to him, albeit in a transfigured mode. He says, "My writing was all about you; all I did there, after all, was to bemoan what I could not bemoan upon your breast. It was an intentionally long-drawn-out leave-taking from you . . ." (87, I). Writing became the most effectively perfected stabilizer in Kafka's mental life.

We shall pause here and turn to Greenacre's (1963) study of gifted and creative individuals, whom she characterized in ways similar to my interpretation of Kafka. She explores "especially the father-son rather than the mother-son part" (p. 14) of the oedipal relationship, and she states that "the eternal search for the father . . . goes on in many artists (using the term in its broader sense) and appears to be an integral part of their oedipal problems" (p. 14). In terms of phase progression in early development, the artist tends "to permit a less decisive closing of the successive libidinal phases of early childhood than might otherwise be true. One result of this intrinsic state of affairs may be a diminished firmness of the barrier between primary-process and secondary-process thinking and imagery, a condition which seems characteristic of gifted individuals" (pp. 15–16). The *Letter* forces this very insight on the reader by its stark persuasiveness, indeed, the evidence contained in the text as a whole.

Greenacre elaborates these thoughts further by saying, ". . . deferment of the resolution of the oedipus complex may result in passive elements in the character being emphasized, and a repetitive, endless search for the ideal father sometimes becomes established" (p. 22). The ultimate futility of this search turns the artist to an "inner acceptance of the creative ability as belonging to the individual himself. It is his own possession; his gift; his fate, burden and obligation; not to be forgiven, sanctioned or lightened by a hypothetical god or god-father" (p. 23).

The *Letter* convincingly demonstrates that no deprecation, no sneering attitude or disregard of his writing or published works by his father, could ever deter him from persevering in his creative endeavor. In all other respects he granted his father the right, indeed the obligation, to dominate his beliefs, values, and actions. However, in the realm of his creative work he was free, even though he declared that "my writing was all about you" (87, I), the father. This enclave of mental freedom in his tortured private world made it possible for him to survive because, quoting Greenacre, "But it is only when the creative person really acknowledges his own ability and accepts the responsibility that it entails, that there is any marked diminution in the dangerous guilt feelings and self-destructiveness" (p. 23). Kafka talks about this enclave of freedom as of a sanctuary he has to take care of at all cost; nothing else seems to matter as long as he remains able to protect this sanctum sanctorum against the destructive forces raging from within and without.*

The second avenue of escape from the persecutory attachment to the father was marriage. Kafka states unequivocally in the *Letter* that "marrying is the greatest thing of all and provides the most honorable independence, it is also at the same time in the closest relation to you" (113, II). To enter the triangle of self, wife, and father is bound to be "punished" by "a touch of madness' (see 113, II). Kafka returned several times in his life to acting on his wish to escape by marriage, but he canceled his plan each time. ". . . the marriage plans turned out to be the most grandiose and hopeful attempts at escape . . ." (97, I). His fear of insanity and his fear of endangering his identity as a writer both loomed on the horizon of marriage and left Kafka no choice but to reso- lutely renounce "Marrying, founding a family, accepting all the children that come . . . the utmost a human being can succeed in doing" (99, II).

The third possible avenue of escape from the insufferable pain of mental imprisonment was one, never as clearly stated or recognized in the *Letter* as the other two outlined above. I refer to Kafka's consumptive illness, which finally caused his death. He tried to avert the spiritual and physical breakdown by being "brutishly complacent" and behaving in "cold indifference" as "the sole defense against destruction of the nerves by fear and by a sense of guilt" (89, I). References to his physical weakness and inadequacy abound in the *Letter*. A hypochondriacal preoccupation with his body's shortcomings —"a little anxiety about digestion, hair falling out, a spinal curvature . . . it finally ended with real illness" (89, I)— is paralleled by a tendency to "wallow" in his observance of their pathetic nature, which it was his lot to bear. They became the source of boundless shame, but his passive acceptance of his body inferiority afforded him small relief. The reification of his body awareness was fol- lowed by somatization. The reading of Kafka's *Letter* strongly intimates that the sequence of undeserved body intactness, its destruction in the course of atonement, and subsequent hypochondriacal obsessions led to the fatal breakdown of his body. His own words give credence to his belief in the inescapable destiny he felt compelled to carry to its fulfill- ment: ". . . naturally I became unsure even of the thing nearest to me, my own body. . . . I was amazed by everything I could still command

* Here André Gide's entry in his journal comes to mind: "A work of art is an equilibrium outside of time, an artificial health". Jean Delay, *The Youth of André Gide* (1963, p. 9).

as by a miracle, for instance, my good digestion; that sufficed to lose it, and now the way was open to every sort of hypochondria; until finally under the strain of the superhuman effort of wanting to marry . . . blood came from the lung. . . . So all this did not come from excessive work . . ." (91, I). The protracted, slow and sorrowful drift toward self-annihilation was the only escape left open after all other efforts to endure life's burdens had come to naught. Kafka was dimly aware of this drift toward physical self-extinction when he said to his friend Max Brod, "My head has made an appointment with my lungs behind my back" (Brod, 1963, p. 76).*

The *Letter* was Kafka's final desperate plea to the father that he come to his help at the moment of physical and mental exhaustion; only his love, care, and acceptance might avert the impending disaster. Having opened his heart to his father in the *Letter,* the son hoped against hope that there could be a word of mutual forgiveness, a sign—no matter how small—of friendliness and love. That hope was in vain. Silence descended, and the passions contained in the *Letter* fell into a void. In this lonely wilderness we hear the echo of words, uttered 2,000 years ago and repeated many times since by men in extremis who "cried out with a loud voice . . . Father, into thy hands I commend my spirit" (Luke 23:46) and "My God, my God, why hast thou forsaken me?" (Matthew 27:46).

Addendum on Freud's Schreber Case**

Anyone who is familiar with Freud's writings must have been reminded of the Schreber case—the most often quoted of his five case histories—in reading the preceding commentary on Kafka's *Letter to His Father.* Freud based his case history on the 1903 autobiographical account by Schreber (1842–1911), entitled *Memoirs of My Nervous Illness.* This document describes in detail the workings of his mind during the years of his psychotic illness, for which he was hospitalized twice.

In both autobiographical documents, those of Kafka and of Schreber, the vicissitudes of the son-father relationship are of focal importance and recorded in the most eloquent of terms; they reveal the private life of their authors' minds with an extraordinary candor and unrestrained self-revelation. The reading of these documents makes it abundantly clear that neither of the two men has acquired in the course of development that modicum of detachment and optimal distance from the dyadic father

* In referring to the circumstances evoking Kafka's remark, Brod writes, ". . . he used these words to describe his disease as a way out, which was not even unwelcome, from the difficulties he was then faced with on the question of the marriage he had been planning."
** S. Freud, *Psycho-analytic Notes on an Autobiographical Account of a Case of Paranoia (Dementia Paranoides)*, 1911.

which normally cancels out the infantilizing influence of intense early father attachment and idealization with its malignant possibility of a regressive fusion. Schreber's attainment of manhood was fragmentary and remained in a state of continuous jeopardy, calling into action all kinds of protective devices to ward off the disintegration of a tenuous self. The entanglement in a perpetual ambivalence toward the father imago blurred his vision of the real father. This condition, similar in both men, rendered them susceptible not only to intense feelings of guilt and their continuous expiation but also to androgynous fluctuations in their sense of self and gender. In these states of conflict and blurred identity the father had become the central figure in relation to whom a confused and disoriented condition of the mind became tenuously stabilized. Any settlement of the relationship to the father had to be abandoned because the son came soon to suspect a mutually seductive complicity between them—mostly of a sadomasochistic nature—which was counteracted by an equally devastating resolution, namely, to seek in the father a protective refuge, a blissful union with the godhead.

Having sketched in broad outlines the general psychological trends recognizable in both documents, we must now admit that their similarity ends at this point of generalization. It is obvious that Schreber's paranoia and his delusional relationship to God, on the one hand, and Kafka's lifelong obsessional preoccupation with the relationship to his father, on the other, are qualitatively quite different. The two men struggle with similar conflicts of a dyadic father attachment but with quite dissimilar weapons. Self-protective psychic accommodations are not only determined by the adhesive power of a given fixation, and consequently a preferred drive orientation, but also by the individual's innate endowment, his unique resourcefulness, creativity, or talent. The function of the latter is well demonstrated in my commentary on Kafka's *Letter to His father.* There he clearly implies that his creative work is to him the ultimate and absolute safeguard against personality disintegration, even though the creative act itself, namely writing, was to his conscious self-experience an act of intimacy with his father: "My writing was all about you; all I did there, after all, was to bemoan what I could not bemoan upon your breast" (87, I). While gratifying infantile emotional longings, Kafka's giftedness—that undefinable quality of genius—kept him in solid touch with the human world; it protected the author from the solipsistic drift into isolation and delusional estrangement from reality. Consequently, the contact with humanity or, more precisely, with his social surround was never lost. He was able to share the uncanny, unreal, dreamlike, and dark side of his inner world with his fellow man in his writing. These remarkable creations seem to me born by the same forces as Goya's "black paintings": they both unhinge irresistibly and fleetingly our sense of "being in this world."

Schreber, in contrast, has lost all ties to the real world. He invented a personal cosmology, an autistic universe of his private design, in which his father, as a real person of his past life, had lost his identity by being projected into the realm of supernatural, ideational constructs. He replaced his father's and his own identity by delusional and hallucinatory creations of his psychotic mind and thus made himself incomprehensible to his fellow man. In this isolation he pursued the tortuous, laborious effort of consolidating his fragmented inner life by putting together his own world order, in which God and he tried in vain to work out a modus vivendi. He was convinced that "a force of attraction emanating from individual bodies—and in my case—from one single human body over such enormous distances . . . may appear quite absurd . . . it is a fact that for me is absolutely unquestionable."* He continues to elaborate the "regular exchange between God and human souls,"* defining the different state of bliss for male and female souls after death. The history, exploration, and verification of such ideas as the ones just mentioned largely constitute the content of the *Memoirs* (Schreber, 1903), on which Freud's case history (1911) is based. To no other reader except Freud could the *Memoirs* at the time of publication have meant more than the bizarre, somewhat piquant self-exposure of a deranged mind.

I take encouragement for juxtaposing the confessions of the two men—Kafka and Schreber—from Freud's remark in his Schreber essay when he says, ". . . we have only to follow our usual psycho-analytic technique . . . and we find ourselves in possession of what we are looking for, namely a translation of the paranoic mode of expression into the normal one" (Freud, 1911, p. 35). This statement affirms the belief that essential aspects of a psychopathological deviation can be traced to a malignant deformation of a stage in normal development and to an abortive attempt to undo the inflicted damage. One such stage, which I explore in this essay, is related to the dyadic father experience in the male child. Freud's above comment, if applied to my purpose of using the Schreber essay to throw additional light on the universality of the isogender dyadic complex in the psychological development of the male child, restricts, however, the comparative review of both documents to a few selected topics. A discussion of Schreber's delusions and constructions in relation to the psychoanalytic theory of psychosis has no place in my present discourse. There are, however, parallels which deserve our attention in an effort to grasp the profundity and ubiquitousness of impact which the imago of the early father exerts on the male child and his subsequent development. The following questions present themselves: what are the transformations which the father imago undergoes in time, what are the residues that become the heritage of this early experience for the remainder of a man's life, and, in which latent or manifest form do they remain

* Schreber (1903). Quoted in Niederland (1974, p. 11).

recognizable to the clinical observer of the life cycle, be he psychoanalyst, anthropologist, or sociologist?

The most startling parallel between the two documents is to be found in the identity of father and God, which runs like a red thread through the autobiographical account of both men. God remains the inscrutable symbol of the other man, or the only other of any consequence; his presence reaches back into the dawn of individual existence and has never since lost the charismatic magnetism of the original father experience. The maturing child who has adhered to this early attachment emotion beyond its time may be looked at as living in an eternal search for his personal Rosetta stone to decipher captivating hieroglyphics and symbolic representations of his own forgotten making. They are projected or transmuted into equivalents of archaic, fixated experiences and expressed on all levels of body and mind. These struggles are the burden of men who are afflicted with the emotional liability of a dyadic father fixation; they live out a never quieted striving for an undefined and undefinable fulfillment; they are torn asunder by puzzlement about the meaning of life; they ceaselessly demand clarification and understanding of the mysteriously unknown in order to loosen or master the stranglehold of the father complex on the mind; this predicament applies to those adolescent or adult males whose dyadic father attachment has never been relinquished in the forward motion of emotional maturation.

In his Schreber essay, Freud has convincingly established the identity of God and father in the mind of the patient. "Of importance to the understanding of the case is Schreber's peculiar combination of worship and admiration toward God on the one hand, and opposition to and disrespect for Him on the other. In assuming a feminine attitude toward God, he believed he was God's wife" (quoted in Niederland, 1974, p. 24). Schreber's never ceasing quarrel with God and the eternal futility of efforts to reach a resolution of his unbearable state of disaffection (except in his delusional cosmology) is paralleled by Kafka's never ceasing effort to come to a mutually respectful recognition between father and son, thus hopefully reaching a state of emotional independence and peace of mind. Kafka accuses his father of having nipped in the bud his zest for life, his self-esteem, and his capacity to love. These are devastating particulars in his long list of filial indictments. Here, Freud's comment on the Schreber autobiography comes to mind: "Through the whole of Schreber's book there runs the bitter complaint that God, being only accustomed to communication with the dead, does not understand living men" (Freud, 1911, p. 25). In order to reach the father-God, one has to surrender one's self-identity and become a body without self-initiated directedness. In Schreber's words of ambivalence, ". . . not even God is or was a being of such absolute perfection as most religions ascribe to Him" (See Niederland, 1974, p. 13).

Kafka blames his father in no uncertain words for having killed his spirit as a small child, having committed a symbolic act of filicide from which no resurrection was ever possible. "Courage, resolution, confidence, delight in this or that, could not last when you were against it or even if your opposition was merely to be assumed; and it was assumed in almost everything I did" (Kafka, I, 23). Yet in spite of accusing his father of having mortally wounded his spirit, the son pronounces with devotion and conviction that he knows; ". . . you are at bottom a kindly and softhearted person" (Kafka, 1966, p. 15). Schreber writes at length about "soul murder." First he accuses his doctor, Professor Flechsig, of it; then he withdraws the indictment by resorting to evasions of complicated cosmological constructs. "Soul murder" is a way of paraphrasing the act of emasculation or bringing about the death of the soul, i.e., of mind, reason, spirit, and identity.

Both documents are replete with endless ruminations, affirmations, and their recantations; they reflect the conviction that God or father is either a monstrous villain with evil power and intention or an incredibly pure and guiltless saint of shining light and inexhaustible goodness. Schreber assigns to God a moral duality; there is an "upper" God and a "lower" God, Ariman and Ormuzd, both projections of his divided self, a superior state of man and an inferior one of woman; the latter he describes as an uninterrupted feeling of voluptuousness to which he is attracted in himself against his will. These alternating perceptions of the father-God, of the "pater noster," reflect the dyadic state of early object relations in which the "good" and "bad" qualities of an object do not belong to the same person. They are part-object relations and therefore preambivalent, since ambivalence by definition presumes that the whole-person concept is established in the child's mind. To the mutually exclusive states of perception and affect, referred to as preambivalent, we should more correctly apply the term "ambitendency" (Mahler, 1975) to avoid confusion.

My next comment refers to the little boy's responsiveness and susceptibility to early bodily manipulations executed by the father and accompanied by his aggressively coercive attitude and selfserving affective involvement. From Niederland's research we have become acquainted with the publications of Schreber's father, a physician, who invented orthopedic apparatuses made of iron, which forced the growing child to lie, to sit, to hold the head, or to carry himself in a fixed so-called natural posture with the purpose of assisting nature in the creation of beautiful children. To this endeavor Dr. Schreber senior, had dedicated his life. This elaborate and, in Germany at the time, widely recognized system of physical education was called by Dr. Schreber "Pangymnasticon." The special exercises and exposure to corrective instruments, applied to the growth of children, comprised a system called "Kallipaedie," literally meaning "beautiful child." (Niederland, 1974, pp. 50–51)* Many of the patient's physical symptoms involving sensations in his head, chest, or coccyx were, in his words, "miracled up" by divine powers. These symptoms, as part of Schreber's delusional system, were concretized experiential references to his father's gadgetry, which Niederland's research, supported by the original illustrations from Dr. Schreber senior's books, has brought to our attention. Schreber describes the "miracled up" states in his visions of world destruction as "in part too of an indescribable splendor" (1903, 17). The physical manipulation of the child by the father's gadgets very likely elicited two extremes of emotional states—horror and enchantment, panic and ecstasy—both surviving as isolated fragments of the early father experience.

The wish of a father for a son is not infrequently coupled with the wish for a "real" boy, namely, strong and handsome; this wish can hardly be called an unconscious or a reproachable paternal desire. However, if it evokes excessive practices to assure its realization or if it coincides too exclusively with the father's need to make up for bodily shortcomings of his own, present or past (father Schreber was supposedly of quite small stature [Niederland, 1974, p. 51]), then the father's efforts are experienced by the son as a blame, a rejection, a degradation of his male identity.

In Kafka's *Letter* we have an example of this reaction. The father wished his son to be "soldierly," to march, swim, and exercise, in short, be a "real" boy. This paternal wish was conveyed mostly by words, such as exhortations, with their accompanying affective innuendo intended to ram the father's wishes into his little son's soul. There is one focal reference in Kafka's *Letter* to an act of his father's bodily manipulation of him, executed with physical force and in a state of angry excitement. Kafka recognizes in this incident a catastrophic moment of his early life. We might refer to it as a specimen memory which compacts, so to speak, the son's early relationship to his father or, more exactly, spotlights a powerful component of it. The *Letter* hints at endless repetitions of this prototypical event, executed in later years in the father's aggressive man-handling of his son's ideational life and value system. Kafka describes in detail "one episode in the early years of which I have a direct memory." The child asked for a glass of water after bedtime. When he did not respond to the repeated request to go to sleep, the angry father picked him up, carried him onto the balcony, left him there, went back into the house, and shut the door. Kafka comments: "I am not going to say this was wrong"; all he wanted to say was that this incident stayed in his memory like a monument of his father's unfathomable powerfulness

* Both terms were extracted from Greek word roots by Dr. Schreber senior, who very likely believed, as educated Germans did at the time, that Greek culture had produced bodies of functional perfection and the greatest beauty.

and his own weak nothingness. To wit, "Even years afterwards I suffered from the tormenting fancy that the huge man, my father, the ultimate authority, would . . . take me out of bed . . . and that meant I was a mere nothing to him" (Kafka, 1966, p. 17). It is worth considering in this connection that the younger the child, the more numerous are physical contact and physical interaction between father and son and the more significant is the role these play in the communication between them as well as in the emotional imprintings of these physical, sensory contact experiences. These imprintings (fixations) of need-fulfilling states, encompassing pleasure and pain experiences, undergo a radical metamorphosis when the child acquires the capability of using the symbolic process, that exquisitely human and powerful mental instrument in man's mastery of the world; its earliest and most spectacular display arrives with the child's acquisition of language and thinking. Their articulation enables the mind to transpose the experience of physical and emotional needs onto a widening internal and social universe created by the symbolic process; we refer to this phenomenon as the growing complexity of the mind and of the expanding inventiveness in social communication.

I have described in Part One the little boy's perception of the dyadic father as the omnipotent protector of the helpless and dependent child. Surrendering to his attendance and sharing by submission or imitation the dyadic father's charismatic presence secures for the child again and again the bliss and security of having averted abandonment. Inevitably the passive posture becomes endowed with pleasant feelings which in the course of development are destined to yield to a masculine identification, which entails an active emotional distancing from the early father. This process goes through many stages of advance and retreat. Often we witness a role playing of "big boy" until the child is able to let go of the familiar and past, ready to move forward. Even then, the forward step in male identity formation often can only be secured temporarily and tenuously by an overbearing turn to noisy motions of self-affirmation. Should this turn or shift in balance from passive to active, from being carried and held to standing on one's own feet and doing one's own thing, be weak or indeed be defeated in the male child, then the passive attachment emotions of the dyadic period prevail beyond their developmental phase. The triadic, or oedipal, stage is consequently deficient in the usual and obligatory conflicts which elicit profound changes in the child's growing personality. With the advent of puberty, or sexual maturation, the never abandoned gender-alien posture becomes linked once more to the sexual drive; this psychophysical constellation is experienced by the male adolescent as a threat of feminization. Entrenchment at this transitional way station leads ultimately to an incomplete or aborted adolescent process. Adolescence requires for its completion the definitive formation of sexual identity. With the resurgence of the father attachment in all the shadings of ambivalence at the time the boy reaches sexual maturity, a transient regression to the dyadic father represents a normal developmental interlude; it opens the door—as regression in the service of development—to the removal of infantilizing residues of bonding to the dyadic father. This completion of unfinished tasks of early childhood is accomplished by bringing to bear the resourcefulness of the adolescent ego, acquired during middle childhood, on the resolution of these tasks, to which the young child had not been equal at the time.

Schreber's preoccupation with feminization, with having been unmanned or with having been transformed into a woman, is a recurrent theme in the *Memoirs* and central to Freud's thesis that homosexual trends, fantasies, and ideation lie embedded in the core of paranoia. "Observation leaves room for no doubt that the persecutor is someone who was once loved" (Freud, 1911, p. 63), namely the father. As the perpetrator of his transformation into a woman Schreber accused alternatively his doctor, Professor Flechsig, the father replication, and God, the deified father image. Flechsig, the man on whom Schreber had formed an "affectionate dependence" (Freud, 1911, p. 42), became the persecutor in his delusional world. By the magic of projection the patient disowns the unacceptable wish and distances it radically from the endangered self. The reversal reads, "it is not me who wants to submit to you, but it is you who wants me to play a woman's role to you." The patient admits in the *Memoirs* to his dishonorable acceptance of possessing a female body, which is the precondition for experiencing "soul voluptuousness," attainable only by women but representing a state of pleasure and fulfillment he envies and wishes to possess.

We recognize in Kafka's *Letter* a lifelong struggle with the same problem of submission and self-assertion, consciously experienced as a feeling of unmanliness as an adult and one of unboyishness, by allusion to girlishness, in his childhood years. All these emotions described in the *Letter* are without fail brought into the realm of his relationship to his father or his father's to him. Kafka's marriage plans came repeatedly to naught because he was convinced that his marriage would disappoint his father by the choice of his wife, even though the father expressed the wish that his only surviving son would prevent the Kafka lineage from dying out. We witness in Kafka's reasoning the projective reversal at work; it reads, "I cannot leave my father without having settled first our tortuous relationship by a friendly reconciliation and mutual forgiveness; furthermore, I cannot leave my father because I know that he could not live happily without me." This is in fact what the *Letter* is all about.

In both cases, the reconciliation motive attains a continuous and forceful, almost obsessional presence. Also in both cases, the accusation of "soul murder" by doctor, father, or God represents the bond that evokes the catacylsmic struggle for release from an emotional prison where the jailkeeper is alternately the prisoner's savior and tormentor. Freud expressed this thought in his Schreber essay: "We are perfectly familiar with the infantile attitude of boys toward their father; it is composed of the same mixture of reverent submission and mutinous insubordination that we have found in Schreber's relation to his God, and is the unmistakable prototype of that relation, which is faithfully copied from it" (Freud, 1911, p. 52).

I have attempted to show that such tragic conditions as recorded in the two autobiographical documents lie essentially in two developmental failures in a boy's life. One of them is the failure of detachment from the dyadic father; the other is to be found in adolescence, when normally the incompleted developmental stage of dyadic childhood is brought to a definitive resolution. Summarily I refer to this task as the deidealization of the infantile father imago. Whether failures along these developmental lines lead to a psychotic illness, to neurotic or characterological personality deformation, or to perversion or deviant patterns of object relations depends on a multiplicity of factors whose considerations lie outside the scope of this discussion.

One comment, however, I intend to make about the divergent outcome of Kafka's and Schreber's father complexes, even though my comment is by necessity speculative. Schreber's father died when the son was in his late adolescence; he was 19 years old (see Freud, 1911, p. 51). Kafka's father was alive as long as the son lived. Kafka, therefore, had a living antagonist with whom he could interact in an ongoing dramatization of his dyadic father complex, at one moment assigning to the great man guilt for his own wrongdoing and evil intentions, at the next moment taking on the entire weight of guilt and badness, declaring his father guiltless, godlike, and beyond reproach. This cycle repeats itself endlessly throughout the *Letter*.

I am fully aware of the fact that the father's personality and despotic behavior in the family, as well as generally in social intercourse, lend a realistic context to Kafka junior's accusations, offering a factual backdrop of daily life to which the particularities of the son-father relationship could be fittingly adapted. From all accounts, Schreber senior's behavior and personality also lent a concrete core to Schreber junior's delusions and accusations, though clearly Schreber junior obliterated the boundary between reality and fantasy, thus making himself the inhabitant of a delusional world.

While Kafka interacted all along with the living representative of his father complex, Schreber, in contrast, had to enact the tragedy of his dyadic father complex entirely on the internal stage of his mind because the father had died. The father had acquired in the son's late adolescence the state of a representational, i.e., internalized, "imago." Here we witness Schreber's distinction between corpses and souls and its elaboration. The mourning process remained at work indefinitely. The father's death separated body and soul: the corpse decays in the earth while the soul is kept alive in heaven where it has become one with God. A protracted mourning occupies Schreber's mind, cast in a concretizing imagery. We might assume that the son's adolescent process was short-circuited by the trauma of a double death: One was the death of his actual father when Schreber was an adolescent, while the other was the death of the father of infancy, which every adolescent boy has to endure in order to become an adult man. The double death might have paralyzed the mourning process or, in other words, mourning could never be brought to its natural termination. In this connection I must mention the importance to Schreber of the date when his father had died. Schreber notes in his Memoirs, 32 years after his father's death (November 10, 1861): "On November 8 or 9th [1893] my illness began to assume a menacing character" (quoted in Niederland, p. 84); the night of November 10 or 11, 1893, Schreber made the first sucide attempt and had himself hospitalized. "He felt he was dead and soon began to believe that he was suffering from ileus (an intestinal obstruction), the very disease to which the father had succumbed" (Niederland, p. 84).

Freud notes, "The patient's infantile attitude towards his father took effect in two successive phases. As long as his father was alive it showed itself in unmitigated rebelliousness and open discord, but immediately after his death it took the form of a neurosis based upon abject submission and deferred obedience to him. Thus in the case of Schreber we find ourselves once again on the familiar ground of the father-complex" (Freud, 1911, p. 55).

The moral dictum "De mortuis nil nisi bonum"* aborted the adolescent task of deidealization of the father in the face of his death. Death, as we well know, invites idealization. An emotional stalemate was thus created in the adolescent boy. The precondition for the son's progression to the state of emotional adulthood was probably forfeited by a virulent ambivalence toward the father. A susceptibility to mental illness was thus laid down early in life; the work of adolescent individuation was catastrophically disrupted and aborted by the father's death. It is possible that the incomplete mourning at adolescence continued in a delusional aggravation during his mental illness, which erupted in midlife. He was first hospitalized at the age of 42 for one year and again, at the age of 51, for nine years; the Memoirs were written during his second hospitalization.

Even though my ideas are speculative, I shall nevertheless pursue this line of thought by saying that in Kafka and in Schreber the normal infantile father complex was incompletely or only defensively and regres-

---

* "About the dead one speaks only well."

sively, i.e., maladaptively, resolved during the adolescent period, which is the appropriate time for the completion of this particular developmental task. Therefore, the normal mourning of the loss of the dyadic father as a corollary of the deidealization of his imago during late adolescence was not lived through by either one of the two men. Schreber resorted to delusional mourning, while Kafka's work of mourning became fused with his lifelong dedication to writing, of which he says, "It was an intentionally long drawn-out leave-taking from you," his father (Kafka, 87.I).

We might apply here what we have so often observed in our clinical work, namely, that fortuitous circumstances, such as death, physical accidents, love disappointments, and many more, especially if they occur at a crucial developmental juncture, tend to give one or another trend of the individual's latent or manifest endowment the upper hand, pushing the course of his life in a certain direction for better or worse.

Hamlet:

75 Years after Ernest Jones

Introductory notes

The idealization of the dyadic father: the "radiant angel"

The struggle of the dyadic male child: submission versus self-assertion: "the dread command"

The "also-mother" of the dyadic stage: "that pernicious woman"

Introductory Notes

Sophocles' *Oedipus Rex* and Shakespeare's *Hamlet* are the two great tragedies of the Western world which are both rooted in the consciousness and mysteries that have governed the son-father relationship through the ages. Yet the two tragedies differ in significant ways, even though they share the central thematic pathos of the son-father experience. The Greek play discloses what has been formulated by Freud as the Oedipus complex, which refers to the little boy's rivalry for the exclusive possession of his mother and to the wish to take the father's place by removing the great, admired, and envied rival from the sphere of his kingly reign. The famous lines from Sophocles' *Oedipus Rex* state this unflinchingly when Jocasta, the mother and the wife of Oedipus, declares, "Before this, in dreams too, as well as oracles, many a man has lain with his own mother. But he to whom such things are nothing bears his life most easily."* *Oedipus Rex*, then, is the tragedy of the oedipal, or triadic, son.

In *Hamlet*, however—despite the oedipal conflict in which the prince

---

* *Oedipus the King;* translated by David Grene, lines 981–984. In *Sophocles.* Chicago: The University of Chicago Press, 1959.

is unmistakably entangled—the dyadic attachment emotions toward the early father overshadow the conflict of the triadic conflict, thus adding an aspect of complexity to the son-father tragedy which is neither explicit nor discernible in *Oedipus Rex*. My proposition that *Hamlet* is the tragedy of the dyadic son I endeavor to support by what follows. In the course of the discussion I hope to throw light on one aspect of Hamlet's behavior, namely, his indecisiveness, which more than any other characteristic of the prince has remained a partial puzzlement even though it has been explored more widely and for a longer time than any other aspect of the play.

The illumination of the Oedipus complex in Freud's early writings has evoked ever since many refinements and modifications; some of them are still not generally accepted. Since Jones built his *Hamlet* interpretation predominantly on Freud's early views, two relevant comments by Freud (1917) shall be quoted: "From this time [of puberty] onwards, the human individual has to devote himself to the great task of detaching himself from his parents and not until that task is achieved can he cease to be a child . . ." (p. 337). He goes on to state that "for the maturing son the task consists in detaching his libidinal wishes from his mother . . . and in reconciling himself with his father if he has remained in opposition to him, or in freeing himself from his pressure if . . . he has become subservient to him." (p. 337). In the classical Freudian view, still prevalent in many quarters, the triadic oedipal situation overshadows all previous vagaries of the infantile mind and has kept the normative and fateful attachment emotions of the male child toward his dyadic father in the darkness of nonrecognition for a long, perhaps too long, a time.

It was Ernest Jones who devoted many decades to establishing a thematic bridge between the two plays mentioned. His first paper on *Hamlet* was published in 1910 (Jones, 1910); his extended and final study on the subject was not published until 1949, when it appeared as a book under the title *Hamlet and Oedipus* (Jones, 1949); a year earlier it had been preceded by a short paper entitled "The Death of Hamlet's Father" (Jones, 1948). These studies took their issue from Freud's conceptualization of the Oedipus complex. Jones expanded on a comment which Freud had made in *The Interpretation of Dreams* (1900): ". . . Shakespeare's *Hamlet* has its roots in the same soil as Oedipus Rex. . . . The play is built on Hamlet's hesitation over fulfilling the task of revenge that is assigned to him. . . . Hamlet is able to do anything—except take vengeance on the man who did away with his father and took that father's place with his mother, the man who shows him the repressed wishes of his own childhood realized" (Freud, 1900, pp. 264–265).

Maloney and Rockelein (1949) were aware of the unfathomed complexity of the Oedipus complex and its early antecedents. Their paper is rich in suggestive ideas in the sphere of early emotional development.

In fact they pose the poignant question to which we later will address ourselves: What did Hamlet fear would happen to him if he would kill Claudius? Was it obligatory for Hamlet to remain passive-submissive? Does his fear of growing up—with all this implies, including the terror of the Queen—paralyze his action and confuse his mind? Does the avoidance of killing Claudius permit him "to return to school, i.e., to become a schoolboy" (p. 95) and in doing so remain a sheltered child of whom he himself speaks with cynical disdain and self-contempt:

> *What is a man*
> *If his chief good and market of his time*
> *Be but to sleep and feed?*

[Act IV, scene iv, 33–35]*

Are not sleeping and feeding the "principal physiological activities of the infant"? (Maloney and Rockelein, p. 97.)

I proceed with the same conviction that guided Jones in his work, namely, the conviction that endogenous givens as well as what is experientially acquired represent the basic structures of the human mind and body from which individual behavior takes its cue. It is true that Jones bases his interpretive approach on the premise that abnormal, i.e., neurotic, aberrations of the instinctual drives and of the defensive organization of the ego contain the etiological explanation of disturbed behavior. Since the days of Jones's Hamlet study, psychoanalytic theory has given to the developmental and adaptive components of behavior a much more prominent place in order to understand motivation within the context of normative stage progression. This point of view has been incorporated by now, more or less solidly, in the body of psychoanalytic theory and has become equivalent to the traditional categories of psychoanalytic metapsychology. Jones took the universality of the Oedipus complex as the base line of his reasoning in the attempt to illuminate, or rather to make sense of, Hamlet's hesitation to avenge his father's murder by his brother, who hastily had married the widowed Queen.

One comment has to be made before I address the essence of my contribution to the "Hamlet problem." In studying the psychoanalytic writings on *Hamlet* I came to realize that each author has added some specific idea to the vast scope of the tragedy in an effort to give persuasive cohesion to the play in its totality. My effort is deliberately more modest and refrains from any textual, historical, and social considerations, as well as from the diagnosis of Hamlet's "madness" or Ophelia's "psychosis." I also abstain from the ambition to render a comprehensive or alternative interpretation of the drama as a whole. With tongue in cheek I quote

* All quotations from *Hamlet* are taken from The Arden Shakespeare *Hamlet,* 1982.

from James Joyce's Hamlet discourse in *Ulysses:* "All these questions are purely academic, Russell oracled out of his shadow. I mean, whether Hamlet is Shakespeare or James I or Essex. Clergymen's discussions of the historicity of Jesus. Art has to reveal our ideas, formless spiritual essences. The supreme question about a work of art is out of how deep a life does it spring . . . the words of Hamlet bring our mind into contact with the eternal wisdom, Plato's world of ideas. All the rest is the speculation of schoolboys for schoolboys" (1961, p. 185). These are arrogant words: Joyce cannot quite abide by them himself. He simply wishes to declare that he elected to use Hamlet as a poetic vehicle to express his own ideas; this seems to me a permissible digression from formalized literary criticism. The departure in his idiosyncratic discourse on Hamlet leads him into the world of Platonic ideas, the essence of which he clinches in his hilarious neologism, "Horseness is the whatness of allhorse" (p. 186). He tries his ideas for fit on the bedazzling creation of Shakespeare. One of his ideas is the intergenerational double, or mirror-image interchangeability between father and son. "Is it possible that the player Shakespeare, a ghost by absence, and in the vesture of buried Denmark, a ghost by death, speaking his own words to his own son's name (had Hamnet Shakespeare* lived he would have been prince Hamlet's twin), is it possible, I want to know, or probable that he did not draw or foresee the logical conclusion of those premises: you are the dispossessed son: I am the murdered father: your mother is the guilty queen. Ann Shakespeare, born Hathaway?" (Joyce, p. 189.)

The untutored reader and audience of *Hamlet* have for centuries been moved by a play as timeless as the human condition, as familiar as the stages of growth from birth to death, inclusive of the uncountable and unaccountable perplexities that lie between them. The play touches each listener deeply and personally. Quoting Joyce again, "But *Hamlet* is so personal, isn't it? Mr. Best pleaded. I mean a kind of private paper don't you know, of his private life. I mean I don't care a button, don't you know, who is killed and who is guilty . . ." (p. 184). The spontaneous audience resonance bears witness to the fact that most personal and private, yet universal human emotions, thoughts, and fantasies are evoked in each listener by this play. It is my hope that my present comment on *Hamlet* will make the audience reaction to the play somewhat more comprehensible. Universal human emotions and the play itself reflect a mutual correspondence which invites our effort to search for significant origins in the common, timeless human experience.

Among these emotions I have elected the son-father experience as

---

* Shakespeare's only son, christened Hamnet in 1585, died when he was nine years old, one year before the play *Hamlet* was composed by his father. (Footnote by P.B.)

the focus of my investigation. There are many more and most of them have been exhaustively discussed by other commentators. The overdetermination of any single aspect of the play is too infinite to possibly do justice to them in one single sweep of interpretation, even though its limited, yet distinct contribution to our enlightenment on *Hamlet* is not to be doubted (see Hutter, 1975). I ask the simple question, where in Hamlet's behavior or utterances can we ascertain reflections of the universal experience of the dyadic, isogender stage, usually referred to as the preoedipal stage, in the emotional development of the male child? In postulating that the consequences or residues of any normative developmental stage can never be lost without leaving some traces in the human mind and, furthermore, in assuming that these traces become constituents of the emotional equipment which determine the individual modality of behavior and thought, an urgent question arises before us: What do these developmental givens contribute to an understanding of Hamlet's perplexing procrastination and, more specifically, to the elective and isolated character of his procrastination and inaction, restricted to the act of revenge, namely, killing his uncle? Hamlet is admirably able to take decisive action in all other matters except this one. Jones was well aware of the early determinants in motivation: ". . . it is often overlooked that childhood is preceded by another period, that of infancy, which is vastly more fateful for the future than anything that happens in childhood" (1949, pp. 84–85).*

In Part One of this book I have developed the proposition of a dyadic isogender stage of rival significance in development to the oedipal stage proper. Since I intend to apply this dynamic formulation to my discussion of the Hamlet problem, I shall at this point review the characteristics of the dyadic stage as well as their pursuant conflicts and resolutions during the adolescent period. From there I shall proceed to trace the residues of these infantile emotions as they survive in the unmodulated, infantile, but beguilingly and histrionically disguised expressions, actions, and utterances of Hamlet, who lingers and loiters in the borderland that lies between youth and manhood.**

* Jones attributes the elucidation of infancy to the work of Freud and especially to that of Melanie Klein and her fellow workers. He makes a distinction between infancy and childhood as two essentially different stages; usually they are referred to in psychoanalytic terminology as the preoedipal and oedipal stages or—as I prefer to call them, with emphasis on the hallmark characteristic of each—the dyadic and triadic stages of infancy or early childhood (Jones, 1949, p. 85).

** The age of Hamlet has been disputed for a long time by critics and actors; they have made him from 18 to 40 years old. Jones recommends that an actor should keep Hamlet's age "within the twenties—preferably the late twenties" (1949, p. 182). Eissler (1968) comments, "Hamlet was about 20 at the beginning of the play" (p. 207). I am in agreement with the latter determination of his age, which seems to me right on the basis of a developmental assessment.

The Idealization of the Dyadic Father: The "Radiant Angel"

The isogender dyadic stage of the boy is preambivalent and precompetitive. The high noon of the male attitudes and strivings which are marked
by ambivalence and competition with the father arrives in the triadic,
or oedipal, period, age three to five, more or less. An overlapping of
the dyadic and triadic stages makes an exact age reference rather arbitrary
and incorrect. Before the oedipal era the father's magnificence constitutes
a source of security and enhances the child's self-esteem; his image is
awkwardly but resolutely appropriated by the boy in imitation and spir-
ited role playing. The father as a figure of importance in comparison
with the mother and the wider world is dimly but luminously perceived
and—for the time being—wildly exaggerated. The elaboration into the
extremes of perfection is proportionate to the toddler's need for a protector
who reinforces his thrust toward autonomy and his resistance against
the infantilizing regressive pull to the symbiotic mother.

One more characteristic of the dyadic stage must be mentioned,
namely, the child's part-object relation. This is referred to as splitting,*
which is to say that the "good" object, in our case the "good" father,
is not comprehended as the same person as the "bad" father who—often
for inexplicable reasons—can suddenly become the source of discomfort
or displeasure. At such an impasse, the child simply walks away from
him or pushes him out of his realm of awareness or perception, turning
to the mother or some other more promising partner at the moment of
need.

The infantile emotions I have just described are paradigmatic for
the little boy's life with his father. They are outgrown with the expanding
awareness of the consistencies in the toddler's surround, pertaining to
persons, facts, and the chronology of events. In this we recognize a growing
sense of reality and predictability. The distortions of idealization, however, survive much longer as an internalized reality and become partially
appropriated by the self. They are part of what we look at as the child's
family support system, in which the father occupies a distinctive shrine
in the little boy's private cosmology. Normally, these beliefs are not cor-
rected until the boy reaches adolescence. Then the process of deidealiza-

* The word "splitting" assumes that a whole exists that is taken apart. This is not
quite correct, since the child starts out with part objects who become unified in due time
to a whole-person concept by the process of sensory and mental maturation. The infant's
object relation starts out with a response to "another" who provides either pleasure or
pain. We speak of a "pleasure object" and a "pain object," in short, a "part object"; both
are devoid of the whole-person concept because each is a separate entity. When the integration of both entities into the whole-person concept is achieved—an achievement that is
slow in coming—we speak of "whole-object" relations. Any splitting that occurs after
this differentiation into whole-object relations, is a falling back on the infantile modality
of object relations, serving a defensive aim and representing a primitive stage in the emotional
life of the individual.

tion becomes the major and most painful task of that period—especially during Late adolescence—which I have conceptualized as the second individuation process of adolescence (Blos, 1967) and have summarized in Part One of this book. I do not hesitate to state here that a progression from childhood to adulthood is beyond the grasp of a youth who has failed to complete the task of adolescence, namely, the deidealization of the dyadic father imago. This theorem will occupy us in the discussion of Hamlet's indecisiveness and procrastination.

The father idealization of Hamlet has not escaped the attention of any spectator or reader of the play. The glorification, the praise, the imputed faultless excellence, the shining virtue and inexhaustible goodness of the dead father tax the bereaved son's language to the utmost in his search for proper expression. To wit:

> *See what a grace was seated on his brow,*
> *Hyperion's curls, the front of Jove himself,*
> *An eye like Mars to threaten and command,*
> *A station like the herald Mercury*
> *New-lighted on a heaven-kissing hill,*
> *A combination and a form indeed*
> *Where every god did seem to set his seal*
> *To give the world assurance of a man.*

[Act III, iv, 55–62]

Only celestial or mythological references, namely godlike images, are elevated enough above the common earthly mediocrity to lend a fitting dignity of expression to the memory of his father. In speaking of his father as a "radiant angel" (I, v, 55)* or—comparing his father with his uncle—"this Hyperion to a satyr" (I, ii, 140), Hamlet mythologizes the father as the sun god of his own internal firmament.** This is impressively confirmed by the awesome pun in Hamlet's opening utterance of the play: "I am too much in the sun" (I, II, 62) (see Gedo, 1972). Transformed and elaborated, this father reference would read, "I have been living too much in my father's blinding brilliance to see any longer reality with convincing clarity or in any reliable proportions." Freud was struck by the probability that Shakespeare's life circumstances might have influenced the development of the son-father theme in the play. He wrote

---

* The "Radiant angel" are the words of the Ghost. To imply that King Hamlet is meant to be evoked by these words presupposes that the Ghost's speech is an amalgam of the father's commanding diction and moral stance as remembered by the son and—in equal measure—of Hamlet's own thoughts, wishes, and judgments, all projected and unified into a coherent texture, the Ghost's words.

** Helius, the sun-god of Greek mythology was also known as Hyperion (see Graves, 1955, p. 249: 154.4).

in *The Interpretation of Dreams* (1900), "For it can of course only be the poet's own mind which confronts us in Hamlet. I observe in a book on Shakespeare by Georg Brandes (1896) a statement that *Hamlet* was written immediately after the death of Shakespeare's father (in 1601), that is, under the immediate impact of his bereavement and, as we may well assume, while his childhood feelings about his father had been freshly revived" (p. 265).

These are just some of the references of idealization in which the play abounds. Even if we account for the fact that mourning evokes the idealization of the dead, the inordinate, almost frenzied form it takes here while failing to arouse the deed of vengeance raises questions of a more complex nature. The residue of dyadic "splitting," to which I have referred above, is recognizable in Hamlet's unrelenting comparison of his father with his uncle Claudius who married his mother. The early split is revived and concretized in King Hamlet and King Claudius, the respective embodiments of celestial purity and base lust. The two men constitute the unreconcilable duality of the archaic father imago. Harold Jenkins comments as follows in his "Longer Notes" in the Arden Shakespeare *Hamlet* (Shakespeare, 1982, p. 438): "The antithesis here between the sun-god [Hyperion], with his majestic beauty, and a creature half man half beast [the satyr] epitomizes in the two brothers the complex nature of man . . . the contrast between the two brother-kings is no less important, *though less often emphasized,* than the revelation of Hamlet's state of mind and his attitude to his mother" (italics mine). In fact, the double father imago's two sides, the pure and the evil, are projections of Hamlet's divided self and as such represent the very essence of an aborted adolescent deidealization of self and object. This unsettled state of part-object relations, if carried forward into adulthood, prepares the emotional ground from which a divided self will sprout. "The idea of man as partaking of both God and beast which thus underlies the play is very much the Renaissance concept" (Jenkins in The Arden Shakespeare *Hamlet,* 1982, p. 438). This virulent conflict is repeatedly made explicit in Hamlet's repetitiveness of feeling guilty for his evilness, followed by atonement and again, for moral weakness with a renewed resolution to act virtuously.

Following up on Jenkins's thought that literary criticism had moved Hamlet's mother complex into the forefront of attention at the expense of the unique role which the father plays in the son's motivations, I have to mention Erlich's Hamlet treatise (1977). He advances an interpretation of the play singularly built around the representation of the father in the child's mind. In this exhaustive study Ehrlich reverses the exclusive attention which Jones and others have given to the maternal issue and applies his Shakespeare scholarship to prove the overwhelming importance of the paternal issue in the play. The title of his book, *Hamlet's*

Absent Father, announces the dominant theme of his argument, which tries to discredit Freud's "misleading hunch." Erlich speaks of a literally absent father during the prince's early life. The residue of father abandonment appears as a lifelong "need for a strong father." This need was exacerbated by the King's death: letting himself be killed (and by a woman at that!), be "absent" from his son again, only attests to the father's weakness and deplorable unfitness as a model for identification. It reawakens the emotions connected to the absence of the father, who, being a pirate and a warrior, was either marauding at sea or fighting in Poland. In fact, when the father-ghost appears on the platform of the battlemented castle, Horatio recognizes him as wearing the same armor he did on the battle-fields of Norway or Poland:

> *Such was the very armour he had on*
> *When he th' ambitious Norway combated,*
> *So frown'd he once, when in an angry parle*
> *He smote the sledded Polacks on the ice.*

[I, i, 63–66]

Might it not be said that the "absent father" became the heroic, strong, overidealized father who served the boy well even as an absent guardian in a dangerous world? We are indeed well acquainted with little boys who form a proud and assuring bond with the father who went away because he had to to go on a "heroic mission." Of course, this does not diminish the child's longing for his presence.

According to Erlich's thesis, the "absent father" needs constantly to be restored. This idea of Erlich expresses in different words and in a different dynamic context what I refer to when I speak of Hamlet's preser-vation of the idealized, dyadic father imago. Erlich therefore disagrees with the psychoanalytic thesis that Hamlet cannot kill Claudius because he would then commit the same crime as Claudius, namely, the crime of patricide by killing his mother's husband, his stepfather, and the crime of incest by procuring her for himself as her lover if the villain were dead. Erlich tends to agree with Maloney and Rockelein (1949) that Hamlet needs Claudius to remain alive as a deterrent to incest (Erlich, p. 48); but even more compelling is to Erlich the son's need to kill the weak father (Claudius) and rescue the strong father (the Ghost-King). This triadic constellation represents "a very specific kind of oedipal crisis, one that has to do with an absent father, a ghostly father" (p. 25). The drama depicts, according to Erlich, "failure of [Hamlet's] striving, unconscious mind to fabricate a strong father" with whom he can identify in order to grow up (p. 50). The extent to which Erlich considers the father figure the hub on which the play turns is best captured in his words, ". . .

the play turns not on Hamlet's identification with Claudius, but on his identification with his father"; therefore, ". . . in *Hamlet* Shakespeare does not deal with repressed patricidal impulses [as Freud and Jones have postulated]* but with a highly complex search . . . for a strong father . . . Hamlet wants his father back" (p. 260). It is true that in the play Hamlet does not mention any concrete memories of his father from childhood which would attest to his presence at home. He refers to him only as to a magnificent apparition, radiating the glow of a charismatic fatherly spirit who infused the child's life with his godlike presence. In contrast, there is Yorick, the court jester, of whom Hamlet speaks with such animated and tender emotions in his conversation with the gravediggers. In these recollections, reaching back into his childhood, we listen to Hamlet's personal, affectionate, playful, and sensual memories in relation to the man Yorick, who had played an unforgettable role in his toddler years and beyond. In the graveyard scene Hamlet takes Yorick's skull from the gravedigger and says: "Alas, poor Yorick. I knew him. . . . He has bore me on his back a thousand times. . . . Here hung those lips that I have kissed I know not how oft. Where be your gibes now, your gambols, your songs, your flashes of merriment . . . ?" (V, i, 178–184.) Are the contrasts between Hamlet's memories of these two men from his childhood due to the distortion of one into an impersonal heroic figure because of Hamlet's conflicted feelings toward him, while the relationship to the other had retained its physical realness in the way he was remembered because no disturbing conflicts had intervened? Or should we conclude that one man, the father, was literally absent, as Erlich postulates, while the other Yorick, was a regular companion-member of the royal household? We do not know what the answer might be; yet we cannot deny the contraposition of the above stated remembrances as expressed in the play.

Jones refers in his study (1949, p. 138) to the splitting into a "good" and a "bad" father, a psychic mechanism called by Jones "decomposition," which plays a role in the formation of myths and dreams. Jones (1949) adds to the two, King Hamlet and King Claudius, a third father figure, Polonius, "the senile babbler, concealed behind a show of fussy pomposity" (p. 154), thus caricaturing traits of Hamlet's real father which, like Claudius' self-seeking villainy, could find no place within his never de-idealized father imago. The three father figures—King Hamlet, King Claudius, and Polonius—live in the son's mind as separate impersonations of disharmonious, unacknowledged, and unintegrated aspects of the original father experience. By this process of dissociation and by concretizing the split-off father imagos, Hamlet kept his father idealization uncontami-

---

* Freud and Jones recognize in Hamlet's conflict and inhibition the manifestation of the classical Oedipus complex, while Erlich recognizes in these traits the passionate but aborted effort to resurrect the idealized father imago.

nated and unaffected by any unworthy and inferior elements. Hamlet carries his paternal idealization further, namely, into his parents' marriage, by extending the dichotomy; thus he perceives his parents' marriage as one between a loving, devoted, faithful, and noble husband and a wife of adulterous, lascivious, and insatiably lustful appetite. Four words in the "tables" soliloquy say it all: "O most pernicious woman!" (I, v, 105.)

Even in death by murder in which the Queen was implicated, the father-ghost pleads with his son to spare his mother from punishment but to kill her lover to salvage her purity from defilement by the incestuous villain. This restriction, in which we see the projection of the son's oedipal wishes, as Jones has convincingly demonstrated, leaves him paralyzed between the choices of matricide and proxy patricide. The first one would take revenge on the "pernicious woman" who has befouled the magnificence and goodness of the dyadic father's marital bed with her seductive sexual greed, while the other would open the gates to his own exclusive and possessive yearnings for the oedipal mother. The latter position with its attendant conflict, guilt feelings, and inhibitions is, of course, Jones's central theme. Within this context he illuminates the fact that Hamlet is more horrified by his mother's adultery and incest than with his father's murder. In other words, his mother's promiscuous and licentious availability to men presents a danger far greater than assuming the role as the executor of his father's command. The danger I speak of is the mother's imputed intent to overpower him with her possessive seductiveness and, furthermore, his own defenselessness before her paralyzing emotional onslaught. We encounter here the archaic configuration of the infant's backward pull to the reengulfing mother and his simultaneous turn to the father as his rescuer from regression. By avoiding his father's assignment, Hamlet forfeits being the autonomous agent of his own moral obligation and duty. I intend to relate these considerations of Hamlet's behavior to the dyadic attachment emotions toward his father. To give this proposition content and persuasiveness, I must turn to the discussion of a particular aspect of the little boy's dyadic father fixation.

The Struggle of the Dyadic Male Child: Submission Versus Self-assertion: "the dread command"

Touching on this aspect of infancy, I shall remark only briefly on what I have discussed at greater length in the earlier part of the book. This seems necessary because these references have a bearing on my contribution to what is summarily called the Hamlet problem.

The infant emerges from an undifferentiated state by advancing to object recognition, which, in its predawn, has been described as the symbiotic state. With the progressive maturation of the sensory-motor equipment, the differentiation between self and human object takes its first step, with the smile as its familiar hallmark expression (process of "separation"; see Mahler et al., 1975). The course of the gradual forward movement toward independent existence, or separateness, is facilitated by the actualization of memory, which comes about through the internalization of the surround as experienced. The infant continues for some time to oscillate between the blissful state of absolute dependency, of oneness with the mother or the breast,* and the forward push toward self-assertion, namely, toward the state of differentiation with increasingly more sharply defined boundaries of the body and later of the self. This process has been described by Mahler (1975) as "individuation." The mother continues for an extended time to be remembered and, therefore, internally experienced as the embodiment of security and of allurement. Her influence or, globally speaking, the blissful state of merger, i.e., the enveloping protection against pain or tension, stands in growing opposition to the forward thrust of development toward self-assertion. This backward pull is summarized by the term "the reengulfing mother."

At this juncture of growth the little boy discovers with mounting excitement the father as a potential ally in his effort to break out of an infantile and confining world of total dependency on the nurturing other. The dyadic father becomes the protector, whose assistance and guardianship is sought by the little boy from now on with avid urgency. Now the once helpless baby not only can stand on his own feet but also can go forward with his father into the wider world, expecting or imagining that both march to the same drummer. This forward step harbors, as do all such developmental turning points in life, the pitfalls of incomplete accomplishments or half-hearted commitments. If one drags one's feet, so to speak, the forward move loses some of its thrust and will fall short of its potential fulfillment. We refer to such developmental fragments as fixations.

A particular consequence of a little boy's ineffectualness in his use of the father as an ally in "individuation" lies in his incapacity to let go of his maternal dependency. Instead of elaborating a temporary paternal dependency based on gender sameness and idealization, he endows the turn to the father with maternal attachment needs. Instead of using the father as a model for imitation and identification, the son enters a relationship to him that contains all the vital elements of a never relinquished identification with the mother. This fact accounts for the feminizing quality which—under these conditions—the little boy's submission to the idealized father entails.

This bifurcation of emotional needfulness into submissiveness and

---

* "Mother" and "breast" are interchangeably used references to denote the infant's response to a caretaking and nurturing person, whoever that might be.

self-assertiveness introduces a source of conflict which will make its fateful presence felt in adolescence and later in a man's adult life. This conflict is reflected in the aversion to, repression of, or overcompensation for feminine leanings. Characterologically, such internal divisiveness becomes manifest in selective, either transient or lasting indecisiveness and ambiguities in action and ideation. This infantile tendency comes often to the fore with irrepressible forcefulness on occasions later in life when heightened emotional states touch on this never settled bisexual proclivity. In other words, regardless of the emotional adherences or residues which survive the period of early childhood and keep isogender dyadic object ties alive beyond their normative timing, the advance to the triadic stage is nevertheless made, for better or for worse, and elaborated, even if half-heartedly, in its own right. However, a certain ambiguity or weakness in any subsequent psychic structure formation remains noticeable; a divided loyalty to conflicting emotional needs continues to persist; both these tendencies carry the legacy of an incomplete and unassimilated early childhood experience into future life. We might say that under such circumstances the thrust of normative developmental stage progression—by its very tentativeness—has forfeited its decisive stride and vigor.

This brief recapitulation of the role of the dyadic father in the life of the little boy shall suffice as the broad formulation from which I shall advance to my comments on Hamlet. They should be read as an addendum to Jones's study and not as an effort to refute his thesis in toto and substitute a comprehensive and different explication of Shakespeare's tragedy.

The play opens with the ghost-father informing his son that he was murdered by his uncle, the father's brother. James Joyce, in his pursuit of "ideas" about Hamlet, refers to the generality of a father representation in the appearance of the Ghost or, in other words, to the internalized father (father imago) in a distorted countenance which is the creative summation of the child's memory traces, need-fulfilling or yearned-for qualities (idealization), as well as of the omissions of ill-fitting observations, derived from the objectively perceived father as a person. This father imago, projected into the outside world of an unsubstantiated reality, is the Ghost. Quoting Joyce, "What is a ghost? Stephen said with tingling energy. One who has faded into impalpability through death, through absence, through change of manners" (Joyce, p. 188).

No sooner is the son informed authoritatively of the nature of his father's death that the idealization of his parents' marriage falls apart:

> . . . *so loving to my mother*
> *that he might not beteem the winds of heaven*
> *Visit her face too roughly. . . .*
> . . . *Why, she would hang on him*

As if increase of appetite had grown
By what it fed on; and yet within a month—

[I, ii, 140–145]

The fact that his mother so hastily married her brother-in-law Claudius points irrefutably to her guilt as an accomplice in the vile deed. His mother's lustful implication in the perpetration of the murder rekindles forgotten memories. He cries out, "O my prophetic soul! My uncle!" (I, v, 41). We can surmise from this shock of recognition that he has always known of his mother's deceptiveness, unfaithfulness, and lascivious surrender to sexual indulgence. The implicit degradation of his father, the double crime committed by his mother, affects Hamlet's mind more profoundly than his father's murder. Matricide is the impulsive course of action by which the son conceives of revenge on the woman who has insulted and destroyed the father's godlike image. Matricide is a deed sternly interdicted by the father's command. May the son's murderous impulse against her have slipped past his vigilance when once in the play he addresses his uncle as mother? (IV, iv, 52–55.) Is not the murderous impulse directed with more elemental forcefulness against the mother who connived in his father's murder than against his uncle who carried out her wish?

Under the influence of infantile logic Hamlet still fears that her ruthless destructiveness might victimize him as it had his father. In the closet scene he comes dangerously near to matricide; he stabs his mother with the deadly foil of words, making her wince and writhe: "I will speak daggers to her, but use none" (III, iii, 387). As his matricidal rage mounts, the son invokes his father's help and control: "Save me and hover o'er me with your wings / You heavenly guards!" (III, iv, 103–104.) The ghost becomes here clearly the impersonation of the charismatic father, who hovers momentarily at the border of reality as a hallucinatory apparition. The sadistic attack on his mother is justifiably called a "verbal matricide" (Hutter, 1975, pp. 430–431). To hurt the mother bodily is sternly prohibited by the ghost-father's edict:

But howsomever thou pursuest this act,
Taint not thy mind nor let thy soul contrive
Against thy mother aught. Leave her to heaven. . . .

[I, v, 84–86]

This paternal command within the storm of his murderous passion leaves Hamlet tossed about in a sea of indecision. His moral self identifies with his father's verdict of Claudius's guilt, demanding his death. However, the idea of executing the father's double command, namely kill the uncle but spare the life of the "pernicious woman," throws the son into the submissive position toward the dyadic father, which he endeavors to oppose with all his might. Hamlet chides himself cruelly for his inaction and his unwillingness to submit to his father's "dread command," which fails again and again to arouse the dedication of an unshakable commitment. Hamlet speaks to the Ghost in the bedroom scene:

Do you not come your tardy son to chide,
That, laps'd in time and passion, let's go by
Th' important acting of your dread command?

[III, iv, 107–109]

These brave words obliterate momentarily the son's urge to take revenge on the mother who has deprived him of his guardian against regression to the reengulfing mother of the symbiotic stage. We should not be deceived by the manifest content of the closet scene simply because it is cast in the terms of the oedipal, allogender complex, i.e., in the heterosexual modality. I have stated before that in the course of its revival infantile fixations are always actualized in the physically mature man on the level of genital sexuality. In Hamlet's case this is enforced by the mother's seductiveness in the bedroom scene.

Hamlet castigates himself helplessly for his procrastination and impassivity. His forceful declaration of his duty to be done turns into "blunted purpose" (III, iv, 111), "Is sicklied o'er with the pale cast of thought" (III, i, 85), and leaves the avenging son "unpregnant of my cause" (II, ii, 563). While the father's voice in him says, "Kill your uncle— spare your mother," the son's version reads, "Resurrect your mother's innocence, kill her lover, and thus undo her evil nuptial tie to the villain." The former is revenge, the latter is salvation of his self. (see Jones, 1949, pp. 109–110). The following quotation from the closet scene gives expression to the son's fervent pleading with his mother to restore her virtuous life of the past:

Queen: *O Hamlet, thou hast cleft my heart in twain.*

Hamlet: *O throw away the worser part of it.*
And live the purer with the other half.
Good night. But go not to my uncle's bed.
Assume a virtue if you have it not.

[III, iv, 158–162]

In the son's paralysis of action appears the unresolved dichotomy of purpose: to restore the madonna mother or avenge the father in filial loyalty. The action I speak of is obviously inhibited or aborted by arrested emotional development, which has affected normative stage progression (i.e., from the preoedipal to the oedipal level) due to the perseverance of contradictory emotional and identificatory aims. This is to say that the infant's attraction to the archaic, symbiotic mother and the fear of her reengulfment is carried forward to the oedipal stage and has endowed the triadic mother with powers of irresistible seductiveness and emasculating subjugation.

Whenever the process of individuation from the dyadic mother is insufficiently or only marginally completed, it is carried forward to the next, i.e., oedipal, stage. We are not surprised to witness then as a consequence, that the growing little boy cannot let go of the idealized father imago as a protection against the seductive and possessive woman in general: should the dyadic mother in the child's mind have never ceased to be the temptress who beckons him into the union of earliest dependency, then the oedipal mother walks in the never obliterated footsteps of bygone days of infancy and becomes the wildly exaggerated and feared seductress to sexual gratification.* Hamlet's words "frailty, thy name is woman" (I, ii, 146) may be paraphrased in sophisticated terms as the quintessence of woman who by her very nature can only live by a self-serving, compromised, and degraded code of ethics. Jones has alluded to the splitting of Hamlet's mother imago into the madonna and the whore: "one of a virginal Madonna, an inaccessible saint towards whom all sensual approaches are unthinkable, and the other of a sensual creature accessible to everyone" (Jones, 1949, p. 97).

The exposure of a bereaved Hamlet to his mother's shamelessly publicized sensuality and incestuous license renders the father's loving presence and protection a condition of his son's emotional survival. No wonder that killing Claudius his proxy father was repeatedly intercepted by the dichotomy of purpose; Hamlet's relinquishment of his procrastination, as viewed in light of the theory here offered, would have equaled an act of suicide by surrendering to the again widowed "pernicious woman." It is my thesis that Hamlet needed his stepfather as a man and the husband of his mother to protect himself from his mother's evil seductiveness, since he had failed miserably in the closet scene in pleading with his mother to be loyal, virtuous and pure. Should she cease to present the danger of her seductiveness, no obstacle would remain for Hamlet to avenge his father and kill his uncle. The mother, however, refused to change her ways and remained for her son "that pernicious woman." To keep his uncle alive is dictated with as much urgency by his horror of the loving, possessive mother who threatens to annihilate his masculinity as it is by the reciprocal urgency to keep his idealized father imago

---

* The dyadic mother of which I speak here appears in mythology as the Siren Circe or the Rhine maiden Lorelei.

alive as the only emotional resource enabling him to survive in the widowed world of his mother. Toward this end he has to keep his father blameless as a loving husband and a virtuous man beyond reproach. Both above-stated determinants of Hamlet's procrastination and inaction weave their way incessantly through Hamlet's words and deeds, expressed innumerable times throughout the play.

The contrast drawn by the son between the devoted love of a noble father and the evil lust of a degraded mother raises suspicions about the genuineness of his rhapsodic incantations. In the closet scene "Hamlet's description of Gertrude's crime as what 'makes marriage vows / As false as dicers' oaths' and 'from the body of contraction plucks / The very soul' [III, iv, 44–45, 46–47] implies, as Kahn has persuasively stated, that adultery" occurred long before the murder was committed (Kahn, 1981, p. 137). The passages quoted reveal Hamlet's awareness of his mother's having cuckolded his father (ibid.). Hamlet the boy could never forgive his father the weakness of letting himself be betrayed or, at the present, for having shown himself unable to keep his wife lovingly and faithfully in the marital bed. Such disappointing and forbidden knowledge of the child became knowledge never possessed, knowledge made to vanish by the magic of idealization. What a horrible thought that his uncle might prove more powerful a man to keep his wife for himself and therefore keep her from preying on her son! Uncle Claudius must be kept alive at any price—even the anguish of moral guilt and the corrosive feeling of shame.

In studying adolescent boys and young men, I have become acquainted time and again with the fact that pubertal maturation forces oedipal issues into the forefront of conflict. Within this process, the relationship to the dyadic father suddenly becomes an acute emotional issue, accessible to consciousness only in disguised form and only intermittently. If this conflict is excessive, we can observe two typical problems: one is the fixation on the dyadic father, manifest in extreme oppositionalism in deed or mind, and the other is the use of the female as a debased partner for sexual pleasure, devoid of tenderness and personal intimacy. I have referred to this latter, often conspicuous behavior of youth as the "oedipal defense"; by this I mean the elaboration of a make-believe sexually mature attitude, a role playing of the oedipal constellation in order to deny and obliterate the need for a dyadic father, as well as the feared domination and possessiveness by a powerful woman, the virago.

Hamlet's love of his girlfriend Ophelia, coupled with fear of her, is devoid of tender emotions; it is largely defensive, namely, an act of feigning manhood. In his cruel and cynical sadism he expresses his basic contempt and revulsion toward women in general and toward her in particular. In a sudden outburst of his misogynous rage he tortures her with his advice: "Get thee to a nunnery, farewell. Or if thou wilt needs marry, marry a fool; for wise men know well enough what monsters you make

of them. To a nunnery, go—and quickly too. Farewell" (III, i, 138–142).
While this sounds like a device to protect her chastity, exactly what
his mother could not do, the double meaning of the advice is revealed
by the fact that in Elizabethan days (as well as later) the word "nunnery"
was used as a slang word for brothel.* Jones notes that "the name 'Convent
Garden' will elucidate the point to any student of the history of London"
(1949, p. 97).

Returning to the theme of Hamlet's misogyny and sadistic vengeance
on Ophelia, we are immediately reminded of a similar scene in the play,
the closet scene, when the son unleashes his passionate outrage on his
mother. After he has removed Ophelia from his life as an extrafamilial
partner in love and sexual intimacy, his sadistic vengeance on women
is thrown back onto the original infantile prototype, the mother. This
unmitigated reenactment of infantile rage at the stage of early adulthood
reinforces the infantile protective craving for the dyadic father. It is often
observed at this stage of life that the loss of a lover can precipitate a
severe state of mental disturbance due to regression; in fact clinical psychiatry is well acquainted with this crisis situation of late adolescence, which
can trigger a psychotic break in personality integration.

Hamlet's emotional attitude toward women, which he revealed in
the dialogue with Ophelia, was rekindled by his mother's unfaithfulness
and murderous conspiracy in pursuit of her lust. His unrestrained reaction
to this event erupted in his relationship to Ophelia, of which Jones re-
marks, "The precise nature of his original feelings for Ophelia is a little
obscure" (1949, p. 91). It is a common observation that young men in
their first tentative love affairs struggle with their residual infantile attitudes toward women, who at this stage of life have acquired a generic
impersonality. The prototypical experience in which this attitude is rooted
leads to the boy's mother or her substitutes in his early life. Hamlets'
conflict becomes further burdened by the "dread command" that overshadows for the moment all other affects of his present life. I refer to the
emotional bond to the father who had died only to become his living
conscience.

In Hamlet, a young man barely beyond late adolescence and still a
schoolboy in Wittenberg, we witness the two conditions alluded to above,
which are typical for the male adolescent who struggles with an acute
father complex. One condition appears in the willful disobedience of
his father's command and the other in his use of Ophelia as a sexual
plaything. In essence, I wish to emphasize the thought again that residues
of the dyadic stage are always worked into oedipal conflicts whenever
these residues were, so to speak, "left hanging" without any workable
resolution. In order to tease out the early or the later and appropriate

* See E. Partridge, *A Dictionary of Slang and Unconventional English.* New York: Macmillan
Publishing Co., 1970.

components of the oedipal conflict, one has to use the instrumentality of the psychoanalytic process. This is comparable to the workings of the spectroscope, which breaks up light, appearing to us of uniform composition, into its constituents, forming a spectrum; thus we are informed of the heterogeneous elements which compose the observation of an apparently homogeneous continuity. Barnett (1975) distinguishes three theories that are hidden in the dramatic texture in the play. They are distinguishable in the spectrum of *Hamlet* and can be summarized in the following themes: "Hamlet as a drama of young adult individuation"; "catastrophic disillusionment with the family ideology"; and "the miscarriage of manhood." My Hamlet discourse touches only on those references within these themes that enlighten us about the dyadic son-father experience and the effect it has on the subsequent life of the son.

There are many allusions in the play to the feminizing submission to his father's will. Hamlet accuses himself of being "unpregnant of my cause" (II, ii, 563); "This is most brave, that I . . . Must like a whore unpack my heart with words . . ." (II, ii, 579–581). Action i.e. following his father's imposition or, inaction i.e. avoiding revenge as dictated by his own moral conviction, both leave Hamlet in the self-contemptuous state of being unmanly; no direction he can take carries a stamp of autonomy. A bisexual dalliance gives this young man on stage a fascinating and unsettled countenance. Here, Eissler (1971) calls our attention to the Hecuba soliloquy: "Hamlet performs a full identification with his mother. The terms he uses for himself actually imply homosexuality: he calls himself a whore, a drab, a male prostitute ('stallion'). . . . Yet this identification with the mother is so offensive to him that it is impossible for him to verbalize his basic conflict directly" (p. 110).*

An effeminate quality in Hamlet's character has been alluded to by many critics. This trait is familiar to us from many protoadolescent boys who carry this bisexual, transient identification with relative equinimity until the either-or urgency of irreversible sexual identity is heralded by the completion of sexual maturation. We may assume that this transitional stage was inadequately mastered by young Hamlet. At any rate, the obliqueness in gender identification which Hamlet projects to audience and reader of the play has rendered his portrayal a most challenging role on stage. Many great actresses have played Hamlet. Elizabeth Powell was the first female Hamlet in London at the Drury Lane in 1796, and Sarah Bartley was the first female Hamlet in America, in New York in 1819. These women were followed by Sarah Bernhardt, Eleanora Duse,

---

* In the Hamlet context the "homosexuality" Eissler refers to should rather be looked at as a late adolescent phenomenon. The young male adult who is making a belated push to overcome his stalemate in sexual identity formation is always drifting about in the boundaryless territory of bisexuality in his effort to transcend it and become an adult. This conflict is typical of late adolescence and is extended in those cases where a dyadic isogender fixation is at work. References to homosexuality in the play are no proof, in my opinion, of an established homosexuality.

Eva LeGalliene, Siobban McKenna, Judith Anderson, and many more. Their impersonation of the prince was accepted by audiences without inordinate emotional or esthetic disquietude. This reaction attests to a general acceptance and fitting portrayal of the bisexual nature of the "melancholy prince." I quote from Joyce's Hamlet discussion in Ulysses (p. 198): "I hear that an actress played Hamlet for the four hundred and eighth time last night in Dublin. Vining held the prince was a woman. Has no one made him out to be an Irishman?" Joyce's quip alludes to the undefined and undefinable personality of young Hamlet who is not yet beyond the molting time of late adolescence, with no unequivocal and final character yet engraved in the countenance of his self. The ambition of actresses to play, and audiences' being willing, if reluctantly, to accept, a transvestite Hamlet tell us that both actor and audience saw in the protagonist's puzzlingly contradictory states of mind the reflection of his ill-defined gender identity, conveyed by his behavior and his words. How absurd an idea it would be to cast an actress in the part of Oedipus Rex! These considerations confirm my characterization of Hamlet as a dyadic and of Oedipus as a triadic son; one still stands with one foot in the immaturities of early childhood, while the other has reached, but not yet stepped over, the threshold to maturity.

Only by his elective procrastination can Hamlet rescue his partially make-believe and still frail self-identity, even though he has to suffer the pain of self-contempt. In this dilemma the only purposeful action he can take lies in forcefully silencing the onrush of his unacceptable emotions, be they dyadic or triadic, and promise himself to obey his father's command:

> And thy commandment all alone shall live
> Within the book and volume of my brain,
> Unmixed with baser matter.

[I, v, 102–104]

Jones bases his argument concerning indecision and procrastination on repressed animosity toward the father, which makes its presence felt in consciousness by its opposite, namely, as "an exaggerated regard and respect for him, and a morbid solicitude for his welfare" (1949, p. 90). "Of the infantile jealousies the most important and the one with which we are occupied, is that experienced by a boy towards his father. . . . The only aspect that at present concerns us is the resentment felt by the boy towards his father when the latter disturbs, as he necessarily must, his enjoyment of his mother's exclusive affection. This feeling is the deepest source of the world-old conflict between father and son . . ." (p. 86). I wish to add to this comment the fact that, at a crucial point in the infant boy's growth, the "deepest source" of enjoyment turns into an equally deep source of perturbance and discomfort by its ominous interference with the child's forward thrust toward individuation and the relinquishment of primary dependencies. At this precarious moment of leave-taking from archaic bonding, the father becomes increasingly important as a novel source and modality of enjoyment and affection which the child experiences in his relationship to him and his supporting function in growing up. For a time, the experience of the father's presence and interaction with him represent an indispensable stimulus for advancement from the self-sufficiency of the early mother-child unit. The intensity of this tie and the sense of security it provides through idealization and attachment emotions can assume abnormal proportions whenever the mother's love and need for the possession of her son fail to keep pace with the child's developmental needs, namely, when she fails to support the child's efforts to loosen his infantile ties. If this transition is forfeited at its normative time, the need for the idealized father imago persists throughout life. Should the individual father be lost by death or be removed permanently from the child's life by desertion, then it is a lucky turn of events if the father imago can be affixed to a substitute and be accepted by him.

This set of propositions must make us wonder why Hamlet calls Claudius "father." Jones informs us that "in the First Quarto Hamlet five times addressed Claudius as father. Shakespeare excised the passages in the Second Quarto and the Folio; they were too near the truth!" (1949, p. 153.) Of course, "the truth" Jones refers to is Hamlet's unconscious wish to kill his father and enjoy his mother's exclusive affection. But is this all there is to be inferred in Hamlet's "Freudian slip"? Was there not also an expression of his wish to have acquired a new father whose presence will permit him to remain the student at Wittenberg, stay there among his friends, be protected from taking on the crushing responsibility of the crown? While I have no quarrel with Jones' explication, I wish to add one succinct component to the complexity of motivations in the Hamlet drama, namely, the need of the bereaved son for his mother's second husband, who protects him from the "pernicious woman" who loves him unmotherly and dangerously. This brings me to the consideration of Hamlet's inability to deidealize the father imago.

The "Also-mother" of the Dyadic Stage: "That Pernicious Woman"

Enough has been written about the character of the Queen and her concupiscence, and what has been written on this score shows such a high degree of consensus that I can expect it to have become general knowledge. Furnivall writes about the Queen, "Her disgraceful adultery and incest, and treason to his noble father's memory, Hamlet has felt in his inmost soul. Compared to their ingrain die, Claudius' murder of his father—notwithstanding all his protestations—is only a skin-deep stain."* When Hamlet speaks with such feelings of revulsion and accusatory condemnation about his mother's infidelity after the ghost-father has informed him of his murder, we can detect in his eloquence a familiarity with the mother's crime, i.e., the uncontrolled pursuit of her erotic avidity. As all early impressions in life such familiarities have a matter-of-fact quality of obviousness. Here, then, lies the unsurmountable obstacle to the deidealization of the father. Only through the preservation of the dyadic father imago can the son rally that protection and security which will help him to ward off catastrophic anxiety over the archaic mother. She, so he senses, has failed him in his effort to gain separateness from her and acquire the autonomy of will which would render his depending on the all-powerful and godlike father imago dispensable.

In the scene when the royal audience settles down to watch the play, the Queen beckons her son: "Come hither, my dear Hamlet, sit by me" (III, ii, 107). In so doing, the mother ignores the fact that her son's girlfriend, Ophelia, is the privileged woman with whom he keeps company and who sits at his side. Hamlet, rejecting his mother's invitation, pointedly replies, "No, good mother, here's metal more attractive. [*Turns to Ophelia.*]" (III, ii, 108.) The Queen had always doted and still does dote on Hamlet, her only child and a son at that, whom she will not let slip away from her embrace of influence. Claudius, not without bitterness and displeasure, says of his wife, "The Queen his mother/Lives almost by his looks" (IV, vii, 11–12). When Laertes challenges Claudius with the question why he does not kill Hamlet who has designs on his life, the King replies that killing Gertrude's son outright would turn her against him and leave him deserted and lost: "She is so conjunctive to my life and soul/That, as the star moves not but in his sphere, I could not but by her" (IV, vii, 14–16). The husband knows that his wife loves her son more than she loves him. This knowledge restrains him from taking action and killing his mutinous nephew and stepson.

"Hamlet had no intention of ever removing Claudius, the second protective father who stood so conveniently between him and the throne" (Maloney and Rockelein, 1949). Paraphrasing the end of this sentence, I would say, stood so conveniently between him and the Queen. Indeed, the authors are clear on this issue, as proven by their comment on the final scene of the play: "Here, first, is the death of the mother-figure whom Hamlet feared . . . Hamlet's response to his mother's death is major psycho-analytic evidence of his terror of the Queen while she was alive." I might add, death has now removed the mother demon—partially, a fabrication or externalization of the little boy's mind—from the outside world, but this has not freed the son from its living memory,

---

* Quoted in Jones, 1949, p. 68.

which exiles him from the life of woman; only in his own death can his mind now find relief and quiescence.

Just as much as Hamlet needs Claudius in the role of an idealized proxy father who protects him by acting as a living shield and deterrent warding off the licentious waywardness of his mother, so Claudius finds assurance in passively enduring Hamlet's presence until, hopefully, by his clever scheming of accidental and inconspicuous circumstances Hamlet will meet his death in England. The failure of this ploy engages Claudius in some other plot. Each man is plotting against the other, and each is restrained, by the desire for self-preservation, from doing away with the other: Claudius to keep his wife's love and Hamlet to avert seduction by his mother should she be widowed a second time.

Let us consider the last scene of the play with these thoughts in mind. It has not escaped the attention of any critical writer on Hamlet that the prince avenges his father and kills Claudius at the moment he realizes that the Queen is dead. Jones argues that Hamlet can kill his uncle at this moment because the object of his oedipal wishes has been removed by fate: ". . . his conscience is free of an ulterior motive for the murder" (1949, p. 100), the ulterior motive being the uncontested possession of his oedipal mother. In other words, the son is now capable of autonomous, guilt-free action. Eissler (1971) notes this newly won freedom by pointing to "the absence of reference to the dread command at the end of the play" (p. 285).

My argument, in the light of the dyadic antecedents which are still potently present in the son's motivation, reads as follows: The Queen's death has laid her menacing and emasculating seductiveness to rest forever; the preservation of her husband is no longer a necessity; he had become suddenly dispensable. This fact enabled Hamlet to spring into action, and fulfill his promise to the ghost-father in the cellary scene at the opening of the play:

> *Haste me to know't, that I with wings as swift*
> *As meditation on the thoughts of love*
> *May sweep to my revenge.*

[I, v, 29–31]

In killing Claudius, Hamlet also fulfills the prediction concerning his own fate which he had in the closet scene:

> *For 'tis the sport to have the enginer*
> *Hoist with his own petard. . . .*

[III, iv, 208–209]*

* In contemporary English line 209 says, "Blown into the air by his own bomb" (see annotation, Shakespeare, 1982).

"This phrase sums up the ironic pattern to be fulfilled in the catastrophe" (Jenkins, in Shakespeare, 1982, p. 332). Hamlet makes himself willingly a companion victim in the family cataclysm, or *Weltuntergang*.

For the sake of assurance that my contribution to the Hamlet problem, formulated within the context of a psychoanalytic developmental psychology, is understood correctly, I wish to state that my argument concerning Hamlet's procrastination and execution of vengeance comfortably accommodates Jones's oedipal motivations as an unconscious determinant. However, I attribute a larger role of determination to the dyadic father in the Hamlet tragedy. I propose that the fear of the archaic mother, a projection of the child's own regressive pull, looms larger in the dynamic configuration of the play than the exclusive oedipal, triadic emotions of love and hate, of conquest and patricide, of incest and guilt.

The son-father tragedy of *Hamlet* displays the complex role which dyadic and triadic residues play in the life of a young man who has arrived at the crossroads of his adolescent personality consolidation poorly prepared for this momentous task. Under these circumstances, the expected and normative time of adolescent closure passes in default, unattended by any developmental vigor and thrust during the early years of manhood. Thus past, present, and future lose their sharp distinctions of import; without this discernment in personal history, maturity, the goal of growing up, remains unattainable and unfathomable; life turns into a mirage of one's beginnings; indeed, life becomes a perennial state of beginnings. If the challenge of adolescence is lost, a man's future is in serious peril—and he knows it in his bones. We have heard it many times from many a young man, bemoaning his loss of innocence and being paralyzed by the responsibilities of adulthood. Hamlet's words echo the helpless despair of every young man who stopped in his track at this crossroad of life:

The time is out of joint. O cursed spite,
That ever I was born to set it right.

[I, v, 196–197]

Epilogue
And what is being done to us?
And what are we, and what are we doing?
To each and all of these questions
There is no conceivable answer.
We have suffered far more than a personal loss—
We have lost our way in the dark.

T. S. Eliot, from *The Family Reunion*

Closing Comment

In writing the essays on Kafka and *Hamlet* and, tangentially, discussing Freud's Schreber case, I applied my thesis about the influence of the dyadic father on the development of the male child; furthermore, I discussed the respective personalities in the light of my assertion that the dyadic complex is, with the Oedipus complex proper, part of what Freud has defined as the "core of the neurosis." In the process I outlined the essential dissimilarity of these two phases of infancy and described their respective contributions to the so-called infantile neurosis. The Oedipus complex proper emerged from these considerations in the aspect of an organizing principle for psychic structure formation at the termination of infancy, proceeding in harmony with the particular mental and physical maturation of this age. Whatever the resolution of conflict is accomplished at the termination of infancy it is always partial and has to be brought to completion during adolescence. In viewing the resolution of the dyadic and triadic complex in a developmental continuum, namely, at the closure of infancy and again at the closure of adolescence, I have paid special attention to this two-tiered task of conflict resolution in discussing the literary figures I set out to study. In my approach to this enterprise I have attributed to the above thesis the validity of a developmental axiom; this I have applied in its specificity of my present formulation to male personality formation and particularly to the reciprocal role of father and son in the dyadic stage of life.

As a psychoanalyst I took this position with the same confidence as Ernest Jones did when he applied as a self-evident universality the Oedipus complex to his discussion of *Hamlet.* In stating the issue in these words, the thought is implicit that—with the still unknown and unpredictable insights into the complexities of psychological development that are to come—my thesis, as it stands now, will be amended one day by psychological formulations which sound at that future moment as self-evident as Ernest Jones's or my own once sounded in the past. One formulation stands on the shoulder of its predecessor, lifted to its new position by the passage of time or, more correctly, by the *Zeitgeist,* which, moving into its ascendancy, makes the familiar appear in a new perspective.

It is not difficult to recognize in novels, poetry, and critical discourse written in consecutive periods of time the changing *Zeitgeist* under whose illumination all previous creations are perceived in a new light. This is certainly true about Hamlet, who has been reinterpreted repeatedly over the last centuries. Both the prevailing philosophy of man and the science of the human mind have clearly influenced the understanding of Hamlet, now as well as in the past. These idiopathic readings by generations have presented to us a broad spectrum of interpretations which over time have repeatedly yielded again and again an unsatisfactory and unacceptable comprehension of the hero's personality, thus keeping the reader's, listener's, and critic's fascination with the Hamlet tragedy ceaselessly alive.

Three broad and distinct versions of Hamlet interpretations, advanced over time, were singled out by Holland (1975). The 17th and 18th century looked at Hamlet as a "Renaissance prince" who represented the noble soul aspiring to man's spiritual harmonization between "God and beast" (Jenkins, in Shakespeare 1982, p. 438) in his earthly existence, transcending the base medieval conflict of morality raging between God and Devil, good and evil. In the late 18th century Goethe's view of the "melancholy Dane" seemed to render his behavior comprehensible. With Goethe's Hamlet discourse in his novel *Wilhelm Meister's Lehrjahre* of 1796 (*The Apprenticeship of Wilhelm Meister*, Fourth Book, Chapter 13) a new interpretation of the hero was advanced.

Goethe's congeniality with an increasingly individualistic and idiopathic view of man, advanced an interpretation of Hamlet which took hold of the European mind of his day and prevailed for a considerable length of time. His explanation of Hamlet's procrastination and paralyzed action of revenge was founded on the concept of a temperamental constitution, which in Hamlet was one of "oversensitiveness."*

The comprehension of personality in general and consequently of Hamlet changed slowly with the progressive dismantling of traditional morality. In the 19th century views of human behavior and its determinants altered with the advance of the natural sciences; to wit, the teleology of Darwinian thought and the concept of the self-regulatory "milieu interieur"** of the physiologist Claude Bernard, to name just two. In addition, we recognize the influence of new philosophies, such as Nietzche's transvaluation of values, and of new insights into human motivation as in the modern psychological novels of Dostoevsky. The synergic confluence of these trends exposed human conflictuality as a determinant of behavior, modifying the concept of free will and introducing the idea of the singular effect of personal history, beginning in early childhood, on individual life. With the advance into the 20th century this concept culminated in the psychological theory of psychoanalysis. The Oedipus complex became its core concept and the cornerstone of the psychoanalytic theory of the neurosis. It was this unique and universal human experience which Ernest Jones in 1910 used as the conceptual foundation of his Hamlet interpretation.

Ongoing and systematic studies in the field of infant and adolescent research brought new aspects of human development to light and forced

* While this view of Hamlet is attached to Goethe's name, it was shared by many leading minds of the period, such as Herder, Schlegel, Coleridge, and many more (see Jones, 1949, pp. 30–31).

** Anticipating the concept of homeostasis and representing the biological paradigm of the psychoanalytic concept "ego."

revisions of existing psychoanalytic theory. I myself being a contemporary of these developments, applied some of them, including the results of my own research, in the literary criticism contained in the above essays. Concerning the Kafka *Letter* we must concede that not enough time has passed yet to have produced a history of successive interpretations which would allow a comparative assessment of them. I hope that my essay on Kafka will evoke sufficient curiosity and inquisitiveness to continue psychological studies of this confessional document in ever greater discrimination and depth.

PART THREE

Toward an Altered View of the Male Oedipus Complex: The Role of Adolescence

CONTENTS

Introduction

I depart now from the narrow focus in which the substantive discussion
of my presentation was carried out and reinstate it in a larger framework
of development. Paying minute attention to the dyadic son-father relationship in relative isolation from the manifold psychic events which
have a bearing on it generated a disproportionate view of that relationship;
in other words, it created by necessity an artifact. This procedure is a
time-honored scientific practice which has as its goal the study of an
isolated structure, unencumbered by the distraction of a larger context
of which it is a part. The effort to reinstate what I have isolated for
study in the totality of personality development will guide the discussion
which follows. This shift to a wider focus is necessary in order to open
up the whole panorama of developmental issues which I had subjected
to a narrow focus of attention for the sake of studying in detail the
specific issue to which this volume is dedicated. This I hope to accomplish
by paying attention to the larger context within which every component
process of life takes it course. To place the reader in a position along
the developmental continuum where he obtains a commanding view of
the life cycle, I have chosen the stage of adolescence. This location opens

up a vast view which stretches back into infancy and forward into adult-hood. From this pivotal vantage point I intend to outline the contextual complexities of development into which the detailed study of the dyadic father in the life of the male can be viewed on a common scale with those other components of development which were in my discourse only peripherally acknowledged. I shall start by taking a look at the history of ideas which are contained in this volume.

The developmental view of the human mind which I have applied to the topic of this volume did not make its appearance fully integrated and clearly conceived, the way Athena sprang forth from Zeus's brow. The process by which my ideas matured and came to fruition was far more laborious, tentative, and experimental. The governing spirit of inves-tigation was one of extended observation. This state of mind prepares a fertile ground—by the sheer fact of growing complexity—for further discoveries and regroupings of new content of observation and thought to be brought forth. It lies in the nature of discoveries, such as new theoretical formulations, that some of the content and many of the expec-tations and speculations built upon them become more or less reduced by self-liquidation to their core essences with the passage of time.

The decades I have spent in clinical research on adolescence have resulted in a harvest of many findings;* they encompass a body of knowl-edge—theoretical and clinical—which I shall present here. In doing so, I intend to clarify especially those of my findings that diverge from the familiar or widely accepted view of the adolescent process. I have chosen adolescence as the nodal nexus in order to clarify and formulate my developmental propositions for two reasons: one, because I have studied this period of human life more extensively and intensively than any other and, two, because this stage reflects in a kaleidoscopic view the entirety of developmental antecedents in one form or another, subjecting them to the gigantic adolescent task of consolidation and integration. Further-more, this stage, by implication, projects a circumscribed, limited, and concentrated range of individual potentialities into what is to follow in life ahead. My analytic work with children and with adults lent the neces-sary perspective to my focus on adolescence, thus averting the danger of too myopic a view of this particular stage. My psychoanalytic investiga-tions have always issued from clinical observations of puzzling phenom-ena, which presented me with intriguing problems of theory and tech-nique.

Before I proceed, a word of caution is in order. I fear I may convey the impression of not appreciating sufficiently the vast research that has so immensely enriched our knowledge of the adolescent process. It is

* In reviewing the history of my research on this subject, I have used some of the following material: Blos, 1974, 1979, 1980.

in many instances quite beyond my faculty to sort out authorship and origins and accord credit to the many suggestive and seminal ideas which, as by a quantum leap, coalesced in a new theorem. I owe more to what I have read and heard over time than I can possibly acknowledge by searching most diligently my memory.

The Recapitulation Theory of Adolescence

The issue I shall discuss first concerns the psychoanalytic recapitulation theory of adolescence. According to this view, the revival of infantile sexuality and the vicissitudes of early object relations is initiated by the biological event of puberty. In accordance with the classical recapitulation theory, the revival and renewed resolution or transformation of the Oedipus complex represent one, if not *the*, essential aspect of the adolescent process. There is no doubt that oedipal issues emerge at adolescence with regularity. But we must acknowledge with equal alertness the revival of dyadic issues which lead to gender-specific constellations in boys and girls. Just because triadic, or oedipal, especially allogender ("positive"), issues occupy the forefront of the adolescent's attention, we are often led to focus on his or her heterosexual behavior, thought, imagery, in short, on the sexual drives and their sublimatory representations; these explicit issues, however, do not have absolute dominance in the adolescent's mind. Quite to the contrary, the fact that other than oedipal issues take such an overriding possession of the maturing child tells us something of import. If we listen attentively and without prejudice, we detect the disturbing invasion of the mind by dyadic (preverbal) emotions and witness either their complete repression or the return of the repressed. When speaking in psychoanalytic parlance with customary singularity of reference to the allogender ("positive") Oedipus complex in adolescence, a corrective amendment is in order, namely, the recognition of its two-tiered origin. Both the dyadic and the triadic stages, when resurfacing in adolescence, fluctuate in the degree of their emotional preponderance, thus contributing additional insight to the time-honored impression of emotional instability, unsettledness, and vacillation during the adolescent period.

The experiential revival of infantile states has to be gauged against the fact that a decisive expansion of the ego has accrued from middle childhood, which has altered, qualitatively and quantitatively, the reexperiencing of oedipal or preoedipal conflicts on the adolescent level. The resourcefulness of the adolescent ego allows it to cope with the revival of infantile object relations in consonance with bodily maturation, thus bringing the state of infantile dependencies to a gradual but definitive closure. This achievement usually, if not always, contains rectifications

or resolutions of conflicts or immaturities carried forward from the infantile period to the adolescent level. In this sense, we speak of adolescence
as a "second chance." This normative developmental advance is forfeited
whenever the child fails to acquire the appropriate ego differentiation
or ego supremacy during the years of middle childhood, the latency period.

What I have foremost in mind when I speak of an impeded ego
development during the latency period are drive fixations on the level
of infantile narcissism. With the expanding perceptive, cognitive, and
critical faculty of the mind, this narcissistic fixation represents the child's
intolerance of having the self-image subjected to the evaluation stringen-
cies of his social surround. Under such circumstances the capacity for
identification, from which the self normally draws immense enrichment
during progressive development, remains woefully deficient. As a consequence, oedipal passions remain weak, their conflict resolution is incomplete, and the superego never gains the autonomous sway over infantile
self-idealization, a necessary precondition for the entry into the latency
period. Looking at this constellation from the side of the ego, one would
refer to the fact that no clear or stable line of demarcation between fantasy
and reality has become part of the latency ego structure; thus the ego's
capacity to critically assess self and object is stunted. "I am what I do"
becomes facilely replaced by "I am what I wish to be" or "I am what
others think I am." Under these conditions it is only natural that the
voice of the self-observing ego remains weak, contradictory, or silent.
The repercussion of this state on reality testing, especially in the world
of object relations, never fails to alert the clinical observer to a developmental anomaly. However, one cannot ignore the fact that regardless of
drive fixation and ego immaturity, some latency children are capable of
the most remarkable cognitive and creative achievements, the defensive
components of which do not reveal themselves until adolescence.

What follows from such a developmental lag is an abortive adolescence or a failure in the autonomous mastery of internal disequilibrating
tensions and in the capacity to use selectively the social surround as a
suggestive source for sublimatory and identificatory adaptations. Under
these circumstances, the social field fails to acquire an age-relevant presence on which to articulate the emerging needs for new object relations
beyond the family matrix; consequently, new object relations within the
peer group show the characteristics of simple object substitutions rather
than those of elaborated replacements. In other words, adolescent development takes its normative course only if the latency ego has progressed
along age-adequate developmental lines. In adolescent therapy, latency
ego deficits often demand our attention above all else, even though sexual
and dependency conflicts occupy the forefront of the behavioral and mental stage. While such conflicts are real enough, they have to be scrutinzed
to identify their defensive aims, which push these typically adolescent

themes into the forefront of the patient's and the therapist's awareness.

I shall now pursue another strand of the recapitulation theory of adolescence. I refer to the conventional implication that the resolution of the Oedipus complex has brought about the closure of the dyadic phase and in its wake the formation of the superego, ushering in the latency period. With the advent of adolescence the conflicts between wish and guilt, typical of the oedipal phase are resuscitated, but so are also the primitive or archaic pleasure-pain polarities of the dyadic phase. Due to the biological condition of physical maturation at puberty, both infantile phases of emotional and physical experiences when revived at adolescence become drawn into the adolescent phase-specific drive modality of genital sexuality. This resuscitation of infantile object relations in conjunction with their emotional and physical sensations is essential in the process of a definitive detachment from the primary love and hate objects of infancy. A regressive circumvention or avoidance of this maturational challenge is forcefully counteracted by a dual danger situation. There is, on the one hand, the dyadic danger of autonomy loss, and, on the other, the oedipal danger of the incest taboo. The developmental conflict and tasks of adolescence in their broadest formulation are identical with the adaptive challenges which ensue from the two danger situations as mentioned.

From Gender Identity to Sexual Identity

From my work with adolescents—male and female—I have gained the impression that the decline of the Oedipus complex toward the end of early childhood represents a suspension of a conflictual constellation rather than a definitive resolution, because we can ascertain easily its continuation on the adolescent level. In other words, the resolution of the Oedipus complex is completed—not just repeated—during adolescence. The same holds true for residues of the dyadic complex. I speak of residues because the major share of emotional and mental investments in that phase have been carried forward to the triadic level in the forward thrust of development. In normal development unmitigated remnants of the dyadic phase are relatively restricted to an idiosyncratic few; these are worked into the adult, mature personality without impeding its renewed self-realization, indeed quite to the contrary, lending it a personal and unique countenance.

My attention was directed to the above considerations by the clinical fact that the isogender, i.e., "negative," Oedipus complex presents a most difficult therapeutic problem in the treatment of the adolescent. The alternation between love and hate of the parent of the opposite sex is always intensified during adolescence. However, a distinction, even if obvious,

needs to be made at this point. The term "oedipal love" implicitly refers
to the sexual component of infantile object relations, in contrast to feelings
of affection, admiration, and loyalty, which never cease to flow in their
asexual, i.e., agenital, modality between the child and both parents. My
observations concerning the isogender Oedipus complex have led me to
the conclusion that oedipal love, directed toward both mother and father,
does not burden the young child with intrinsic contradictions or mutual
exclusiveness as it does in adolescence when the polarities of masculinity
and feminity reign supreme. Their coexistence cannot easily be tolerated
by the sexually maturing individual. In other words, the state of bisexuality is tolerated in the prelatency child without the catastrophic disharmony
it evokes at puberty. It is the allogender, i.e., "positive," Oedipus complex
that falls under repression or finds its resolution through identification
and the regulatory influence of the superego at the termination of the
oedipal phase. It remains the task of the adolescent oedipal resolution
to transmute the isogender ("negative") Oedipus complex, namely, the
sexual love for the parent of the same sex. This transmutation is accomplished by the desexualization of infantile dyadic, isogender ("negative")
attachment emotions and their deflection onto ideational, ego-syntonic
structures such as the adult ego ideal, which is independent from object-
libidinal enmeshments. I shall return to the issue of transformation in a
section exclusively devoted to it.

Clinically, this aspect of the oedipal constellation appears at adolescence in a paradoxical disguise; it is in evidence whenever a drive fixation
on the isogender ("negative") oedipal position is interwoven with symptom formation or characterological defenses. Such pathological development is often not recognizable on first sight, especially when the adolescent
pushes heterosexual behavior and fantasies into the center of his life in
general, or of his therapy in particular. The urgency of, and the preoccupation with, sexual affects and urges during adolescence are familiar to
us. In fact, their attendant conflicts, anxieties, and defenses play a large
part in our therapeutic work. It has been my experience that, alongside
the adolescent effort to reach a heterosexual identity, we also have to
reckon with an intrinsically defensive element in this striving which aims
at keeping the conflicts of the isogender ("negative") oedipal love in repression. I have called this adolescent maneuver the oedipal defense.

Anyone who works therapeutically with adolescents can easily verify
the fact that, for example, with a male adolescent (of middle and late
adolescence), it is, relatively speaking, less laborious to deal with the
defenses against sexual and erotic fantasies and feelings in relation to
girlfriend, mother, or sister than to male peers, father, and brother. The
affects directed toward the female remain in the realm of a gender-appro-
priate position and are ego-syntonic. In contrast, the uncovering of the
isogender oedipal fixation leads at adolescence inescapably into the realm

of homosexuality, latent or manifest, and into the center of sexual identity problems. Should these remain unaltered by the adolescent process, we may speak of a secondary adolescent fixation. In that case, the adolescent choice of defense will determine the adult character consolidation, and, due to the unaltered infantile libidinal position, this fixation will engender disharmonious affects and moods in the love life of the adult. The adolescent's usual dread, horror, and ego-dystonicity of homosexuality or perversion in general are often voiced quite directly by the adolescent girl or boy and constitute in many cases the first productive approach to the problem of sexual identity. Since the resolution of the isogender Oedipus complex is one of the tasks of adolescence, the coming to terms with the homosexual component of pubertal sexuality is an implicit developmental task of that period. In fact, we might say that sexual identity formation is predicated on the irreversible outcome of this process. Gender identity, namely the clear knowledge that "I am a boy" or "I am a girl," is established during the earliest years of life, even though the sexual function of each gender remains a vaguely conceived and interchangeable notion for a considerable length of time. Adolescents in general and adolescent patients in particular always display the twofold oedipal strivings—isogender and allogender—with a sense of their basic incompatibility as to gender-defined object choice and sexual self-definition; this predicament brings the maturing individual up against an either-or of decisive finality. When we speak of this sorting out of roles in their personal as well as sexual and social meanings, we refer to the concept of identity, which receives its irreversible imprimatur in adolescence. The more or less conflictual state in which the compound identity is attained has to be viewed as a normal and expectable aspect of growing up and is not, in and by itself, a sign of an abnormal adolescent passage.

The drive vicissitudes just alluded to can be reflected in such common adolescent complaints as a sense of vocational indecision or noncomitment, of floundering or academic failure in college. These problems are just as often outgrown by the passage of time but given too quickly and randomly the stigma of wasted time. They may reveal themselves to be in the long run incapacitating adjuncts of a symptom complex which we, as therapists, are called on to unravel. On first sight, defeats of this nature look like oedipal inhibitions, especially whenever a boy sets out to follow in the vocational footsteps of his father or, generally, when the young person feels called upon to fulfill the ambitions which one or both parents harbor passionately for their offspring. The oedipal factor plays, no doubt, a decisive role. But juxtaposed to it—as we see in so many cases of gifted boys—is the infantile tendency to renounce oedipal competition and envy in exchange for the regressive contentment derived from standing in the glow of shining grandeur that radiates from the imago of the oedipal father. By appersonation the son transcends infantile passive dependency and temporarily takes a share in the father's active presence; if this should be wanting, the little boy will conjure it up. However, in accordance with the polarities of infantile positions, he pursues with equal avidity the pleasures—pervasive but hardly acknowledged—of the submissive passive position in relation to his father. In this connection we must remember that every boy once—fleetingly or more lastingly—identified with the role of the envied and admired procreative woman: the mother. I have observed how these trends in the small boy become pathologically aggravated when his father, disillusioned in his conjugal life, shifts his need for emotional fulfillment from his wife to his son. Whenever I hear a father say in the consultation preceding the treatment of his son, "The only one I love in this world is my son," I feel alerted to the central complex of the patient. In following such cases in treatment, I have been repeatedly impressed by the emergence of the Janus-faced oedipal passions and of the alternating conflicts they inexorably contain. Should the conflicts attached to the incest taboo and bisexuality remain critically beyond resolution, the adolescent patient protects himself against their repetition by a stubborn denial of any self-limitation. Thus the grave affront to infantile narcissism is circumvented. We see here once again how ego maturation takes its cue from drive maturation. The fact that a "facilitating environment" (Winnicott, 1965, p. 223), such as a work opportunity for self-realization and participation in the adult world, is preconditional for the process of growing up should be self-evident. However, it needs emphasizing in this context that the creative use any individual makes of such social opportunities remains predicated on drive and ego maturation or, in other words, on the unimpeded forward movement of the adolescent process.

A Comment on Bisexuality

It is a time-honored and generally accepted tenet of psychoanalytic theory that the Oedipus complex is reactivated during adolescence. In conjunction with regression in the service of development, this reactivation leads to the loosening of infantile object ties and initiates the second individuation process of adolescence. Progressive ego dominance as well as the characterological stabilization of defenses can be observed during the process of adolescent psychic restructuring. The similarities of this stage to that of the transition from the oedipal to the latency stage are striking and have attracted the attention of many psychoanalytic observers. It has been my impression that the first decline of the Oedipus complex at the stage of sexual immaturity forces the allogender ("positive") component of the complex into repression and into identificatory transformations (superego), and that this is accomplished by more absolute and stringent measures than appears to be the case with the isogender ("negative") component of the complex. The little boy's passive love for the father and his identification with the mother seem to find a bypass, often apparent as characterological trait or split-off fantasy, during the resolution of the Oedipus complex and the solidification of the superego. The feminine component of the little boy's instinctual life becomes restrained, restricted, or rejected, far more forcefully by narcissistic injunctions, manifest in shame and contempt, than by superego interdictions. The mastery of his world by aggression always skirts close to the modality of mastery by passive surrender to moral principles, namely, to the father, or by externalizing the dilemma as one between the self and the outer world.

It is a well-known fact that the boy's relationship to his father is never better, i.e., less conflicted or more positive, than it is at the dawn of pubescence. The boy enlists the father's assistance in his defense against the regression to the preoedipal, the archaic mother. It can be observed how this phase affects the resuscitation of the Oedipus complex, regardless of earlier fixations, and how this phase complicates, in some fashion, its adolescent replication as well as resolution. It is my contention that adolescence not only is faced with the revival of the oedipal conflict but that the definitive resolution of the total complex is the inherent task of adolescence. This task involves the irreversible renunciation of infantile object ties to both parental figures, i.e., to both their dyadic and triadic imagos. An adjunctive or corresponding resolution pertains in many cases to an incestuous tie of the adolescent boy to his sister and of the adolescent girl to her brother.

For the young child, the bisexual position is less conflictual, allowing a host of compromises, than is the case for the adolescent who has attained sexual maturity. The resolution of the isogender Oedipus complex as an object involvement of a sexual nature confronts the adolescent boy with a relatively novel conflictual experience and task. Displacement to an isogender nonincestuous extrafamilial object can never be a satisfactory solution because this would only extend the complete oedipal constellation beyond its developmentally appropriate time, into bisexual or homosexual object attachments of adulthood. The only road open for the boy lies in the deinstinctualization of the dyadic, isogender, narcissistic, i.e., homosexual, object tie, leading to the formation of the ego ideal in its final form. In the process, all ego-ideal trends that have accrued over time, from primary narcissism to symbiotic omnipotence and, later, from narcissistic identifications to the stage of isogender, i.e., homosexual, idealizations, such as seen in the well-known highly emotional adolescent friendships between boys or between girls with pronounced passions of possessiveness, jealousy, and envy, become integrated in the permanent ego ideal that coalesces during the terminal stage of adolescence. From here on, the ego ideal remains an unalterable psychic structure which extends its influence on thought and behavior over a much larger sector of the personality than was the case before adolescence. This shift has to be viewed as a collateral to those changes that the adolescent superego undergoes at the same time and is familiar to us in the proverbial adolescent rebelliousness. Of course, the process of emotional emancipation, of the consolidation of individuality and of the selective affirmation of parental or societal values and principles to live by, can proceed either stormy or quietly, as far as the subject himself or the outside observer is concerned. Psychologically these changes indicate that ego and ego ideal are taking over some of the superego's controls by delimiting its rigid scope of influence in mental life (Blos, 1962).

The Second Individuation Process of Adolescence

In observing adolescents, we notice that development does not advance in a steady or in a straight and forward-moving line. For a considerable time an alternation between progressive and regressive movements is the rule rather than the exception. We are accustomed to recognize in regressive phenomena a normative adolescent characteristic. A shift in emphasis, however, has been noticeable ever since infant research has so vastly extended our knowledge of the dyadic, or preoedipal, child. The reflection of earliest structure formation on the adolescent process has become an integral aspect of adolescent psychology. The vicissitudes of preoedipal object relations and the varied traumatizations of normal childhood are, to a great extent, offset in their noxious potential by subsequent ego development and by the stabilization of psychic structures. These achievements are predicated on maturational advance in the symbolic process of language development, memory function, and internalizations such as superego formation and identifications. However, the preoedipal phase can never be discounted in its effect on the oedipal stage—on its formation, conflict, and resolution. There is no doubt that preoedipal components have increasingly engaged our attention in the treatment of the adolescent child.

Viewing this developmental move from the vantage point of adolescence, I have referred to it as the second individuation process (Blos, 1967). One crucial developmental advance to be accomplished at adolescence deals with the self-divestiture of infantile dependencies. Obviously, at this advanced stage, they are of an internalized nature; we refer to them as object representations or imagos. Should they be persistently externalized or projected onto the outer world during adolescence, the disengagement from infantile dependency objects is thwarted or precluded. This kind of adolescent pathology is well known. In the first —the infantile—stage of individuation the young child gains relative independence from the physical presence of the mother through internalization. Once the small child has acquired a representational world of his physical and emotional surround, his maturational potential—motoric, sensory, and cognitive—dashes forward in an outburst of new faculties and masteries.

I have paid explicit attention to the individuation process of infancy because of its relevance to an understanding of adolescent individuation. The first step in infancy accomplishes a relative independence from external objects, while the second, the adolescent step of individuation, aims at the independence from internalized infantile objects. Only when this last process is completed can childhood be transcended and adulthood be attained. This internal change comes about through normative adolescent regression, which is nondefensive; thus I have called it regression in the service of development. At no other developmental stage is regression an obligatory condition of growth. It is by way of nondefensive regression that the adolescent comes in contact with lingering infantile dependencies, anxieties, and needs. These are revisited with an ego equipment infinitely more resourceful, stable, and versatile than the one the small child had at his disposal when originally confronted with such disquieting and taxing conditions. Furthermore, the ego of this advanced stage is, as a rule, sufficiently reality-bound to forestall a regressive engulfment within the undifferentiated stage, namely, in a state of ego loss or psychosis. It is a well-known fact that the adolescent process and the eruption of adolescent psychotic illness are related by a developmental risk, which, in my opinion, lies in the individual's capacity or lack of it to keep the nondefensive regression of this age within bounds, i.e., to stay on the advanced side of infantile development which is to say, beyond the undifferentiated stage. It is only through a delimited regression that infantile object dependencies can be overcome. It remains a constant challenge for the therapist to differentiate between what in the clinical picture is defensive regression, causing developmental arrest and symptom formation, and what is regression in the service of development, which we have come to identify as a prerequisite for progressive development to take its course and sustain its momentum. I know that the chaotic and inconsistent behavior of the adolescent often defies our wish for clear-cut differentiations, but I also know that relevant clues are forthcoming if the clinician's patience and attentiveness hold out.

The Transformations of Dyadic, Isogender Attachment Emotions

Psychoanalytic theory has shown us in great clarity the course which the allogender ("positive") oedipal attachment follows from early childhood through adolescence to adulthood. All along this course there re-

mains one unaltered characteristic, namely, its implicit gender appropriate-
ness; the object remains one of the opposite sex. We have come to consider
gender polarity along the shift from infantile to adult sexuality as a developmental axiom. Some amendments, however, become plausible and exi-
gent when we follow the developmental course of the isogender ("negative") oedipal constituent. Its gender-inappropriate nature is bound to
reach an impasse at puberty when sexual maturation can no longer accommodate infantile isogender strivings derived from the dyadic phase of
development. Obviously, there is no displacement of these object-directed
drive components available within the sexual identity, whose definitive
formation is acquired during adolescence. One might relegate the transformation of the isogender drive component entirely to neutralized, i.e.,
desexualized, emotional attitudes, to character traits, or to sublimatory
endeavors. This would be the logic by which the classical psychoanalytic
theory explicates the resolution of the isogender, i.e. negative, Oedipus
complex. The dynamics of these transformations are by no means self-
evident or self-explanatory even though observation tells us that the
isogender infantile attachment emotions fade into oblivion with the closure of adolescence. The dynamics by which the isogender complex attains
its adolescent-specific resolution have been the subject of my research
for many years. I became soon aware that male and female adolescents
pursue different paths toward, and attain different resolutions of, their
respective isogender dyadic complex.

The traditional, psychoanalytic schema has only partially been borne
out in my therapeutic work with adolescents. I have found it necessary
to postulate an intermediate step in this developmental pathway. Freud's
(1914) ideas concerning narcissism and ego ideal are here brought to bear
on the adolescent process. I shall present a condensed version of the
proposition which my clinical observations suggested and which were
confirmed over the years. The isogender—preoedipal and oedipal—attachment is to a large extent a narcissistic object tie; at adolescence, the libido
invested in this tie becomes desexualized and thus initiates the narcissistic
structure of the adult ego ideal. From an adaptational or psychosocial
point of view one might speak of this process as the socialization of
infantile and oedipal narcissism. At the adolescent juncture to which I
call attention here, the infantile ego ideal of self-aggrandizement, as an
always attainable gratification and self-esteem regulator, becomes transformed into the adult ego ideal, which, constitutes a drive toward perfection. The infantile belief in the realizability of perfection becomes replaced
during late adolescence by the urge toward its approximation. This urge,
by its very nature, remains a lifelong endeavor, since the process of approximation can remain active only as long as life lasts. Its intention
and direction are ego-syntonic and always unequivocal; by implication
there is no place for doubt or second thought. Whatever the edict that

emanates from the adult ego ideal, it is self-evident to the rational mind as well as to the emotional being. Should this not be the case, we very likely deal with superego issues, which resemble so often those of the ego ideal. This dubious accountability is one more reason for outlining differentiating criteria that lie beyond the well-known reactions of guilt or shame as indicative of superego or ego-ideal neglect.

The above thoughts are derived from clinical observations which have demonstrated to me that the resolution of the negative oedipal conflict in adolescent analysis effects a personality change of a particular nature; we recognize this change in an emerging self-determination, in a projection of the self into a realistic adult life, and, last but not least, in the tolerance of self-limitations. The intrinsic precondition for this developmental advance to adulthood lies in the deidealization of self and object or, in more general terms, in the acceptance of life's existential imperfections, ordinariness, repetetiveness, and incongruities.

The gradual tolerance of values as guiding principles of conduct and aspirations, rather than of anticipated and promised perfections of self and object yet to come, is a signal characteristic of the maturing adolescent. This characteristic, when observed in the analysis of adolescents, stands in such marked contrast to a patient's preanalytic life that it has become to me a trustworthy indicator of the adult ego ideal *in statu nascendi*. I have credited the decline and paling influence of the infantile ego ideal or, conversely, the emergence and structuralization of the adult ego ideal to the analytic work which has brought about in these cases the resolution of the isogender ("negative") dyadic and triadic complex.

A Note on Idealization

Before pursuing the theoretical implications of what has been said, I must say a word about adolescent idealization in general. These comments apply to boy and girl in equal measure, even though their idealizations are different in content and organization as to the qualities of rigidity and flexibility. A good reason exists for making a distinction between the idealization of the self and the ego ideal as such. Even though idealizations have their roots in infantile narcissism, we cannot ignore the fact that the advent of sexual maturation draws these early narcissistic formations into the instinctual turbulence of adolescence. Here we encounter them either in the area of object relations or in a regressive enhancement of narcissism as seen in self-idealizations. These formations are unstable and subject to rapid fluctuations; they are primitive regulators of self-esteem. Self-idealization can provide, at least temporarily, a gratification on the order of infantile need gratification. The ego ideal, in contrast, provides only approximations to fulfillment; it involves the states of delay and anticipation; it is a ceaseless journey without arrival; it is a lifelong striving for perfection. Superego demands can be fulfilled with a subsequent sense of well-being. Ego-ideal strivings can never be fulfilled or "lived up to." They are a sustained striving for perfection that furnishes a sense of well-being or, better, of being "on the march."

The ego ideal has its deepest roots in primary narcissism. Yet every stage of subsequent development enlarges its scope in terms of content and function. Both ego ideal and superego begin to develop early in life, long before they assume the structure of a psychic institution. They originate in response to the external world and remain, therefore, prone to reexternalization. Here I want to emphasize the fact that the ego ideal is subject to qualitative changes during the course of development. That is to say, the ego ideal can easily become enmeshed with new drive modalities, as well as with new ego competencies, as both emerge at different developmental stages. By virtue of this fact, we can expect the ego ideal to become drawn into the ferment of the libidinal and aggressive drives of adolescence. The adolescent reinstinctualization of those psychic structures that derived from the internalization of object relations encompasses the ego ideal as well. Its narcissistic core attaches itself to the narcissistic object libido that finds a renewed outlet within the resurgence of the isogender complex. Its resolution brings the mature ego ideal into existence as the desexualized, i.e., transmuted, survivor of the isogender complex. Even though the early steps, as well as the final ones, of ego-ideal development are different in male and female, the adolescent structuralization of the ego ideal determines, for both sexes, the end phase of the adolescent process; in other words, it marks the termination of psychological childhood.

From the Infantile to the Adult Ego Ideal in the Male

The developmental history of the ego ideal and its implications for an understanding of adolescent personality consolidation emerged slowly but clearly from my work with adolescent boys. Clinical observation led me to recognize the fact that the origin of the adult ego ideal in the boy reaches back into the archaic past of individual psychic life. These insights were attained by a slow and circuitous route; I hope the reporting of its itinerary will not prove too laborious an account to the reader.

I shall open this topic with the observation of several male patients in their late adolescence who shared one prominent symptom complex. They had high ambitions, yet they were unable to pursue them; they were aimless and dejected, given to extreme mood swings, to sporadic but short-lived spurts of enterprising action and an unfailing return to monotonous dreams of glory: nothing ever congealed into a purposeful pursuit, a sustained experimentation, or the visionary excitement of a realizable goal. These are typical adolescent characteristics; they acquired the specificity of a symptom complex only by their static, repetitive, and involuntary nature. Thus they affected perniciously the common challenges to youth, such as vocational choice, job performance, academic achievement, and the pursuit of gratifying object relations with boys, girls, and adults alike. The irrefutable evidence of failure rendered the present dismal and the future ominous. Flight into rebellion, lethargy, or compensatory schemes carried out in action or fantasy led only further into the quicksand of helplessness. Yet any effort to transcend painful negativism could never be sustained. Occupational goals or short-term objectives were easily lost in indecision and doubt; they were often and abruptly abandoned despite a seemingly strong motivation that brought them into being. These and related phenomena have been widely described in the literature, and in fact are very well known generally. Among the various dynamic and genetic explanations, the male adolescent's rivalry with the oedipal father stands out as the standard model. Defenses against castration anxiety seem to have barricaded all roads to progressive development. There can be no doubt that this theme reverberates through the adolescent struggle of the male. There is always an abundance of direct expressions or associations, ideas, and affects leading in this direction. However, interpretations along these lines rarely resolve, in my experience, the symptomatology of such pervasive inhibitions and developmental arrests as described above. Obviously, there are some other forces at work, the origins and dynamics of which have hitherto eluded our grasp.

It occurred to me that the complementary complex of the male's rivalry with the father, namely, his love of him and his wish to be the passive recipient of his affection and inflated admiration, presented an obstacle to the formation of realistic goals and their active pursuit. In fact, such passive aims directed toward the father rose to the surface repeatedly and without fail, even though these aims clashed with conscious ambitions and were subject to severe self-criticism. They obviously persisted because they secured gratifying gains, such as a sense of security, self-confidence, and the avoidance of anxiety and shame. A comparable gain can be achieved by the transient instinctualization of ego and superego functions during adolescence. We only have to think of the irrational passion with which an adolescent boy may devote his exclusive attention to a gadget, most commonly a car, to an idealized activity, most commonly in the field of sports or music, or to the defense of some moral, political, or religious conviction. These common observations convey to us the highly personalized overvaluation of the object of his dedication. In this connection I shall cite a male student whose vocational ambitions were the same as those which his father had set for his son. Failure had to prevent success because of a four-pronged conflict: as a success he was either offering himself as a love object to the father (castration wish), or he was annihilating him by usurping his position (patricide); on the other hand—turning to the other two conflict components—as a failure he was renouncing his ambitions, and thereby he was inducing the father to treat him like a contemptible girl—so, at least, the son conjectured. Paradoxically, in failure he established his autonomy, even if a negative one, by repulsing the father's seductiveness and not becoming his best-loved, ideal son. The complexity of this constellation is due to the fact that both the isogender and allogender ("negative" and "positive") Oedipus complexes come into play again at the terminal phase of adolescence. The final resolution of both is always decisively influenced by the fixation points in early object relations and by the implicit bisexual orientation of childhood in general.

Observations of this kind have convinced me that the ego ideal remains an immature, self-idealizing, wish-fulfilling agency, resisting any transformation into a mature, namely, abstracted, goal-intentional, and action-motivating force, as long as the young man's isogender complex cannot be drawn sufficiently into the normal developmental thrust or, when therapeutic assistance is sought, into the therapeutic work. I am certain that analysts know from experience how impenetrable this aspect of the defensive organization remains in the analysis of the male adolescent. Only after the analysis of the fixation on the isogender, dyadic and triadic, complex has been accomplished can the formation of an age-adequate, workable ego ideal take its normal course. The dynamics of this structural innovation at adolescence led me to say that the adult ego ideal, as it emerges at the termination of adolescence, is "the heir to the so-called negative oedipus complex" (Blos, 1965, 1972). By inference, I assume that adolescent psychic restructuring which progresses unaided by therapeutic help follows a similar course.

The Idealization of the Self

I shall now return briefly to self-idealization and the ego ideal in adolescence, because the conceptualization of the adolescent ego-ideal formation permits a more precise differentiation between the two. The acquisition of ideals is not identical with an ego-ideal structuralization. One can neither speak of ego ideals nor of superegos in the plural. Yet one frequently encounters the term "ego ideals" in the literature. Both superego and ego ideal denote a cohesive structure, representing a system, identifiable by its function, rather than an aggregate of isolated traits, patterns, or mental-emotional personality proclivities. Self-idealization is a typical aspect of adolescence; it displays, quite unmistakably, its narcissistic origin and function as a regulator of self-esteem. Concurrently with an extended dependence on it, we discern a more or less malignant impairment of reality testing, objectivation, and mature object relations. At the point where narcissistic aims of self-idealization are externalized, they are easily confused with the manifestation of the ego ideal. Indeed, the adolescent's uncompromising ideals, expressed in word or action, are often mistaken as evidence of a strong ego ideal. My clinical impressions of some of the angry or opinionated late adolescents, often encountered among college students, who seek the establishment of a perfect society, of harmonious family or love relationships, have convinced me that the belief in an absolute and perfect world is rooted in an archaic belief in parental perfection. The idealized parent imago, when externalized, lends a fanatical vision to the striving for such a perfect world, while the narcissistic rage, a response to parental disillusionment, finds a belated expression in the irrationality of violence. An imperfect world must either yield to correction or it must be destroyed. This kind of all-or-nothing principle is repeatedly and in varying forms demonstrated with particular virulence in excesses, individually or in groups, in the social behavior of adolescents or young adults. We must be careful not to subsume all youthful, so-called idealism and utopianism under the category of replication of infantile wishes and in so doing devalue the socially invaluable potential contained in youthful aspirations, expressed with passionate, though often poorly reasoned, dedication and candor. If we apply discriminatory scrutiny to our observation of youthful behavior, we shall have no difficulty in discovering those conditions under which the violent correction, in thought or action, of an evil world reflects the externalization of the lost parental perfection; such reactions demonstrate how extraordinarily painful the effort is to transcend the loss of the idealized self and object.*

Psychoanalytic theory has always emphasized the close connection between the ego ideal and the narcissistic losses of infancy. In accordance with its origin, which also influences its function, the ego ideal is basically averse to object-libidinal involvement. Its roots lie in primary narcissism or in self-sufficient satiation by merger with an idealized real or fantasy object, shaped by the need for a tensionless state. A recourse to such merger states is activated by the infantile condition of tension intolerance; it perpetuates, so to speak, an eternal approximation to the narcissistic self-perfection of infancy. If we follow the course which the ego ideal takes from infancy to adulthood, we can trace a continuous adaptation of its basic function to the increasingly complex system by which the self measures itself as it progresses along developmental lines. Thus the

---

* We find the prototypical ancestors of this mood in the nihilist students depicted in Arcady and Bazarov in Turgenev's novel *Fathers and Sons* (1862). Arcady eventually settles down in marriage and an ancestral life pattern, while Bazarov, in a triumph of self-idealization over a thwarted romance, commits suicide.

ego ideal gets further and further removed from primitive efforts to restore narcissistic self-sufficiency at the price of reality testing and reality adaptation. In fact, the ego ideal functions as a psychic institution, at least in its mature form, only as long as its goal remains beyond its grasp. Its precondition is the competence to tolerate tension and resolve conflicts in an adaptive, age-competent manner. Whatever man accomplishes, imperfection remains an everlasting constituent of his endeavors; yet this fact has never held man back from renewing his efforts. While the superego is an agency of prohibition, the ego ideal is an agency of aspiration. "Whereas the ego submits to the superego out of fear of punishment, it submits to the ego ideal out of love" (Nunberg, 1932, p. 146). Many decades later we read again, "Our ideals are our internal leaders; we love them and are longing to reach them. . . . We are driven by our ambitions, [but] we do not love them" (Kohut, 1966, p. 251).

In my work with the male adolescent, I was often struck by how intensely his self-idealization is cultivated by him as an aim in itself, without being followed up by an act toward realization or achievement. The comparison of this attitude to a fixation on forepleasure is convincing, especially when we observe repeatedly the decline of this mode of functioning with the ascendancy of genitality and mature object relations. This thought, already contained *in nuce* in the clinical starting point of my deliberations on the process and function of adolescent deidealization, can now be restated: the ego ideal emerges from its infantile state only when, in late adolescence, the narcissistic object attachment to which the infantile ego ideal became joined has lost its libidinal bonding. This libidinal detachment acquires a mounting degree of urgency at adolescence because the revival of infantile object attachment and the affects involved in this bond become sexualized by virtue of pubertal maturation. In the case of male isogender attachment emotions a homosexual potential is either fleetingly or more lastingly evoked. This disquieting emotion is diverted by the formation of the adult ego ideal, which by its consolidation affirms its roots in the narcissistic sector of the personality and carries it forward as a self-acknowledged system of guiding principles devoid of object libido. This task is accomplished by the male adolescent in his resolution of the isogender dyadic and triadic complex.

Approaching the Adult Personality Formation

These deliberations on preoedipality in relation to adolescent psychic restructuring permit me to say that the dyadic (preoedipal) stage of object relations rivals the oedipal stage in its contributions to adolescent personality formation. However, there are good reasons to designate the oedipal stage as the *primum inter pares*, because at that particular juncture a forward step in psychic organization has been reached which reflects an entirely new, namely triadic, complexity of conflictual object relations. Their resolution is memorialized in the definitive structure of the ego which is attained at this point and designated as the superego. I make here a distinction between object relations as need-gratifying expressions and psychic structure formation as an organizational element of personality growth. Within this developmental context the phase-specific, so-called infantile neurosis makes its transient appearance but is self-liquidating in the normal course of development. Whenever neurotic psychopathology prevails in childhood or adolescence, it has been my observation that noxious dyadic remnants have been carried forward and have worked their way into oedipal formations.

In order to lend support to the statement I just made, a clinical illustration may be welcome, especially since the thesis I advance diverges from the currently held theory. As a caveat I preface the case by stating my belief that any presentation of case material is a prejudicious act, contingent on a set of criteria which are based on the reporter's observational selectivity and his interpretive summation; they, in short, determine how we choose to record clinical data and how we attribute specific meaning to them. The ultimate test of what I report in the following lies in a consensual validation, namely, in the reader's recognition of a congruent meaningful experience.

The young man was 22 years old when he started analytic treatment. He is an artist of considerable talent without any dependable work discipline, always searching for and temporarily finding dependent, heterosexual relationships at the price of surrendering his personal autonomy and his sense of pride. He had been an extremely anxious young child with sleep disturbances, nightmares, delayed sphincter control into latency, and a reluctance to go to school. A turbulent and unsuccessful school career led him finally into drugs. At the present time, due to his limited earning power he still lives at home. He is seriously engaged in the analytic work and is determined to get his life "on the road." I will report his first analytic session after summer vacation, when he started his fourth year of analysis.

He begins by telling me that his summer has been good, that he has worked well without drinking and, of course, without drugs, which he gave up two years ago. He then states emphatically, "Now, I must get out of my parents' house!" He continues: "I can't get it together when I try to deal with my parents as whole persons. My father being a drinker—that nice guy who loves to go out with me for dinner, whom I like so much, who is so sweet—and then behaves like a tottering fool. It confuses me, it confuses my thinking and the way I see my life and myself. With my mother I have an easier time; I know she can be pretty weird, but I can appreciate the strong and supportive side of her. She annoys me, but she does not confuse me the way my father does."

The next thought follows abruptly: "I was terribly anxious last night.

I was scared of my first analytic session tomorrow when we would open a new can of worms. The only thing to calm me down was to make love to Jennifer, the woman I have lived with all through the summer. I told Jennifer casually of my desire, not letting her know how terribly anxious and scared I was. She said, 'No, not tonight.' I said nothing but I felt devastated, lost, angry, confused. Then I had a dream, really a nightmare. I dreamed that Jennifer and I are somewhere in a desolate country, way out in nowhere. We are in two separate cars; both are standing still. A helicopter hovers above us with a man in it. He has a rifle to shoot us as soon as we would try to get out of our cars. There was no escape. There were bushes around to dive into, but they stood near a 2,000-foot precipice. Whatever we would do, we had to die. I was frightened. I woke up. In the morning when I told Jennifer of my anxiety, she said, "Why didn't you tell me? I would have helped you." He continues: "It's my old problem all over again: When I was a child I could never tell my parents about my terrible anxiety in the present tense, always in the past tense; then they felt relieved and would say, 'Let's talk it over.' I always had to protect them from falling apart. Only then could I be sure that they would take care of me and I would not die. It was a Catch 22. They needed me and I needed them. They never wanted me to be close to anybody except to them. They are such needy people, just as I am."

Let us look at the manifest material of this session as a comprehensive, integrated statement. Analytically and developmentally speaking, the patient is actively engaged in the consolidation phase of late adolescence and postadolescence. The motto of his day is "I have work to do," including the analytic work, which cannot proceed without, in his words, "opening a new can of worms." Liquor or drugs have become ego-alien, or antithetical to his present identity. He struggles at the moment with dyadic fixations which are actualized via dyadic modalities. These the patient verbalizes in associated memories about maternal and paternal experiences in early childhood. These specific associations will now be reported; they were obviously elicited by last night's rejection and the anxiety dream which followed.

He first recalls his mother's unavailability in moments of anxiety. He says, "I was three; I was in a night panic; I went to my mother's bed to put my head against her when she suddenly stiffened and turned into a silent stone." And again, "When I was a little older I still had nightmares; one night my father came to my bed and lay down next to me; he did it many times; my anxiety left me; no more nightmares." In the transference the patient is groping forward toward the postdyadic transition to the triadic, i.e., oedipal, stage, which is expressed in his deidealization attempt via the critical, ambivalent assessment of his father. Yet at the same time, his turn to the rescuing father, his analyst, presents a threat of regression at the moment when he is still under the spell of last night's panic, so reminiscent of his early childhood. The "can of worms" represents the anxiety-provoking, regressive pull to infantile dependency and ego dissolution. Panic mounts whenever he finds himself under the sway of the archaic, reengulfing (symbiotic) mother, the paradigmatic imago who refuses—so he feels—to assuage the little boy's night terror. In his bewilderment and helplessness he turns to the analyst-father as the replication of the dyadic rescuer. Here the analyst becomes the pivotal agent in the demarcation of the self and in the deidealization of primary object relations. Both processes promote the ego's active distancing of itself from infantile dependencies.

The dream presents itself as a typical oedipal dream, at least in a superficial overview of its manifest content; the expected setting is there with the two lovers locked in separate cars, preventing physical contact and furthermore, with the only escape via death, while the scene is watched over and totally controlled by a threatening man with a rifle, etc. This cliché of a scenario depicting the oedipal triangle is, however, contradicted by the patient's associations, which dispell such a monomorphic interpretation and permits, quite to the contrary, a biphasic or double-tiered comprehension of it. In fact, this clinical material is presented to demonstrate this theoretical point in observable terms.

One more detail of the session has to be mentioned. The patient is convinced that the man with the rifle is himself; it is his own aggressive affect which kills the frustrator, namely the woman he loves who refused him and with whom he merges in death. We might indeed be permitted to go beyond this and conclude that the patient is incapable of turning aggression against the object without becoming his own victim. This sado-masochistic attitude is clearly observable in his intolerance of ambivalence, in his gentle adaptability to the demands of others, and in his tender and caretaking solicitude toward them. These attitudes appear in his professional life as inhibited self-assertion, as fragmented capacity to work, and as an agitated perseverence on the threshold of becoming somebody who could seriously matter to himself and others. In a cynical self-ridiculing mood he said of himself, "All my life I struggled to be the most gifted underachiever." He now realizes that he must leave his family if he is ever to become what he fervently aspires to be, namely a genuinely creative artist, a man, a husband, and a procreative adult.

The symptoms dealt with in this patient's analysis are representative of the end phase of adolescence, when dyadic and triadic (oedipal) residues are worked through and integrated into adult sexuality, character structure, and work identity. The analysis—as so often happens—delays by its nature and purpose the closure of adolescence, extends a typical adolescent psychic plasticity, and permits treatment to accomplish what the adolescent process normally accomplishes unaided. The process of therapy encompasses an oscillating focus of dominance in relation to one or the other of the infantile stages of object relations. A prominent pathological component of this case lies in the ease with which the patient oscillates between the respective infantile phase-specific positions; in fact, this oscillation as an adaptational device or a state of being had acquired for this young man the familiarity of a life style, a resigned, almost comfortable acceptance of an outgrown wardrobe. Continuing the metaphor, I might say that acquiring new and fitting clothes while abandoning the old ones is, for this patient, as momentous a step to take as it is for the toddler to do without his security blanket or his teddy bear.

The Adult Ego Ideal

Even though we consider the ego ideal to be part of the superego system, they do not evolve from the same conflictual matrix, nor are they overlapping entities at the time of their emergence. Quite to the contrary, their origins are heterogeneous, their starting points are not synchronous, their contents are not identical, and their functions are disparate. What they have in common is their motivational influence on behavior, and their regulatory function of the sense of well-being. We can "distinguish between the superego, as the later and more reality-syntonic structure, and the ego ideal as the earlier more narcissistic one" (A. Reich, 1954, p. 209). However, the chronology of their definitive structure formation is reversed: the superego is established earlier, namely, at the decline of the oedipal phase, while the ego ideal does not reach its definitive, i.e., adult, structure before the terminal stage of adolescence.

It has often been noted that the narcissistic nature of the ego ideal draws, at an early age, the body image into its realm. It is therefore no surprise that the course of ego-ideal formation is not identical for boy and girl. However, for both sexes the function of the early, or infantile, ego ideal can be recognized in its aim, which is to repair or wipe out a narcissistic hurt caused by comparison with or slight by others or, simply, by the state of immaturity, dependency, and relative physical littleness and weakness of the child. Each child has passed through these stages and walked away from them with idiosyncratic affinities to certain anxieties; be they insignificant or disturbing, they evoke in either case habitual strategems to counteract, as thoroughly as possible, their interference with the sense of wholeness. The narcissistic recourse to a state of illusory self-protection induces a sense of well-being, which is, however, maintained after infancy only at the price of a certain degree of reality distortion. As ego development progresses, such isolated but lasting distortions extend an insidious influence on the adaptive resourcefulness of child, adolescent, or adult.

The first step in ego-ideal development leads from primary narcissism to delusional omnipotence shared with the mother and, beyond that, to narcissistic identifications with idealized objects. These identifications become progressively tempered by the reality principle, which takes a forward leap at the time it is called upon to aid in the resolution of the Oedipus complex. The consolidation of the superego keeps flights into omnipotence and aggrandizement in check. The recourse to the state of infantile omnipotence becomes definitively relegated to the world of fantasy. In fact, the creative aspect of fantasy and its expressive modalities (such as play or pictorial and verbal imagination) reflect, on a metaphorical plane, the potency and power of the procreative, dyadic (preoedipal) mother, who has always aroused, to various degrees, to be sure, the envy of the male and the female child. This envy which the little boy harbors is defeated in the bud; however, the momentum of this infantile envy does not just vanish in thin air, but is transposed into other modalities of realization. This might throw light on the observation that adolescent boys so frequently pine for creativity, originality, and fame. Girls, indeed, have similar aspirations, but these remain more forcefully attached to the yearnings for a fulfilling relationship. This opinion has been generally expressed by observers of the gender differences in the aspirations and wishes of adolescent boys and girls. The fact that a greater portion of humankind's creative efforts and achievements in the sciences and the arts is identified with men than with women can only partially be attributed to cultural influences. Reverberations of male awe and envy of female procreation can still be detected in the male adolescent's urge to create, be this a gadget, a fortune, a molecule, a poem, a song, or a house. Such wishes fall far short of any characteristic we attribute to the ego ideal, yet they furnish the material for repetitive daydreams and usually remain shackled to these nether regions by strong inhibitions. To illustrate, I shall relate an incident from the analysis of a late adolescent male patient. He reported one day that he had heard himself say aloud, as talking to himself, "Now, Chris, don't be a woman." At the time, he was languishing in daydreams, blissfully hoping that all would turn out for the best. He was startled by his own words, which revealed both his wish and its refutation—or, more pointedly, his emotional conflict. Should the conflict over such disquieting, bisexual issues of identification not be dealt with effectively during adolescence, their continuation is bound to burden the life of the adult.

If the infantile need for oneness with the archaic mother remains overly strong, the Oedipus complex falls under the shadow of this fixation. A regressive component in the resolution of the boy's Oedipus complex can be discerned in the narcissistic identification with the archaic, omnipotent, phallic mother. To some extent, this compromise seems to be a rather normal aspect of the male Oedipus complex that reaches its final resolution, rather belatedly, during its adolescent resuscitation. Whenever the preoedipal fixation on the phallic mother weakens the rivalrous, phallic assertion of the boy, the Oedipus complex is destined to remain incomplete. This abnormal condition certainly becomes evident during adolescence, if it did not already do so during the latency period. The time for the outbreak of the neurosis lies, usually, in the period of late adolescence (Blos, 1972), when the adolescent's increase in sexual libido, while welcomed as an ally in the struggle to counteract his "childish ways of life," especially passivity, easily becomes an overworked, defensive activation of reassuring but short-lived effectiveness (A. Freud, 1958, p. 266).

One characteristic remnant of the regressive component, embedded paradoxically in the Oedipus complex, is to be found quite universally in the young adolescent boy's castration anxiety in relation to the phallic woman in general (Blos, 1962, 1965). This powerful apprehensiveness causes the boy to idealize the father or men in general, seeking protective and reassuring peership. Sharing the idealized paternal power and superiority becomes a transient source of narcissistic grandeur that will last until the sexual impulse of puberty threatens the arousal of homosexual object libido. At this point, we can observe how the ego ideal again becomes fatefully enmeshed with object-libidinal strivings due to the relatively incomplete resolution of the Oedipus complex. Adolescent psychic restructuring normally, even if belatedly, loosens preoedipal libidinal adhesions, i.e. dyadic fixations. This move opens the path to mature ego-ideal structuralization and adult personality formation.

The structuralization of the mature ego ideal reduces excessive self and object idealizations to the level of more realistic self and object appraisal. The capacity for objective judgment serves as a check against any inopportune aggrandizement of the self. Thus it sustains the inexorable "striving for perfection," which is the source of narcissistic sustenance, removed and remote from the vicissitudes of object relations. The adult ego ideal of the male enshrines, so to speak, its history from primary narcissism to the merger with maternal omnipotence and, beyond, to the attachment emotions which the little boy experiences in his relationship to the dyadic father. The latter stage of these infantile object relations is transcended during adolescence in ego-ideal formation. Only in terms of this last and decisive step, which integrates the various epochs of the ego-ideal history in its mature structuralization, can we speak of the male ego ideal's being the heir of the isogender complex.

It is implicit in the nature of adolescence that at this age the primitive state of self-idealization, including the vast spectrum of magic, omnipotence, and grandiosity, becomes challenged as never before. The realization of oedipal aspirations could, at the young age of physical immaturity, still find a modicum of perfection, even if only a borrowed one, in simply being the object of parental expectations. Expressions of parental overestimation of the child, derived from their own narcissistic needs, are easily taken by the child as reliable promises or predictions, which never fail to be called into question by reality assertions during adolescence. It is true that postoedipal superego criticism of the self counterbalances the primitive powers of self-idealization and prevents them from ever totally dislodging objectivity; however, they are never extinguished. The normal state of a partially integrated but still externally regulated ego ideal of childhood undergoes a radical and lasting change during adolescence. A throwback, in the face of adolescent challenges, to the infantile ego ideal is a rather common occurrence before the mature appraisal of object and self becomes irreversible. The second individuation process and the consolidation process of adolescence render existing self and object representations less rigid but more stable and realistic. If the attendant disappointments, compromises, and losses cannot be tolerated, the adolescent process is doomed to miscarry. "The exclusive production of fantasies that aim at one's own aggrandizement reveals a serious disturbance of the narcissistic balance, particularly when these fantasies persist *after puberty*" (A. Reich, 1960, p. 296; italics mine). It is no exaggeration, in this context, to say that adolescence is comparable to a continental divide that determines, once and for all, the direction in which the ego ideal will flow from here on: either it will revert to its familiar source of origin, or it will seek a new course, untested and unknown.

The extent to which the demands or expectations of society, in conjunction with adolescent psychic reorganization, are growth-promoting seems contingent on the concurrent formation of the mature ego ideal. Of course, commitments undergo change over time, but in order to change, they must first have existed. The critical time of life in which they attain mature form and content is late adolescence. Whatever the complications in the forward move to the state of commitment may be, most maturing persons reach a workable compromise which bears the marks of their uniqueness, be they strengths or weaknesses, assets or liabilities. If all goes reasonably well, the life space once declared as one's own provides a fitting or balancing physical, social, and personal environment, which must suffice to take care of the complexities of the individual. If, however, the adolescent fails in this task and becomes a patient, then one discovers that there always was a more or less extensive ego-ideal pathology present. Focusing on the ego ideal alone in assessing a patient's abnormality in functioning grossly restricts our view of the dynamics involved in any case. With this proviso clearly stated, I think there is no reason that prevents us from singling out the ego ideal for intensive study. In fact, the scrutinizing focus on this structure is particularly suggestive in relation to late adolescence, because we deal here not only with a normative structure formation, but with one that represents a critical factor within the maturational process and exerts a temporarily disequilibrating influence on personality functioning.

More about Idealization: Applied Psychoanalysis

The distinction between a primitive and a mature ego ideal is widely accepted. The prominent role of ideals in adolescence has been recognized since the times of Aristotle,* but the genetic antecedents of this adolescent characteristic have still to be explored. The adolescent-specific proclivity to idealization is observable in self-idealization and its externalization. The adult ego ideal operates outside of the mental sphere of volition; due to this fact, we speak of its automatization, a mode of operation it shares with the function of character. While character traits are observable from early childhood on, character as an integrated system of behavior shares with the ego ideal the time of its structuralization, which is adolescence (Blos, 1968). The decisive role of the ego ideal in the maintenance of the narcissistic balance, experienced as self-esteem, is a generally held tenet of the psychoanalytic theory of personality.

In the field of applied psychoanalysis, the ego-ideal concept has been employed in the discussion of literary figures. Among these Prince Hal has been widely studied in depth and portrayed in terms of the idealization of object and self, as well as the adult-ego-ideal consolidation of late adolescence. This Shakespearean character in *Henry IV* displays the enigmatic contradictions of youth—debauchery and high idealism—in a flamboyant fashion. All along the course of his bewildering actions, Prince Hal never loses touch with his inner struggle of growing up. The consolidation of the ego ideal lies at the center of this struggle, in which he first fails, but finally succeeds by reconciling the idealized father imago he loves with the imperfect, if not downright evil, father person he hates. Had his father, the King, not murdered his own cousin, Richard II, whom Hal had followed to Ireland as a boy, whom he had idealized, and whose favor he had won?

Ernst Kris (1948 p. 273), interpreted Prince Hal's conduct within the framework of the Oedipus complex and the ambivalence conflict that vacillates between obedience, flight, and parricide. In the effort to transcend the infantile conflict, the defensive and adaptive role of ideal formation is clearly present. The Lichtenbergs (1969) shifted the focus to that "aspect of adolescent development by which a particular adolescent achieves the formation of his ideals" (p. 874). Prince Hal was made again

* See Aristotle, *Rhetoric,* ed. W. D. Ross, in Aristotle, *Selections.* New York: Scribner, 1927, p. 323–325.

the subject of a study by Aarons (1970), who viewed the son-father conflict in relation to the vicissitudes of the ego ideal. The two components central to this theme are those of object love (the isogender Oedipus complex) and object deidealization, as I had described them in their intrinsic connection to adolescent ego-ideal formation (Blos, 1962, 1965). Prince Hal is indeed a dramatic character of extraordinary plausibility when viewed by Aarons within the context of the ego-ideal concept. The author illuminates Prince Hal's flight from royal dignity at the court to carousel at the tavern by pointing out that through peer relationship the "tie of dependence is broken" and a "recathexis of the ego ideal for which the father stood" is made possible. Aarons calls this the "renewal" of the ego ideal and defines it "as the rescue and reaffirmation of the ego ideal— a sublimation of the love for the father" (p. 332f.). In surveying the psychoanalytic studies of Prince Hal, from 1948 to 1970, we notice a gradual shift of focus from oedipal strivings to idealization and disillusionment, namely, to the problem of adolescent ego-ideal formation and the process of deidealization. Falstaff, a split-off father imago, in conjunction with the peer world, the prince's drinking companions, reconstituted a proxy family which—by a grand detour—assisted the troubled youth in the formation of the mature ego ideal and the assumption of his princely identity. These tumultuous late adolescent events illustrate the renewed object enmeshment or the reinstinctualization of the idealized object, from which the mature ego ideal emerges.

Studies in literary criticism like the ones I have mentioned exemplify the usefulness of concepts developed in this treatise on son and father. Prince Hal in particular demonstrates the developmental thesis in regard to late adolescence in his transformation from a "drop-out" prince into the utmost royal dignity of a king. The dramatic demonstration of his conflict resolution in relation to his father's conduct of life can easily be scaled down to plebian proportions or contemporary conditions without losing a shred of persuasiveness. Indeed, Prince Hal invites some of the comments which follow.

In its mature form, the ego ideal weakens the punitive power of the superego by taking over some of its function; equally, ego aspects become engaged in its service. The realm of the ego ideal, borrowing Nietzsche's words, lies "beyond good and evil." Piers and Singer (1953), speaks of the ego ideal as a "magic belief in one's invulnerability or immortality to make for physical courage and to help counteract realistic fears of injury and death" (p. 26). Potentially, the ego ideal transcends castration anxiety, thus propelling man toward incredible feats of creativity, heroism, sacrifice, and selflessness. One dies for one's ego ideal rather than let it die. "Here I stand, I cannot do otherwise" were Luther's words at the Diet of Worms, when he was urged, under great peril to himself, to recant his belief. The ego ideal is the most uncompromising influence on the conduct of the mature individual: its position always remains unequivocal. The consolidation of the adult ego ideal in the course of adolescent and postadolescent development is an achievement of momentous import, not only for the single individual but also for the maintenance of a cohesive society and its communal organization.

The adolescent patient needs to be exposed—gradually and repeatedly—to a disillusionment in self and object. Over time, this leads to a tolerance of imperfection, first in the object and finally extending to the self. How difficult and painful the process of deidealization of object and self is for the adolescent never ceases to impress me. Indeed, I feel inclined to say that the deidealization of object and self represents the most distressful and tormenting single aspect of growing up—if any such generalization can be made at all. The magnitude of this step at adolescence is comparable to the Copernican revolution, which deprived man of his place in the center of the universe—a truly sobering, existential consciousness. Having made this cosmic analogy, I might mention in passing a concomitantly emerging sensitivity, namely, that not until adolescence a true sense of the tragic emerges; this is part of the mature faculty to accept the human condition. In contrast, the young child tends to fix blame on caretaking people and thus experiences feelings of sadness, fright, anger, or abandonment. Mourning follows a different pathway before and after the second individuation process and the deidealization of self and object. For the work of mourning to take its course, the attainment of what I shall call "mature ambivalence" is essential; otherwise, a split in the ego of the postadolescent personality occurs. This split is between the acceptance and the denial of the finality of death. The irreconcilability of these positions threatens the cohesiveness of the psychic organism and weakens the ego's integrative function in all aspects of life.

As a common example, I mention the "abandonment malaise" of the adolescent who tells us in endless variations of his conviction that "nothing will ever work out" in his love relationships or that he "will never accomplish anything great the world needs, admires, and loves." So many encouraging beginnings so frequently fall apart during late adolescence. The roots of such dysphoric moods are of preoedipal origin, even though we usually encounter them amalgamated with oedipal anxiety, guilt, and inhibitions. Excessive indulgences in food, liquor, or drugs reveal preoedipal fixations, even though a pseudo-oedipal stance is often forcefully and frantically maintained, only highlighting the intensity of the struggle to reach emotional maturity. As an aside I remind the reader of Prince Hal's attachment to Falstaff, a semifather, and of the prince's debauchery in food, drink, and the mixed company of the tavern.

We have learned from clinical work with adolescents that the persistent, irrepressible psychic irritants of a preoedipal nature make their appearance in treatment, demanding therapeutic interventions which, hope-fully, are able to reach the primitive emotions and infantile needs which confront the therapist in all kinds of sophisticated disguises. In practice, treatment veers constantly between preoedipal and oedipal realms on the one hand and the adolescent's present life on the other; should one of these periods dominate too exclusively the therapeutic scene, the thera-pist attempts to relate it to the ignored or underplayed stage of the life cycle. The respective vehicles of these efforts are—in ascending levels of abstraction—advice, judgment, explanation, interpretation, and recon-struction. Preoedipal components in adolescent therapy often lie concealed behind the patient's guarded, critical, and suspicious attitude or behind his unshakably trusting expectancy of the good life the therapist will deliver. A precious sense of security and safety derives from being part of an idealized object, be this the preoedipal mother or dyadic father, either one or both, alternatively reified in the person of the therapist. Parenthetically I might mention that fathers as idealized maternal imagos appear more frequently in contemporary adolescent patients than in those of the past, because many more parents have shared, of late, the caretaking of their small children. Be this as it may, the revival of the idealized parent imago in the person of the therapist, man or woman, demands a most delicate work in bringing about object deidealization. The best out-come of this process we refer to as trust, wellspring of a therapeutic alliance and, in a more mutual, permanent, and broadly shared human connection, the bedrock of genuine personal and intimate relationships.

Modifications in the Theory of Female Development

Since the central theme of my investigation concerns son and father, little has been said about any comparable or collateral developmental lines in the development of the girl. Some comments follow in order to lend a broader gender perspective to what has been explicated at great length. We have arrived at a fitting moment to relate a pertinent piece of psychoanalytic history. Freud's "Fragment of an Analysis of a Case of Hysteria" (1905) is a time-honored specimen of oedipal pathology in a late adolescent girl by the name of Dora. The very diagnosis of hysteria and its definition, as used at the time, implies the presence of a sexual conflict characteristic of this neurotic illness. The patient's symptoms—in this case conversion symptoms—reflect the pathological elaborations of an unresolved, virulent Oedipus complex at adolescence. The case history portrays in greatest clarity how the affective and sexual conflicts of Dora's love for her father became fatefully interwoven with the life of a married couple, Herr and Frau K., who were friends of her family. Dora's father had started an affair with Frau K., whose husband Herr

K. was enamored with Dora, then an adolescent girl of 16. At 18 Dora started treatment with Freud. How ingeniously Freud pieced together the details of fact and fantasy, conscious and unconscious, in the course of the treatment is too well known to require any comment here.

When Dora suddenly disrupted the analysis after three months, Freud searched for the emotional currents that had caused this impetuous action. What furthermore puzzled Freud was the unsatisfactory relief from symptoms, despite the clarifications and interpretations he had offered the patient, which undoubtedly were correct. What was amiss in the work that left it incomplete on two accounts? As to the disruption, Freud concluded that "I did not succeed in mastering the transference in good time" (1905, p. 118). Dora—a hysteric of 18—might well have responded to the man who discussed with her most objectively and in detail sexual matters of the greatest delicacy in the same way she had responded once before to the seductive intimacy of Herr K., from whom she had fled in panic and vengefulness.

Be this as it may, it is quite another aspect of the case history that I want to bring to the reader's attention. This aspect concerns the preoedipal fixation on the dyadic isogender relationship, which, on the oedipal level, led to a revival and the subsequent repression of the isogender oedipal tie. A fixation on this preoedipal attachment, when resuscitated at adolescence, is frequently silenced—in life as well as in treatment—by the diversionary display of heterosexual wishes, actions, denials, conflicts, and agitations. I have alluded to both these issues in my discussion of the normative homosexual conflict in relation to adolescent sexual identity formation and, furthermore, when I spoke of a specific adolescent reaction which I have termed oedipal defense. By quoting from the Dora case, I wish to demonstrate that Freud was fully aware of both these issues, but kept them confined to his commentary on the case. He never alluded to them in the treatment, where he pursued with single-minded pertinacity the "positive" (allogender) oedipal theme in Dora's acting out of her wish for and rejection of Herr K.'s attempted seduction (1905, p. 25). In fact the case has been—and still is—read without attributing to preoedipal issues the overriding developmental prominence they deserve in the patient's psychopathology.

While working on the Dora paper, Freud wrote to Fliess (letter of October 14, 1900) that in the case at hand "the chief issue in the conflicting mental processes is the opposition between an inclination towards men and towards women" (Freud, 1887–1902, p. 327) in an adolescent girl. Dora declared, after her conflict was seemingly understood, that she couldn't "forgive him [her father] for it [the affair with Frau K.]" (1905, p. 54). She complained, "I can think of nothing else" (p. 54). Freud postulated that "this excessively intense train of thought must owe its reinforcement to the unconscious" (pp. 54–55). This comment he clarified by saying, "For behind Dora's supervalent train of thought which was concerned with her father's relations with Frau K. there lay concealed a feeling of jealousy which had that lady as its *object*—a feeling, that is, which could only be based upon an affection on Dora's part for one of her own sex" (p. 60). Freud concluded that the girl was jealous of her father and not of his mistress; in other words, she wished to be the object of the woman's love.

Freud viewed this attachment in the context of adolescent boys and girls, who "show clear signs, even in normal cases, of the existence of an affection for people of their own sex" (p. 60). Once more, in the Postscript to the Dora case, Freud returned to this crucial and central complex in Dora's pathology; here we read, "I failed to discover in time and to inform the patient that her homosexual (gynaecophilic) love for Frau K. was the strongest unconscious current in her mental life" (p. 120n). Thus Dora's two dreams, especially the second, in which the Sistine Madonna figures prominently as an association (p. 96), might be understood differently and unhesitatingly today in terms of that "strongest unconscious current in her mental life."

The two women Dora had loved finally betrayed her. The girl discovered that "she was being admired and fondly treated [by her governess] not for her own sake but for her father's" (p. 61). As a repetition of this, Frau K., with whom "the scarcely grown girl had lived for years on a footing of the closest intimacy" (p. 61), "had not loved her for her own sake but on account of her father" (p. 62). We can confidently assume that at the bottom of Dora's sense of betrayal lay a sense of emotional abandonment by the mother, even though the case history tells us nothing factual or reconstructed about it.

Dora's thwarted love for the two women became forcefully removed from her conscious affective life, while the heterosexual drive was histrionically pushed into the forefront of her mind. Freud referred to this as "noisy demonstrations to show that she grudged her [Frau K.] the possession of her father; and in this way she concealed from herself the contrary fact, which was that she grudged her father Frau K.'s love" (p. 63). With scientific objectivity Freud explained that he would not "go any further" into this important subject . . . because Dora's analysis came to an end before it could throw any light on this side of her mental life" (p. 60). In a final opinion on this case which for a long time has typified the psychopathology of repressed heterosexual libido, Freud stated that the mortification in betrayal by the two women whose maternal love Dora craved "touched her, perhaps, more nearly and had a greater pathogenic effect than the other [case], which she tried to use as a screen for it,—the fact that she had been sacrificed by her father" (p. 62). Their expression came too late or was postponed too long to benefit the patient.

I must confess that I myself did not read the Dora paper in the present light until I became aware through my own clinical work of the concepts presented earlier in this discussion. Even though in the Dora case Freud stated as contingent observations such conclusions as I have endeavored to highlight, these were never systematically incorporated in the classical psychoanalytic theory of female adolescence. While I present here my own conceptualizations about adolescent development, I also want to show that some of them were contained *in nuce* in the Dora paper. To do homage to Freud's genius, I have presented a neglected aspect of the Dora case, in the hope of stimulating its rereading with an altered and broadened focus of attention.

Dyadic, Gender-specific Constellations

The revisitation of the Dora case lends itself to the introduction of a topic I have explored for many years. I refer to my efforts to trace the divergent developmental lines in male and female adolescence, sorting out, as it were, their inherent similarities and intrinsic differences. I shall not dwell on the male and female oedipal constellation because it is a topic so well known and so firmly established that it needs no comment here. However, some words about the preoedipal period of both sexes are in order, because the reverberations of these early object relations determine, to such a large extent, the adolescent-specific relations to male and female and to people generally, as well as to the world at large, to abstract thought, and to the self.

From therapeutic work with adolescent girls and young women we know of the powerful regressive pull to the preoedipal mother, leading to symptom formation and acting out. Overeating and nibbling or over-dieting and food abstinence as quasi-addictions of an episodic, transient nature are common enough ideosyncrasies of the female adolescent. Weight, i.e. eating, problems, such as bulimia and anorexia, are symptoms almost exclusively restricted to the female adolescent. When the girl goes through the preadolescent phase, we recognize in her object relations the regressively revived imagos of the good and the bad mother. The reflections of this phase appear in merger fantasies and violent distancing behavior. Their enmeshment with oedipal issues is always part of the clinical picture. The infantile tie to the mother, however, remains for the girl a lasting source of ambivalence and ambiguity, because it contains by its very nature homosexual components; these are bound to be reinforced by puberty. We discover in the heterosexual acting out of the adolescent girl—especially the young adolescent girl—two aims; one leads to the gratification of infantile, tactile contact hunger, while the other seeks to strengthen the girl's still infirm sexual identity. Both these aims are entangled in the young adolescent girl's—initially defensive—attachment to the opposite sex. Her advance to adult genitality occurs only gradually and often remains incomplete, without, however, necessarily endangering the healthy personality integration of the woman. The future capacity for, and pleasure in, mothering are, to a large extent, facilitated by the mature female's unconflicted and open access to the integrated good and bad mother imagos. Adolescent emotional development determines in a decisive way the outcome of this ambivalence struggle. In my opinion, there is no treatment of the adolescent girl in which the features of this regressive pull and the ambivalent emotions toward the early mother are not issues of central importance. We can always detect in the woman the remnants of that primordial love in her relations to members of her own sex. The fact that the girl, but not the boy, has to change in later life the gender of the first love and hate object, the mother, renders the psychological development of the girl more complex than that of the boy.

In contrast, the boy's infantile tie to the early mother remains throughout the phase of adolescent regression sexually polarized and, consequently, a source of conflict essentially different from that of the adolescent girl. The girl tends to extricate herself from the regressive pull toward merger by a forward rush onto the oedipal stage. The small boy, on the other hand, normally goes through a stage in which the fear of the archaic castrating mother—the original caretaker and organizer of the infant's body orifices and functions—forms the nucleus of the male's apprehensiveness vis-à-vis the woman. This formation is most convincingly demonstrated during male preadolescence when we observe this apprehensiveness either in the avoidance of the opposite sex and hostility toward girls in general or in the sexual bravado of juvenile machismo. These conflicts of early childhood and adolescence, universal as they are, never cease to affect the relations between the sexes throughout life.

Dusting off the accumulation of years, we readily admit that the question which Ernest Jones asked in 1935 is still relevant and provocative, even though it still remains unanswered to everybody's satisfaction. In his paper "Early Female Sexuality" Jones (1935) took issue with Freud's view of penis envy and its role in the development of femininity. His closing sentence reads, "The ultimate question is whether a woman is born or made." However, he was sure of three facts, namely, that a woman is not an *homme manqué*; that preoedipal little boys and girls are not, psychologically speaking, both masculine; and, last but not least, that femininity is not a defensive formation at its origin. "On the contrary, her [the little girl's] femininity develops progressively from the promptings of an instinctual constitution" (Jones, 1935, p. 495). Whether a primary femininity exists is still a controversial issue, but contemporary evidence leans strongly toward the conclusion that woman is born and not made, and certainly that femininity cannot be defined or understood by its negative apposition to the male. This opinion does not deny the fact that cultures

introduce distortions in this process by imposing socially sanctioned phal-
locentric models of feminine normalcy.

At this point our investigation will best be served by stating briefly
the classical Freudian concept of female development before we turn our
attention to modifications of the psychoanalytic psychology of the adolescent girl. This detour into the early years of life, into the origins of what
is to follow later, is essential for an understanding of female adolescence.
Obviously, the psychosexual component of development stands at the
center of our attention when the psychological differentiation in the development of boy and girl is under scrutiny. In Freud's view, infantile psychosexual development of the female and the male initially follows an identical course, namely, one of male valence; in other words, there is only
one genital for both sexes, namely, the male one. Freud concludes that
the phallic phase* of the girl is one of complete concordance of genital
orientation in the little boy and girl. I shall quote his opinion to which
he adhered throughout his life: "With their entry into the phallic phase
the differences between the sexes are completely eclipsed by their agree-
ments. We are now obliged to recognize that the little girl is a little
man" (Freud, 1933, p. 118). Freud goes on to say that masturbation during
this phase is carried out on the "penis equivalent," that is, the clitoris.
When the girl discovers her "genital inferiority" (as it was called then),
the masturbation of boy and girl follows different lines. With the advent
of this critical divergence in psychosexual development arises the division
into "male equals active" and "female equals passive." This point of
view has led to much confusion, simplification, and acrimonious debate.
To quote a key sentence from Freud; "Along with abandonment of clitoral
masturbation a certain amount of activity is renounced. Passivity now
has the upper hand . . ." (Freud, 1933, p. 128). Up to this stage in Freud's
psychosexual theory of development the vagina remains undiscovered
by both sexes. Indeed, Freud (1933) was of the opinion that the girl
does not discover her vagina until puberty; therefore—so the argument
goes—a full sense of femaleness cannot exist at any earlier age. At puberty
the leading role of the clitoris recedes with the ascendancy of the vagina
as the excitable organ, thus ushering in femininity. In order to accomplish
this progression in psychosexual development, "The clitoris should wholly
or in part hand over its sensitivity and, at the same time, its importance
to the vagina" (p. 118). In the very next sentence, Freud states that "the
more fortunate man" does not have anything analogous to the "handing-
over" with which the would-be woman has to contend. What the disad-
vantage of possessing two organs of sexual sensitivity and excitability
might be is never considered or debated. At any rate, the little girl remains

* The term "phallic phase"—in its classical definition—reflects the opinion that the
universality of the penis as a body part of both genders represents the zonal focus for
boy and girl around which this stage of psychosexual development is organized.

a little boy until she discovers that she does not possess a penis. The realization of her sexual identity is supposed to occur at the decline of the phallic phase.

The ensuing castration complex consolidates penis envy, which, in turn, becomes the ultimate propellant force toward a female body image and the girl's acceptance of her physical state as castrated. Consequently, femininity supposedly has its origin in a defensive position; it is not genuine but constitutes a secondary formation. With the ascendancy of the reality principle the little girl transcends the inescapable disappointment in her body—and her mother's as well—by turning to the father. Thus, in a jealous identification with the mother she obtains the paternal phallus and by proxy gives a baby to the father just as her mother had done. This procreative achievement must be left dormant in wishful thinking due to her physical immaturity. The oedipal experience brings penis envy to a relative decline because the oedipal baby supposedly represents a restitution of the penis which she had either lost or never possessed. Thus goes Freud's conceptualization of female development. A question never elucidated in Freud's writing pertains to the fact that the wished-for oedipal baby in the little girl's doll play is always female—the world over—from time immemorial, while the commonly wished-for baby of the mature woman is a boy: "A mother is only brought unlimited satisfaction by relation to a son" (Freud, 1933, p. 133). Doll play reestablishes the little girl's sense of bodily completeness as well as the awareness of the female procreative faculties which she shares with her mother. We cannot but ponder whether the so-called oedipal baby (female doll) is not an amalgam of the experience of preoedipal mothering in its active and passive forms and, secondarily, of oedipal strivings which contain earliest maternal wishes. The fact that mature women usually, but not always, prefer a baby boy reflects, in part, powerful sociocultural influences, but beyond this, we recognize in this preference for the penis bearer an effort of the mature woman to stem the everlasting regressive pull to the preoedipal mother imago, a pull and counterpull, expressed in being alternately baby and mother in doll-play to which the little girl has once in the past given herself over with such abandon.

The Origins of Gender Identity

The above considerations bring us back to the question we considered earlier, namely, is gender identity due to innate (biological-genetic) or learned (cultural-environmental) factors, or what combination of both is of determinative valence? Let us start with the much discussed Freudian dictum, "Anatomy is destiny." This declaratory statement removes the influence of social factors on the shaping of femininity or of masculinity into the realm of almost trivial epiphenomena. We must admit that this classical psychoanalytic position has been slowly turned around, and to-day many of its aspects stand quite securely on their heads. This is to say that, on the basis of clinical evidence, we can attribute to parental and wider social influences as well as cultural attitudes toward the female baby and young child a significance for gender-identity formation that tends to outweight biological givens (Stoller, 1976, p. 73; Ticho, 1976, p. 141). Paraphrasing Freud's dictum, Stoller (1974, p. 357) adds an elegant twist to it, indeed a most convincing one, by saying, "Anatomy is not destiny; destiny comes from what people make of anatomy."

Gender-identity formation seems to occur much earlier than previously thought. Stoller has advanced the plausible opinion that core gender identity has its roots in the first year of life. Child observation supports the assumption that an innate male-female dimorphism is a biological given which permits us to speak of a primary femininity and masculinity. Sex differences can be observed in the neonate before we can speak of learned behavior, even though we do not know exactly when and how learning, imprinting, and conditioning affect decisively and lastingly the process of differentiation within the core gender identity. At any rate, there exists an appreciable body of data which lend weight to the opinion that neonates show observable differences linked to their gender. Any unprejudiced observer of young children has no difficulty in noticing early manifestations of sex differences in behavior, be these in motility, posture, play patterns, investigative curiosity, or fantasies. Gender identity on the level of mental awareness, sensed as "this is me," receives formative and lasting influences from the infant's social surround.

The vast and varied infantile experience of body incompleteness (smallness, helplessness, dependency) leads in boy and girl to different mental representations of self and object. We know, for instance, that the little boy resists more aggressively than the girl the demand for sphincter control and behavioral restraints in general. He is usually more difficult to train and to manage than the girl, who tends to contain her aggression toward the mother more globally by deflecting it toward the acquisition or possession of a body part, the penis, which merges symbolically with the representation of the lost breast;* both body parts gain the nature of perfection through idealization. The little boy's wish for a baby in his attempt to achieve body completeness is seldom as concretely expressed as the girl's wish for a penis. The adolescent boy's defensive reaction toward passive sexual strivings or fantasies far exceeds in intensity anything we witness in an adolescent girl who might sense or become

---

* The expression "lost breast," as used here, refers to the memory trace or concretized feeling state in relation to a part object loss which is identical with the function of the early nurturing caretaker.

aware of such feelings in relation to another woman. Two observations shall exemplify what has been said:

1. Freud (1909, pp. 86–87) records the following dialogue between the five-year-old Hans and his father:

> *Hans: I am going to have a little girl.*
> *I: Where will you get her, then?*
> *Hans: Why, from the stork. . . .*
> *I: You'd like to have a little girl.*
> *Hans: Yes, next year, I am going to have one. . . .*
> *I: But why isn't Mummy to have a little girl?*
> *Hans: Because I want to have a little girl for once.*
> *I: But you can't have a little girl.*
> *Hans: Oh yes, boys have girls and girls have boys.*
> *I: Boys don't have children. . . .*
> *Hans: But why shouldn't I?*

The little boy's envy of the female procreative function will in time yield to the reality principle by way of the transmuting process of substitution, sublimation, and the symbolic sharing in parturition (couvade).

2. A three-year-old girl went to the toilet of her nursery school with a boy her age. When she saw his penis she demanded, "Give it to me," repeating her request in threatening crescendo. The boy took to his heels in fright, but the girl pursued him, shouting, "Give it to me." At home she demanded that her mother buy her the "little toy" which the boy possessed. The mother's explanation that she could not buy it at a store left the little girl unconvinced and unconsoled.

Similar observations, perhaps less dramatic than the ones I mentioned, are so common that we look at them as typical. Penis envy appears as a two-layered phenomenon: The girl's wish for the mother's breast becomes shunted onto a masculine track in her effort to avoid regression to primary passivity; in this process she deflects the aggressive impulse from harming the mother by directing it greedily toward the male genital. Should a fixation on this level occur, the foundation for the development of a masculinity complex is prepared. This constellation often appears in full bloom at adolescence and never fails to reveal in treatment an unresolved and severe ambivalence conflict with the dyadical mother.

For an example, I refer to an analytic patient, a late adolescent girl with wildly untamed masculine wishes. She furiously brushed any reference to "penis envy" aside by saying, "Nonsense, I don't want my brother's penis; I don't want *him* to have one." Needless to say, the brother was the mother's admired and favored child. What the girl desired was the mother's exclusive attention and love, both intrinsically associated with the possession of a penis and the girl's own belief in the superiority of boys. Parenthetically, I want to mention that this girl entered analysis with the absolute conviction that her problem lay in the unsettled and confused relationship with her father; to her great surprise she came to realize that her mother complex lay at the center of her neurotic illness. This observation is an illustration of what I have called the oedipal defense.

I recall another patient, a late adolescent girl who used to assign to all physical objects in the world a male or female designation. For example, big books were male, pictures were female, and so forth. During a college course this girl once made a comment which was responded to by the teacher as being extremely intelligent. At this moment she had the hallucinatory physical sensation of having a penis. Being a dedicated member of the women's liberation movement, the reported experience aroused in her fury, disgust, and a sense of humiliation. This incident deserves mentioning because it occurred at a time in her treatment when the analytic work had reached the repressed and frustrated childhood cravings for her mother's physical affection, which at this juncture in her late adolescence surfaced in fantasies of a lesbian relationship and the thought of playing with the breast of her girlfriend. Since the resolution of dyadic fixations and of the isogender Oedipus complex constitutes one of the obligatory tasks of adolescence, the emergence of so-called penis envy in conjunction with lesbian trends should be considered a transient but normal, though quantitatively and qualitatively variant, epiphenomenon of the process of psychic restructuring during female adolescence.

As we know from Freud's writings about femininity, he was never convinced that any of his developmental propositions were telling the whole story. He had come early to the conclusion that the course by which the oedipal stage is reached and the Oedipus complex resolved is not analogous for the male and female child. Contemplating the girl's resolution of the Oedipus complex, Freud (1931) was struck by the fact that "at this point [of inquiry] our material—for some incomprehensible reason—becomes far more obscure and full of gaps." In the perplexing pursuit of this problem Freud came to realize that the dyadic stage exerts an influence on the emotional development of women that equals or even exceeds the influence of the oedipal stage. He finally went so far as to throw doubts on one of the cornerstones of psychoanalytic theory when he wrote, "It would seem as though we must retract the universality of the thesis that the Oedipus complex is the nucleus of the neurosis" (1931, p. 226). The last word in the discussion of these matters has not yet been spoken. The definitive teasing out of the specific factors which, in their intermeshing dynamics, compose the whole panorama of male and female development has not yet acquired sufficient luminosity and consistency in observation and reasoning to satisfy our curiosity. The factors I have been talking about in this volume are of a most heterogeneous nature; a grasp of their synergic organization and function remains still the object of search. The science of human development aims at coordinating the influences of constitutional givens, of earliest irreversible imprintings, of object relations and their effect on psychic patterning, and, last but not least, of sociocultural determinants in their ceaseless changeability over history. I hope I have succeeded in sharpening our awareness of those still obscure regions where investigative work awaits impatiently our attentive presence.

References

AARONS, Z. A. (1970), Normality and abnormality in adolescence. *Psychoanalytic Study of the Child*, 25:309–339. New York: International Universities Press.

ABELIN, E. (1971), The role of the father in the separation-individuation process. In McDevitt, J. B., and Settlage, C. F. (eds.), *Separation-Individuation*. New York: International Universities Press.

ABELIN, E. (1975), Some further observation and comments on the earliest role of the father. *Int. J. Psycho-Anal.*, 56:293–302.

ABELIN, E. (1977), The role of the father in core gender identity and in psychosexual differentiation. Abstracted by Prall, R., *J. Amer. Psychoanal. Assn.*, 1978, 26:143–161.

ARISTOTLE, *Selections*, ed. Ross, W. D. New York: Scribner, 1927. Pp. 323–325.

ARLOW, J. A. (1981), Theories of pathogenesis. *Psychoanal. Quart.*, 50:4, p. 505.

BARNETT, J. (1975), Hamlet and the family ideology. *J. Amer. Acad. Psychoanal.*, 3:4.

BENEDEK, T. (1959), Parenthood as a developmental phase. *J. Amer. Psychoanal. Assn.*, 7:389–417.

BIBRING, G. L. (1964), Some considerations regarding the ego ideal in the psychoanalytic process. *J. Amer. Psychoanal. Assn.*, 12:517–521.

BLOS, P., *The Adolescent Personality*. New York: Appleton-Century-Crofts, 1941.

BLOS, P., *On Adolescence: A Psychoanalytic Interpretation*. New York: Free Press, 1962.

BLOS, P. (1965), The initial stage of male adolescence. *Psychoanalytic Study of the Child*, 20:145–164.

BLOS, P. (1967), The second individuation process of adolescence. *Psychoanalytic Study of the Child*, 22:162–186. New York, International Universities Press. Reprinted in Blos, P., *The Adolescent Passage*. New York: International Universities Press, 1979.

BLOS, P. (1968), Character formation in adolescence. *Psychoanalytic Study of the Child*, 23:245–263. New York: International Universities Press.

BLOS, P. (1971), The generation gap. *Adolescent Psychiatry*, Vol. I, eds. Feinstein, S. C., Giovacchini, P., and Miller, A. A. New York: Basic Books.

BLOS, P. (1972), The function of the ego ideal in adolescence. *Psychoanalytic Study of the Child*, 27:93–97. New York: Quadrangle Books.

BLOS, P. (1974), The genealogy of the ego ideal. *Psychoanalytic Study of the Child*, 29:43–88. New Haven, Conn.: Yale University Press. Reprinted in Blos, P., *The Adolescent Passage*. New York: International Universities Press, 1979.

BLOS, P. (1976), The split parental imago in adolescent social relations: an inquiry into group psychology. *Psychoanalytic Study of the Child*, Vol. 31, New Haven and London, Yale University Press.

BLOS, P. (1979), Modifications in the classical psychoanalytic model of adolescence. In *The Adolescent Passage*. New York: International Universities Press. Pp. 473–497.

BLOS, P. (1980), Modifications in the traditional psychoanalytic theory of female adolescent development. *Adolescent Psychiatry*, 8:8–24. Chicago: University of Chicago Press.

BLUM, H. (1977), The prototype of preoedipal reconstruction. *J. Amer. Psychoanal. Assn.*, 25:757–785.

BROD, M., *Franz Kafka*. New York: Schocken Books, 1963.

DELAY, J., *The Youth of André Gide*. Chicago: University of Chicago Press, 1963.

EISSLER, K. R. (1968), Fortinbras and Hamlet. *Amer. Imago*, 25:3.

EISSLER, K. R., *Discourse on Hamlet and "Hamlet."* New York: International Universities Press, 1971.

ELIOT, T. S. (1939), *The Family Reunion*. New York and London: Harcourt Brace Jovanovich.

ERIKSON, E. (1981), The Galilean sayings and the sense of "I." *Yale Rev.*, 1981, p. 331.

ERLICH, A., *Hamlet's Absent Father*. Princeton, N.J.: Princeton University Press, 1977.

FREUD, A. (1958), Adolescence. *Psychoanalytic Study of the Child*, 13:255–278. New York: International Universities Press.

FREUD, A. (1965), *Normality and Pathology in Childhood*. New York: International Universities Press.

FREUD, A. (1970), The infantile neurosis: Genetic and dynamic considerations. In *The Writings of Anna Freud*, VII. New York: International Universities Press, 1971.

FREUD, S. (1900), *The Interpretation of Dreams*. Standard Edition, 4. London: Hogarth Press, 1958.

FREUD, S. (1887–1902), *The Origins of Psychoanalysis: Letters to Wilhelm Fliess, Drafts and Notes*, eds. Bonaparte, M., Freud, A., and Kris, E. New York: Basic Books, 1954.

FREUD, S. (1905), *Fragment of an Analysis of a Case of Hysteria*. Standard Edition, 7:7–122. London: Hogarth Press, 1953.

FREUD, S. (1909), *Analysis of a Phobia in a Five-Year-Old Boy*. Standard Edition, 10:5–149. London: Hogarth Press, 1955.

FREUD, S. (1911), *Psycho-analytic Notes on an Autobiographical Account of a Case of Paranoia (Dementia Paranoides)*. Standard Edition, 12. London: Hogarth Press, 1958.

FREUD, S. (1914), *On Narcissism*. Standard Edition, 14:73–102. London: Hogarth Press, 1957.

FREUD, S. (1917), *Introductory Lectures on Psycho-Analysis*. Standard Edition. London: Hogarth Press, 1963.

FREUD, S. (1921), *Group Psychology and the Analysis of the Ego*. Standard Edition, 18. London: Hogarth Press, 1955.

FREUD, S. (1923), *The Ego and the Id*. Standard Edition, 19. London: Hogarth Press, 1961.

FREUD, S. (1924), *The Dissolution of the Oedipus Complex*. Standard Edition, 19:173–179. London: Hogarth Press, 1961.

FREUD, S. (1925), *Some Psychological Consequences of the Anatomical Distinction between the Sexes*. Standard Edition, 19:243–258. London: Hogarth Press, 1961.

FREUD, S. (1927), *The Future of an Illusion*. Standard Edition, 21. London: Hogarth Press, 1961.

FREUD, S. (1931), *Female Sexuality*. Standard Edition, 21:225–243. London: Hogarth Press, 1964.

FREUD, S. (1933), *Femininity.* Standard Edition, 22:112–135. London: Hogarth Press, 1961.

GEDO, J. E. (1972), Caviare to the general. In "K. R. Eissler's Discourse on Hamlet:" A symposium. *Amer. Imago,* 25:3.

GLOVER, E., *The Technique of Psychoanalysis.* New York: International Universities Press, 1955.

GRAVES, R. (1955), *The Greek Myths.* Baltimore, Maryland, Penguin Books.

GREENACRE, P. (1957), The childhood of the artist: Libidinal phase development and giftedness. *Psychoanalytic Study of the Child,* 12:27–72. New York: International Universities Press.

GREENACRE, P. (1963). *The Quest for the Father.* New York, International Universities Press, Inc.

GREENACRE, P. (1966), Problems of overidealization of the analyst and of analysis. *Psychoanalytic Study of the Child,* 21:193–211. New York: International Universities Press.

GREENSON, R. R. (1968), Disidentification from mother. *Int. J. Psycho-Anal.,* 49:370–374.

HAYMAN, RONALD, *Kafka: A Biography.* New York: Oxford University Press, 1982.

HERZOG, J. M. (1980), Sleep disturbance and father hunger in 18- to 20-month-old boys. *Psychoanalytic Study of the Child,* 35:219–233. New Haven: Yale University Press.

HUTTER, A. D. (1975), The language of Hamlet. *J. Acad. Psychoanal.,* 3:4.

INHELDER, B. and PIAGET, J. (1958), *The Growth of Logical Thinking from Childhood to Adolescence.* New York, Basic Books.

JONES, E. (1910), The oedipus-complex as an explanation of Hamlet's mystery: A study in motive. *Amer. J. Psychol.,* Vol. 21.

JONES, E. (1935), Early female sexuality. In *Papers on Psychoanalysis.* Boston: Beacon Press, 1961.

JONES, E. (1948), The death of Hamlet's father. *Int. J. Psycho-Anal.,* 29, 3.

JONES, E. (1949), *Hamlet and Oedipus.* New York: Doubleday, 1954.

JOYCE, JAMES, *Ulysses.* New York: Random House, 1961 (new printing of the first American edition, published in 1934).

KAFKA, F., *Letter to His Father.* New York: Schocken Books, 1966.

KAHN, C., *Man's Estate: Masculine Identity in Shakespeare.* Berkeley: University of California Press, 1981.

KARME, LAILA (1979), The analysis of a male patient by a female analyst: The problem of the negative oedipal transference. *Int. J. Psycho-Anal.,* 60:253–261.

KINSEY, A. C., et al., *Sexual Behavior in the Human Male,* Philadelphia: Saunders, 1948.

KOHUT, H. (1966). Forms and transformations of narcissism. *Journal of the American Psychoanalytic Association,* 14.

KRIS, E. (1948), Prince Hal's conflict. In *Psychoanalytic Explorations in Art.* New York, International Universities Press, 1952 (p. 273).

LICHTENBERG, J. D., and LICHTENBERG, C. (1969), Prince Hal's conflict. *J. Amer. Psychoanal. Assn.,* 17:873–887.

LOEWALD, H. W. (1951), Ego and reality. *Int. J. Psycho-Anal.,* 32:10–18.

MACK BRUNSWICK, R. (1940), The preoedipal phase of libido development. In Fliess, R., *The Psychoanalytic Reader.* New York: International Universities Press, 1948.

MAHLER, M. (1955), On symbiotic child psychosis. *Psychoanalytic Study of the Child,* 10. New York: International Universities Press.

MAHLER, M. S., PINE, F., and BERGMAN, A., *The Psychological Birth of the Human Infant.* New York: Basic Books, 1975.

MALONEY, J. C., and ROCKELEIN, L. (1949), A new interpretation of Hamlet. *Int. J. Psycho-Anal.,* Vol. 30.

NIEDERLAND, W. G. *The Schreber Case,* New York: Quadrangle Books, 1974.

NUNBERG, H. (1932), *Principles of Psychoanalysis.* New York: International Universities Press, 1955.

PIERS, G. and SINGER, M. B. (1953), *Shame and Guilt.* New York, Norton, 1971.

REICH, A. (1954), Early identifications as archaic elements in the superego. In: *Psychoanalytic Contributions.* New York, International Universities Press, 1973, pp. 209–253.

REICH, A. (1960), Pathological forms of self-esteem regulation. In *Psychoanalytic Contributions.* New York: International Universities Press, 1973, Pp. 288–311.

ROSS, J. M. (1977), Toward fatherhood: The epigenesis of paternal identity during a boy's first decade. *Int. Rev. Psycho-Anal.,* 4:327–347.

ROSS, J. M. (1979), Fathering: A review of some psychoanalytic contributions on paternity. *Int. J. Psycho-Anal.,* 60:317–327.

ROSS, J. M. (1982), Oedipus revisited: Laius and the "Laius complex." *Psychoanalytic Study of the Child,* 37. New Haven, Conn.: Yale University Press.

SCHREBER, D. P. (1903), *Memoirs of My Nervous Illness,* translated by Ida Macalpine and Richard A. Hunter. London: Dawson, 1955.

SHAKESPEARE, W., *The Arden Shakespeare* Hamlet, ed. H. Jenkins. New York: Methuen, 1982.

STEVENS, WALLACE, *Opus Posthumous.* New York: Random House, 1982.

STOLLER, R. (1974), Facts and fancies: an examination of Freud's concept of bisexuality. In Strouse, J., ed. *Women and Analysis.* New York, Grossman.

STOLLER, R. (1976), Primary femininity. *Journal of the American Psycholanlytic Association,* 24 (5).

STOLLER, R. J. (1980), A different view of oedipal conflict. In *The Course of Life,* Vol. I, eds. Greenspan, S. I., and Pollock, G. H. Mental Health Study Center, U. S. Department of Health and Human Services, 1980.

TICHO, G. R. (1976), Autonomy in young adults. *Journal of the American Psychoanalytic Association,* 24 (5).

TURGENEV, I. (1962), *Fathers and Sons.* New York: Farrar, Straus & Giroux.

WINNICOTT, D. W. (1965), *The Maturational Process and the Facilitating Environment.* New York: International Universities Press.

WINNICOTT, D. W. (1969), The use of an object. *Int. J. Psycho-Anal.,* Vol. 50.

Index